WITH CHRIST AFTER THE LOST

▲

WITH CHRIST AFTER THE LOST

A Search for Souls

By

L. R. Scarborough, B. A., D. D.

Revised and Expanded by

E. D. Head, A. M., Th. D., D. D., LL. D.

BROADMAN PRESS

Nashville, Tennessee

Copyright, 1952
BROADMAN PRESS
Nashville, Tennessee

4262-03

ISBN: 0-8054-6203-1

Printed in the United States of America

To

B. H. CARROLL, D.D., stainless soul, matchless preacher, immortal teacher, conquering kingdom leader, who was the founder of the Chair of Evangelism in theological education, and has entered into a deathless reward; and to the treasured students in our classes in evangelism and personal work who have gone, and who will go, out to win and build souls for Christ, this volume is cheerfully dedicated in the hope of a fadeless immortality.

FOREWORD

This book is wrought out of the author's soul in twenty-one years in pastoral, teaching, and personal evangelism. For twelve years in two pastorates he sought, in his own churches and hundreds of other churches, to turn men to Christ. For many years as professor of evangelism in the Southwestern Baptist Theological Seminary, in classes in personal work and in evangelism, he sought to impart the method, spirit, and doctrines taught by the Master and his apostles in soul-winning; to inspire, and to lead in seeking and finding the compassion for souls and the power of the Spirit, hundreds of men and women under his tutelage. In these years of teaching, each year he led in from eight to fourteen special evangelistic meetings and in many soul-winning conferences. He believes that every preacher, every missionary, and every Christian should seek to win souls to Christ.

The author herein acknowledges a debt of gratitude to the immortal B. H. Carroll, under the influence and inspiring example of whose evangelistic ministry he was placed for many years; to his devoted preacher father, under whose soulful sermons and inspiring life he learned to love lost men; to a sainted mother, whose prayers were answered in his call to preach and by whose efforts he was led to see himself a sinner and to find Christ as Saviour; to a devoted, faithful, and unselfish wife, through whose prayers, love, faith, and sacrifice he has been able to give much of his time and powers to soul-winning; to Dr. George W. Truett, the compassionate and powerful pastor-evangelist, under whose example he has been led to value the soul-winning life; to Doc Pegues, now with the Saviour, whose tireless zeal in going after the lost, as an untrained layman, fanned into flames the holy fires of evangelism in his soul; to the hundreds of pastors, laymen, and women who have invited him to aid in soul-winning campaigns; and especially to the co-operant and Christ-loving members of the Baptist churches at Cameron and Abilene, Texas, whose co-operation, prayers, and patient efforts in his two pastorates enabled him to gain the passion for souls, build evangelistic churches, and go out in hundreds of evangelistic meetings. The debt he owes to the prayer groups in these two churches he will never be able to pay in time or eternity. He is deeply indebted to Dr. R. A. Torrey, whose invaluable book, *How to Work for Christ*, he has taught through many years.

This book is meant for preachers to read and to teach to soul-winning bands in their churches. It is designed for use in study courses in Sunday schools, young people's organizations and mission bands, and in classes in personal work and evangelism in theological seminaries, missionary training schools, and Bible departments in Christian schools. It seeks to give scriptural knowledge in winning lost souls to Christ, to give a knowledge of the best methods in evangelism, and to give inspiration, compassion, and power to all whose hearts turn to a search for lost souls and the power of God in unselfish service for Christ Jesus.

L. R. SCARBOROUGH

FOREWORD

For Revised Edition

Since Dr. L. R. Scarborough wrought this book out of his soul fired with compassion for the lost, other methods of evangelism have come into being. Because of the desire to include these more recent methods in one textbook and also to adapt the book for more effective teaching procedure, I have ventured upon its revision after seventeen years of experience in teaching it in Baylor University and in Southwestern Seminary. Even with such a justifiable objective, I approached the task with great hesitation. This hesitation was due mainly to the fact that I realized the signal danger of removing from it the personality of its inimitable author. I have striven earnestly, therefore, to keep alive his unique emphasis, even the forms of expression which were so manifestly characteristic of him, thus preserving the author's original style, even his throbbing heart of love for a lost world—that heart throb which pulsates through these pages.

Among the changes which have been made in this revision, the following may be mentioned: First, the numerous pertinent passages of Scripture have been recorded in the order of the books of the Bible from which they are taken. Second, the material in certain of the chapters has been more systematically organized, and a few chapters which contained considerable repetition have been condensed into one comprehensive chapter. Third, a somewhat extensive list of the best books on evangelism and related themes has been included for the convenience of those who may desire to pursue the subject further.

For the completion of the revision of this classic text, I am indebted to many who have helped and encouraged, Two efficient secretaries, Miss Mamie Storrs and Mrs. Paul

A. Robertson, have typed the material, with Miss Storrs doing further extensive research in matters of detail. Dr. Ray Summers, professor of New Testament and now also professor of evangelism, has edited the manuscript, making valued suggestions, rewriting part of the materials, and bringing it to its final form for publication.

It is our earnest prayer that as this book goes forth in its present form, it may continue to kindle fires on heart altars, to the end that multitudes may be won from sin to salvation, from darkness to light, from futile gnawing on the bread that perishes to accepting him who is the Bread of life.

E. D. HEAD

Fort Worth, Texas

CONTENTS

Introduction—The Task Universal 1

PART ONE—Some Spiritual Prerequisites

1.—The Winner's Soul and Life 11
2.—The Winner's Prayer Life 16
3.—The Winner's Faith and Convictions 21
4.—The Winner's Compassion 29
5.—The Winner's Heavenly Unction 34

PART TWO—Some Inspiring Examples

6.—The Matchless Winner 43
7.—The Apostle of Holy Fires 47
8.—The Pentecostal Preacher 51
9.—The Topmost Evangelist 55

PART THREE—The Way to Win

Section A—*Perennial Evangelism*

10.—The Evangelistic Church 61
11.—The Soul-winning Pastor—Priest, Preacher, Evangelist 73
12.—Visitation Evangelism 81
13.—Music in Evangelism 86
14.—Evangelism in the Home 91
15.—Educational Evangelism 96
16.—The Spiritual Value of Money 103
17.—Conserving Results 107

Section B—*Seasonal Evangelism*

18.—Revivals—How to Promote Them 113
19.—Simultaneous Crusades 121
20.—Youth Revivals 128

21.—Brotherhood Revivals 136
22.—Evangelism in the "Highways and Hedges" 141
23.—Drawing the Net 145

PART FOUR—Personal Work

24.—Suggestions to Winners 153
25.—How to Deal with Children 157
26.—How to Win the Unconcerned 162
27.—How to Reach the Deceived and Deluded 166
28.—How to Win Skeptics and Doubters 186
29.—How to Win the Moralist 193
30.—How to Win the Pleasure-loving 199
31.—How to Meet the Lost Man's Difficulties 203
32.—How to Deal with Those Under Conviction 230

PART FIVE—Scripture Passages for Workers

33.—Vital Scriptures for the Heart of the Soul-Winner 241
34.—The Unbeliever's Peril and Destiny 245
35.—God's Attitude Toward the Lost 249
36.—God's Provision for the Sinner's Redemption 252
37.—The Salvation of the Soul 260
38.—The Salvation of the Life 269
39.—The Christian's Heavenly Rainbow 280

Conclusion—The Call of the Cross 283

Bibliography 287

Introduction
The Task Universal
God's Pungent Words to His Children

PROVERBS 11:30. The fruit of the righteous is a tree of life; and he that winneth souls is wise.

EZEKIEL 33:7-8. So thou, O son of man, I have set thee a watchman unto the house of Israel; therefore thou shalt hear the word at my mouth, and warn them from me. When I say unto the wicked, O wicked man, thou shalt surely die; if thou dost not speak to warn the wicked from his way, that wicked man shall die in his iniquity; but his blood will I require at thine hand.

DANIEL 12:3. And they that be wise shall shine as the brightness of the firmament; and they that turn many to righteousness as the stars for ever and ever.

MATTHEW 4:19. And he saith unto them, Follow me, and I will make you fishers of men.

MATTHEW 9:37-38. Then saith he unto his disciples, The harvest truly is plenteous, but the labourers are few; pray ye therefore the Lord of the harvest, that he will send forth labourers into his harvest.

MATTHEW 22:9. Go ye therefore into the highways, and as many as ye shall find, bid to the marriage.

MARK 16:15. And he said unto them, Go ye into all the world, and preach the gospel to every creature.

JOHN 4:35. Say not ye, There are yet four months, and then cometh harvest? behold, I say unto you, Lift up your eyes, and look on the fields; for they are white already to harvest.

JOHN 20:21. Then said Jesus to them again, Peace be unto you: as my Father hath sent me, even so send I you.

ACTS 1:8. But ye shall receive power, after that the Holy Ghost is come upon you: and ye shall be witnesses unto me both in Jerusalem, and in all Judaea, and in Samaria, and unto the uttermost part of the earth.

1 CORINTHIANS 9:22-23. To the weak became I as weak, that I might gain the weak: I am made all things to all men, that I

might by all means save some. And this I do for the gospel's sake, that I might be partaker thereof with you.

GALATIANS 6:9. And let us not be weary in well doing: for in due season we shall reap, if we faint not.

JUDE 23. And others save with fear, pulling them out of the fire; hating even the garment spotted by the flesh.

REVELATION 22:17. And the Spirit and the bride say, Come. And let him that heareth say, Come. And let him that is athirst come. And whosoever will, let him take the water of life freely.

THE MAGNITUDE OF THE TASK

The most gigantic undertaking God has laid out for Christian men is to lead lost souls to Jesus Christ. The salvation of the world cost God more, and requires more from man, than any other movement in human or divine history. To make a world he had only to speak the word (Heb. 11:3); to save the world he had to crucify his only begotten Son (Isa. 53:10). In this saving program he requisitioned all the powers of his triune deity, and he calls for the co-operation of every saved man. Christ emptied himself in sacrificial libation on God's altar to redeem us, and God requires us to offer to him our best and our all in witnessing to others of this redeeming grace (Luke 10:27; Phil. 2:7). The highest in heaven and the lowest on earth should combine in this imperial task.

THE INCLUSIVENESS OF THE TASK

The divine obligation of soul-winning rests without exception upon every child of God. The Christian receives the essence of this obligation and call at the time of his salvation. Regeneration demands reproduction in kind. The fruit of a Christian is another Christian. To witness for Christ is a spontaneous and natural expression of the newly saved child of God. The worldwide mission principle is present in germ in every case of spiritual regeneration. The hope of evangelism on the human side is found in this embryonic principle. Some men are divinely called to preach to a lost world; some women are called to give life and power in home and foreign fields to teach a redeeming gospel. Every Christian is called in the hour of salvation to witness for Jesus Christ. Nothing in heaven or on earth can excuse him from it. God gives no furloughs from this heaven-born obligation. Not ignorance, or poverty, or environment, or difficulties of any kind—nothing—can exempt or excuse any child of God from its pressing daily importance. The difference between the preacher's and the layman's call is one of extent and degree. They are both called to win men to Christ.

The Appeal of the Task

Above all other motives to the truly saved man, as a spur to service and an incentive to soul-winning, is the cross of Christ. Christ calls from Calvary for us to carry the saving efficacy of his cross to a lost world about us. Paul said, "The love of Christ constraineth us" (2 Cor. 5:14)—his love for me expressed in his death for me; my love for him expressed in my life of winning service. The nail-torn hands, the thorn-pierced brow, and his dying cry, "My God, my God, why hast thou forsaken me?" (Matt. 27:46), appeal to the soul of every child of God to be a fisher of men, a winner of men. We imperil every joy of heaven by neglecting to heed these calls to service.

The appeal comes from *above*. God calls with a fatherly love, Christ pleads with a Redeemer's compassion, and the Holy Spirit urges with a constant intercessory insistence. The Bible repeatedly presses this universal duty upon us. To refuse to witness of a saving gospel to a lost world day by day is nothing short of high treason, spiritual rebellion, and inexcusable disobedience to God's holy commands.

The appeal comes from *beneath*. The doomed in eternity are anxious that their lost relatives and friends shall not share their destiny. Have you heard in your deepest soul the tragic words of the rich man as in hellish torment he beseeches Abraham: "Send him to my father's house: for I have five brethren; that he may testify unto them, lest they also come into this place of torment" (Luke 16:27-28)? If you refuse the voice of God and the pleading of the Spirit, if you heed not the perils of lost men about you, if you drown all the longings of your own soul to win someone to Christ, do not turn away from the intercessions of the rich man in hell. His brothers still live next door to you. Testify to them today.

The appeal comes from *within*. The saved soul itself longs to win someone. Soul-winning fires burn in the depths of every child of God. Andrew cannot long abide with Christ without thinking of and going after his brother Simon. These inner compassions and spiritual longings call us out to the ripening fields. Christ said to his disciples as they offered him bread after he had won the fallen woman at Jacob's well: "I have meat to eat that ye know not of" (John 4:32). He had an inner hunger which soul-winning alone would satisfy.

The appeal comes from *without*. Man's need, his perils, his undone and ruined state of soul, his imminent doom in a Christless eternity, press this call upon our hearts. The unconscious cry of a lost humanity comes to greet the listening ear of every saved man. To go along unheeding this cry is to court the death of the lost and to be guilty of a world's spiritual ruin. The unsaved in home, shop, school, store, street, everywhere, demand attention at our hands every hour.

The Responsibility of the Task

God says: "Son of man, I have made thee a watchman unto the house of Israel: therefore hear the word at my mouth, and give them warning from me. When I say unto the wicked, Thou shalt surely die; and thou givest him not warning, nor speakest to warn the wicked from his wicked way, to save his life; the same wicked man shall die in his iniquity; but his blood will I require at thine hand" (Ezek. 3:17-18).

Can parents with unsaved children, wives with unsaved husbands, teachers with unsaved pupils, preachers with unsaved all about them, read this tragic message of lost men's blood on their hands and rest in peace without doing their utmost to win them to Christ? What is it to stand at God's judgment with the blood of the unwarned lost on our hands? Paul said, "I am pure from the blood of all men" (Acts 20:26). But he also said: "I say the truth in Christ, I lie not, my conscience also bearing me witness in the Holy Ghost, that I have great heaviness and continual sorrow in my heart. For I could wish that myself were accursed from Christ for my brethren, my kinsmen" (Rom. 9:1-3). To live in a world filled with the unsaved and not try to win them to Christ; to be saved by God's free grace and go to meet him with no sheaves, nothing but leaves, a barren life, a crownless life—this is an unspeakably horrible thing to do. You can do better. Win someone. Begin today. Take the blood of the lost off your hands.

The Rewards of the Task

Evangelism has its shining rewards, its spiritual compensations for the expenditure of blood, energy, time, talent, and life. "And they that be wise shall shine as the brightness of the firmament; and they that turn many to righteousness as the stars for ever and ever" (Dan. 12:3). "And he that reapeth receiveth wages, and gathereth fruit unto life eternal: that both he that soweth and he that reapeth may rejoice together" (John 4:36). "Henceforth there is laid up for me a crown of righteousness, which the Lord, the righteous judge, shall give me at that day: and not to me only, but unto all them also that love his appearing" (2 Tim. 4:8)—this thought encouraged the aged Paul as he faced the endless life beyond death.

The soul-winning life is not an easy life. It is full of sacrifices, deprivations, separations, and disappointments. Yet it is a happy life, a joyous service, which fills all the avenues of the soul with peace and joy in the Holy Spirit and sets all the joy bells of the heart to ringing.

Soul-winning is a deathless business. Its rewards accumulate with the passing centuries. The fruit multiplies. Think of Stephen and Ananias as they doubtless shared in Paul's coming to Christ. Paul's victories have just begun, and these winners share in his endless labors. Think of the increasing glory of the simple cobbler who won Spurgeon to Jesus, as Spurgeon's labors go on reaping harvests for Christ. Think of the man who won John Wesley and the woman who won Charles Wesley, the merchant who won Moody, the street preacher who won Sunday. Their crowns are growing as the labors of these winners multiply in the salvation of others. Think of the growing crowns of the mothers who won their sons and daughters—sons and daughters who in every quarter of the globe and in every phase of life live to extend Christ's kingdom, exalt the Name above every name, and lead a lost world back to God's light. Surely all who love our Christ should enter the holy calling of winning souls. No other life has a greater reward than has that of the soul-winner.

1. The peace of soul realized in doing God's will is one of the richest rewards of the soul-winner.

2. Soul-winning widens the vision and lifts the spiritual horizon for a larger look at God and his program.

3. It fattens the soul and makes it grow by leaps and bounds in the grace and knowledge of Jesus Christ.

4. It enriches one's future and lays up heavenly treasures. The storehouse above is filled with "angel's food" for the soul's other and larger day.

5. It brings joy to three worlds. It brings joy to the world of the sinner's heart, to the world of his loved one's soul, and to the hearts of the heavenly group. This joy

in seeing others come to know Christ in saving grace is the fullest and richest joy known to man. To help change a destiny in the heavenly way, to turn an immortal life into the comradeship of God, to change its abiding place from one of an eternal hell's doom to a blissful home with Christ and the angels—this is life's highest reward.

6. It assures a heavenly companionship. It brings one into closest touch and fellowship with the Father, the Saviour, and the Holy Spirit, whose eternal task is seeking and saving the lost. Christ said: "Go ye therefore, and teach all nations, baptizing them in the name of the Father, and of the Son, and of the Holy Ghost: teaching them to observe all things whatsoever I have commanded you: and, lo, I am with you alway, even unto the end of the world" (Matt. 28:19-20). Soul-winning is always blessed by Christ's enriching presence.

7. It is the surest way to the enduement of the Holy Spirit's power. It is the straightest road to Pentecost.

8. Its chief reward is the crown it brings to Christ, the glory it puts on his exalted head. The truest winner of men is not seeking a crown for himself, a diadem as fadeless as the stars for his own brow; but rather he seeks such a diadem to replace the crown of thorns on Christ's head. It is to make him Lord of lords and King of kings that spurs us on to win men from sin.

Part One

SOME SPIRITUAL PREREQUISITES

1

The Winner's Soul and Life

PSALM 24:3-4. Who shall ascend into the hill of the Lord? or who shall stand in his holy place? He that hath clean hands, and a pure heart; who hath not lifted up his soul unto vanity, nor sworn deceitfully.

PSALM 51:7-13. Purge me with hyssop, and I shall be clean: wash me, and I shall be whiter than snow. Make me to hear joy and gladness; that the bones which thou hast broken may rejoice. Hide thy face from my sins, and blot out all mine iniquities. Create in me a clean heart, O God; and renew a right spirit within me. Cast me not away from thy presence; and take not thy holy spirit from me. Restore unto me the joy of thy salvation; and uphold me with thy free spirit. Then will I teach transgressors thy ways; and sinners shall be converted unto thee.

MATTHEW 5:8. Blessed are the pure in heart: for they shall see God.

JOHN 17:16. They are not of the world, even as I am not of the world.

ROMANS 12:1-2. I beseech you therefore, brethren, by the mercies of God, that ye present your bodies a living sacrifice, holy, acceptable unto God, which is your reasonable service. And be not conformed to this world: but be ye transformed by the renewing of your mind, that ye may prove what is that good, and acceptable, and perfect, will of God.

2 CORINTHIANS 6:17. Wherefore come out from among them, and be ye separate, saith the Lord, and touch not the unclean thing; and I will receive you.

GALATIANS 2:20. I am crucified with Christ: nevertheless I live; yet not I, but Christ liveth in me: and the life which I now live in the flesh I live by the faith of the Son of God, who loved me, and gave himself for me.

GALATIANS 5:24. And they that are Christ's have crucified the flesh with the affections and lusts.

GALATIANS 6:14. But God forbid that I should glory, save in the cross of our Lord Jesus Christ, by whom the world is crucified unto me, and I unto the world.

EPHESIANS 5:11. And have no fellowship with the unfruitful works of darkness, but rather reprove them.

2 TIMOTHY 2:21-22. If a man therefore purge himself from these, he shall be a vessel unto honour, sanctified, and meet for the master's use, and prepared unto every good work. Flee also youthful lusts: but follow righteousness, faith, charity, peace, with them that call on the Lord out of a pure heart.

1 JOHN 2:15. Love not the world, neither the things that are in the world. If any man love the world, the love of the Father is not in him.

The Assurance of a Saved Soul

The primary and basic prerequisite for soul-winning is that the soul-winner have in his deepest soul an experiential knowledge of Jesus Christ as his own personal Saviour. He must have looked at Christ through eyes of repentance and faith and have accepted him as Lord and Master. He must know the way over which he would lead others. Spiritual regeneration precedes acceptable service in God's plan. Assurance of salvation is a condition of constant and successful soul-winning. Doubt about his own salvation will limit the doubter's power in leading others in the way. Great confidence in God and conviction of the truth should characterize the testimony of the soul-winner. The blind cannot lead the blind without direful results to both, and especially is this true in eternal and spiritual matters. To know Christ in forgiving, redeeming, delivering, and keeping power is essential to successful evangelizing. Paul's spiritual powers were greatly reinforced by the fact that he could say: "I know whom I have believed, and am persuaded that he is able to keep that which I have committed unto him against that day" (2 Tim. 1:12).

The Separateness of a Consecrated Life

All those who aspire to win souls must be set apart by divine consecration. Not only is a saved soul necessary, but also a redeemed life. Those who handle the vessels of the

Lord must have pure hearts and clean hands. "Holiness unto the Lord" must be on the skirts of God's spiritual priests today. "Consecrate yourselves to day to the Lord" (Ex. 32:29) is God's command to those who would win souls to him.

Separation from the world's mind, method, and way is another prerequisite to victory in spiritual harvesting. "Be not conformed to this world: but be ye transformed by the renewing of your mind, that ye may prove what is that good, and acceptable, and perfect, will of God" (Rom. 12:2). "Wherefore come out from among them, and be ye separate, saith the Lord, and touch not the unclean thing; and I will receive you" (2 Cor. 6:17). "Love not the world, neither the things that are in the world. If any man love the world, the love of the Father is not in him" (1 John 2:15). "In the world, but not of the world" is Christ's standard for us. "Let us lay aside every weight, and the sin which doth so easily beset us" (Heb. 12:1). "If thou take away from the midst of thee the yoke" (Isa. 58:9)—any yoke of sin or worldliness—then there is the promise of blessing and power. Worldliness or secret sin clogs the power ducts from God to our souls. Indulgence in worldly pleasures is death to our influence in winning men to Christ, and the harboring of secret sins is spiritual paralysis to our power with God. "Your body is the temple of the Holy Ghost" (1 Cor. 6:19), and God's temple should be untainted.

The Obedience of a Yielded Life

"And we are his witnesses of these things; and so is also the Holy Ghost, whom God hath given to them that obey him" (Acts 5:32). "And he said unto them, Cast the net on the right side of the ship, and ye shall find" (John 21:6). "Behold, to obey is better than sacrifice, and to hearken than the fat of rams" (1 Sam. 15:22). There is no salvation in obedience, but there is much joy and power. To be a winner worth while, we must adopt Christ's map of the world and be willing to go anywhere with him. We must say with Peter, "At thy word I will let down the net" (Luke 5:5). "Woe unto him that striveth with his Maker!" (Isa. 45:9).

We must be more than obedient to God; we must be supple and pliant in his hands. The ideal is to be "as the clay is in the potter's hands" (Jer. 18:6), to be molded as pleases him. Gideon won his victory over the Midianites because he was a garment in the hands of the Holy Spirit. "The Spirit of the Lord clothed itself with Gideon" (Judg. 6:34 ASV marg.). We must be reliantly and pliantly willing to do his will anywhere before we can confidently claim his power in our kingdom tasks. "For one is your Master, even Christ" (Matt. 23:10). We should be subject to his orders. Spiritual reliance carries us far toward victory in evangelizing for Christ.

The Compassion of an Aspiring Life

A spiritual hunger for righteousness, a longing for a deeper and richer fellowship with Jesus Christ, and an aspiration for a higher comradeship with God, are a necessary part of the soul-winner's inner equipment. When Christ gave his soul-enriching beautitudes, such as "Blessed are they which do hunger and thirst after righteousness," he was preparing his hearers to be "fishers of men" (Matt. 5:6; 4:19). Andrew had not long "abode" with the Saviour until he thought of Simon and "brought him to Jesus" (John 1:39-42). Paul was gaining equipment for larger service when he said, "Forgetting those things which are behind, and reaching forth unto those things which are before, I press toward the mark for the prize of the high calling of God in Christ Jesus" (Phil. 3:13-14). Jesus was preparing Peter for Pentecostal victories when he probed his anxious soul with the question, "Lovest thou me more than these?" and Pentecost was in promise when Peter answered, "Yea, Lord; thou knowest that I love thee" (John 21:15-16).

Not only should our inner life reach out for God, but our hearts should also reach out for lost men. We must see with our inner eyes what Jesus saw when from Olivet he wept over Jerusalem. We should know something of what thrilled the Saviour's loving heart when he had "compassion on the multitude." It was this holy, spiritual compulsion of soul which caused him to leave heaven's throne and take up Calvary's cross for our redemption. We should know something of Paul's longing and burden of heart when he said: "I have great heaviness and continual sorrow in my heart. For I could wish that myself were accursed from Christ for my brethren, my kinsmen according to the flesh" (Rom. 9:2-3). We should know something of Isaiah's meaning when he said, "If thou draw out thy soul to the hungry, and satisfy the afflicted soul; then shall thy light rise in obscurity, and thy darkness be as the noon day: and the Lord shall guide thee continually, and satisfy thy soul in drought, and make fat thy bones: and thou shalt be like a watered garden, and like a spring of water, whose waters fail not. And they that shall be of thee shall build the old waste places: thou shalt raise up the foundations of many generations; and thou shalt be called, The repairer of the breach, The restorer of paths to dwell in" (Isa. 58:10-12).

Compassion for the lost brings heaven's power upon our efforts and equips us for "taking men alive."

2

The Winner's Prayer Life

Isaiah 38:5. Go, and say to Hezekiah, Thus saith the Lord, the God of David thy father, I have heard thy prayer, I have seen thy tears: behold, I will add unto thy days fifteen years.

Jeremiah 33:3. Call unto me, and I will answer thee, and shew thee great and mighty things, which thou knowest not.

Matthew 6:6. But thou, when thou prayest, enter into thy closet, and when thou hast shut thy door, pray to thy Father which is in secret; and thy Father which seeth in secret shall reward thee openly.

Mark 11:24. Therefore I say unto you, What things soever ye desire, when ye pray, believe that ye receive them, and ye shall have them.

Luke 11:13. If ye then, being evil, know how to give good gifts unto your children: how much more shall your heavenly Father give the Holy Spirit to them that ask him?

1 Thessalonians 5:17. Pray without ceasing.

James 5:16. Confess your faults one to another, and pray one for another, that ye may be healed. The effectual fervent prayer of a righteous man availeth much.

The Habit of Prayer

An essential condition to the soul-winner's success is the development of a prayer life, the establishment of a habit of prayer. Prayer is the Christian's most glorious privilege, most enlarging opportunity, and most essential obligation; for it opens the door to communication with God, makes easier his access to men, and is the surest way to bring God and men together in saving and keeping relationship. The prayers of Abraham, Jacob, Moses, Nehemiah, and Daniel, marked turning points in the history of nations. The kingdom of heaven swings on the pivot of Christ's and Paul's prayers. Jesus, the Son of God, and Paul, his greatest apostle, had well-developed prayer habits. They allowed no intrusions into their prayer life and no substitutions for their supplications. Prayer was as essential to their spiritual ongoing as was food to their physical well-being.

Jesus and Prayer

Christ's prayer life is one of the most impressive parts of his earthly ministry. Most of his public deeds of any consequence were accompanied by a season of prayer: when he was baptized (Luke 3:21), before he called his disciples (Luke 6:12), as he raised the dead (John 11:41), before his trial (John 17), before his betrayal (Luke 22:42), before his death (Luke 23:46), and in many other cases. The following things can be said about Jesus and prayer:

1. He prayed often. Prayer filled his life.
2. He almost always prayed before he faced any great task or trial.
3. He prayed in public.
4. He prayed in secret—often all night, sometimes alone and sometimes with his disciples.
5. He put a high premium on secret prayer (Matt. 6:6).
6. He practiced intercessory prayer (John 17:9-26).
7. He promised the power of the Holy Spirit in answer to prayer (Luke 11:13).
8. He taught that a sinner could pray for his own salvation (Luke 18:13).

Soul-winners should not miss the power of Christ's example in the matter of making a prayer plan and establishing a prayer life.

Paul and Prayer

Prayer was a pre-eminent factor in the life and ministry of the apostle Paul. He prayed during the time of his conversion (Acts 9:11) and started his Christian career by a season in Arabia praying unto God and getting from him his message of the gospel (Gal. 1:12, 16-17). The record of his prayers in jails, in synagogues, on streets, in private homes, on river banks, on seashores—everywhere—is a thrilling and inspiring part of his wonderful career. His recorded prayers are specimens of deepest devotion to, and communion with, God, and evidences of deepest religious and spiritual convictions. His ringing injunctions to all Christians, "Pray without ceasing" (1 Thess. 5:17) and "Be careful for nothing; but in every thing by prayer and supplication with thanksgiving let your requests be made known unto God" (Phil. 4:6), come to us today as a mighty call to a worthy prayer life. "Praying always with all prayer and supplication in the Spirit" (Eph. 6:18) was with him a large part of the Christian's armor. It was by prayer that he received salvation; escaped dangers; foiled his enemies; preached the gospel; built churches; sent out missionaries; opened cities, continents, and nations to the gospel; broke out of jails; and died a triumphant death.

Others and Prayer

Christian history in all ages is luminous with examples of the prayer life of spiritual heroes. Luther and Knox, reformers, prayed down the walls of caste and traditions and opened new empires to truth and righteousness. John Wesley and Finney, evangelists, started soul-saving movements and won men by the thousands. Their influence will last until the King comes again. They won by their prayers and faith. Charles H. Spurgeon and Dwight L. Moody, mighty preachers and institution-builders, by prayer wrought wonders in Christ's name. Broadus and Carroll, teachers, preachers, and leaders of men, by prayer and faith wrought in kingdom enterprises a work which will outlast the stars. Livingstone, Carey, Judson, and many other missionary heroes, by prayer opened doors of opportunity to the gospel in heathen lands, through which millions are coming to Christ. Prayer works wonders. The prayer life is a source of joy and power to winners incomparable to any other source.

Suggestions for Prayer

1. We should make much of secret prayer. Nothing should crowd it out. Nothing should be substituted for it.

2. We should have a special time for secret prayer. It should be made a habit and become as vital and as necessary as our meals.

3. We should seek to be in prayer groups with prayer-believing, devoted Christians. "If two of you shall agree on earth as touching any thing that they shall ask, it shall be done for them of my Father which is in heaven" (Matt. 18:19).

4. We should put away from our hearts everything which is a foe to our prayer life and power. "If I regard iniquity in my heart, the Lord will not hear me" (Psalm 66:18). "That your prayers be not hindered" (1 Peter 3:7) is Peter's caution to winners. We should put away from our lives—

(1) All compromise in conduct inconsistent with the high standards of Christian living set out by the New Testament.

(2) All worldliness and the pleasures which feed the carnal and hinder the spiritual.

(3) Every personal habit in thought, appetite, passion, word, or deed that slows up or bars the operation of divine grace and sanctification in our lives. "Put off . . . the old man" with all his ways (Eph. 4:20-32). Remember what God says about our bodies: "Know ye not that your body is the temple of the Holy Ghost which is in you?" (1 Cor. 6:19). God has a right to a clean and untarnished temple. We should not grow in our lives any of the "works of the flesh," as seen in Galatians 5:19-21.

(4) All spirit of unforgiveness. God will not hear us if we are unforgiving (Matt. 6:14-15; Eph. 4:32). Read carefully Ephesians 4:20-32.

5. We should encourage everything which will grow, strengthen, and enrich the prayer life. We should—

(1) Devotionally study God's Word, claiming the promises, feeding on the hidden manna.

(2) Read spiritual books, and study the biographies of God's men who have won in his kingdom.

(3) Seek the companionship of men and women of faith and piety, those who live close to God, many of whom live in quiet places unknown to the headlines of our papers, or are perhaps shut in by sickness or other limitations.

(4) Seek in every way possible to produce in the inner life the fruit of the Spirit, "love, joy, peace, longsuffering, gentleness, goodness, faith, meekness, temperance" (Gal. 5:22-23), and to crucify "the flesh with the affections and lusts" (Gal. 5:24). "Put on the new man, which after God is created in righteousness and true holiness" (Eph. 4:24).

6. We should have a prayer list—the names of the unsaved among our acquaintances or loved ones. These names should be carried, if not in a book, certainly in the memory; and a time should be given each day to special prayer for them. Some day God will say, "I have heard thy prayer, I have seen thy tears" (Isa. 38:5).

3

The Winner's Faith and Convictions

MATTHEW 15:28. Then Jesus answered and said unto her, O woman, great is thy faith: be it unto thee even as thou wilt. And her daughter was made whole from that very hour.

MARK 9:23. Jesus said unto him, If thou canst believe, all things are possible to him that believeth.

LUKE 5:4-5. Now when he had left speaking, he said unto Simon, Launch out into the deep, and let down your nets for a draught. And Simon answering said unto him, Master, we have toiled all the night, and have taken nothing: nevertheless at thy word I will let down the net.

ACTS 4:12. Neither is there salvation in any other: for there is none other name under heaven given among men, whereby we must be saved.

ACTS 4:19-20. But Peter and John answered and said unto them, Whether it be right in the sight of God to hearken unto you more than unto God, judge ye. For we cannot but speak the things which we have seen and heard.

ROMANS 1:16. For I am not ashamed of the gospel of Christ: for it is the power of God unto salvation to every one that believeth; to the Jew first, and also to the Greek.

GALATIANS 1:8. But though we, or an angel from heaven, preach any other gospel unto you than that which we have preached unto you, let him be accursed.

GALATIANS 2:20. I am crucified with Christ: nevertheless I live; yet not I, but Christ liveth in me: and the life which I now live in the flesh I live by the faith of the Son of God, who loved me, and gave himself for me.

EPHESIANS 4:11-15. And he gave some, apostles; and some, prophets; and some, evangelists; and some, pastors and teachers; for the perfecting of the saints, for the work of the ministry, for the edifying of the body of Christ: till we all come in the unity of the faith, and of the knowledge of the Son of God, unto a perfect man, unto the measure of the stature of the fulness of Christ: that we henceforth be no more children, tossed to and fro, and carried about with every wind of doctrine, by the sleight of men, and cunning craftiness, whereby they lie in wait to deceive; but speaking the truth in love, may grow up into him in all things, which is the head, even Christ.

2 TIMOTHY 1:12. For the which cause I also suffer these things: nevertheless I am not ashamed: for I know whom I have believed, and am persuaded that he is able to keep that which I have committed unto him against that day.

HEBREWS 11:6. But without faith it is impossible to please him: for he that cometh to God must believe that he is, and that he is a rewarder of them that diligently seek him.

THE SOUL-WINNER'S FAITH

Faith in God through Jesus Christ is not only the initial factor in obtaining life for the soul, but is also the mightiest lever of power for service. Without faith it is impossible to please God. Faith is the cup in which the begging lost soul receives life from God (John 1:12). It is the wire bearing to the soul the current of heavenly grace (Eph. 2:8). It is the key that unlocks God's treasures and granaries, and the spiritual guide which leads us into God's "green pastures" and "still waters." It leads into lands of peace and hidden fountains (Rom. 5:1). It is the outstretched hand of a sinner, which the big hand of our Heavenly Father takes to keep us from falling and fainting as we go the weary ways of the earthly life (Isa. 41:13). It is the delicate needle with which God vaccinates and sanctifies our souls against deadly sins and doubts.

It is God's spiritual tonic for character. It puts iron in the blood and steels the soul for battle. It made a Moses laugh at Pharaoh and at the barriers of sea and desert. It bridged swollen Jordans and demolished Jerichos for a Joshua, and held back setting suns that victory might crown his day while fighting God's battles. It took the rage out of lions' dens and made them safe places for a Daniel. It took the destroying elements out of fire when the Hebrew children stood true to their God. It made heroes like John the Baptist, Paul, Luther, Knox, and thousands of others. With it weaklings are conquerors, and without it giants are pygmies. It is a divine necessity to all who would win for God. "This is the victory that overcometh the world, even our faith" (1 John 5:4). "The people that do know their God shall be strong, and do exploits" (Dan. 11:32).

If our faith is to make us conquerors, it must possess certain spiritual ingredients.

It must be reliant. "Commit thy way unto the Lord; trust also in him; and he shall bring it to pass" (Psalm 37:5). We must depend with a holy and trustful reliance on God's strength if we are to become great winners. An invalid spiritual motherhood will bear deformed or weak children. Paul's stronghold in evangelism was, "I . . . am persuaded that he is able to keep that which I have committed unto him against that day" (2 Tim. 1:12).

It must be unstaggering. "He [Abraham] staggered not at the promise of God through unbelief; but was strong in faith, giving glory to God" (Rom. 4:20). "Without doubt" is the key to God's promises.

It must persist in the face of God's denials and delays. The Gentile mother pressed her case and won her daughter's deliverance from the devil by persistent faith. Christ and the disciples rebuked her time and time again, but she worshiped and in remarkable humility trustfully pressed her suit until Christ said, "O woman, great is thy faith: be it unto thee even as thou wilt" (Matt. 15:28).

It must look above difficulties at God and know that he is greater than their number, size, or combinations. Moses did this at the Red Sea. Elijah did it at Mount Carmel with Ahab. Paul did it in facing the devil's emissaries wherever he went. You and I must do it if we are to win lost souls to Christ.

It must remember God's hidden resources and count his promises at heaven's valuation of them. God has manna never yet distributed, quails never yet sent out of his poultry yard, and fountains never yet opened to his thirsty Israel. God has recruits for all his armies. Elisha showed God's other army to his servant at Dothan, his squadron of "angel airplanes" at the order of faith (2 Kings 6:13-18). God never broke a promise, and there is no record where a promise ever failed to be fulfilled if faith gripped it.

It must remember its true and only source of supply. Let us look "unto Jesus the author and finisher of our faith" (Heb. 12:2). Peter's miraculous walk on the water failed when he took his eyes off Jesus (Matt. 14:28-31). So will our faith fail if we do not constantly feed on him. "They drank of that spiritual Rock that followed them: and that Rock was Christ" (1 Cor. 10:4). Christ is faith's manna and meat (John 6:48-58).

The Soul-Winner's Convictions

In the work of winning men to Christ there are certain fundamental doctrines to which every winner should heartily subscribe and which should become an essential part of his spiritual machinery. He should become "rooted and grounded" in the basic principles of the gospel. Some of these are as follows:

1. *The deity of Christ.*—Christ is God's Son (Matt. 16:16-17; Luke 1:35, 42-43); he is the brightness of God's glory, the express image of God's person, very God of very God, the visible image of the invisible God (Heb. 1:3). We should accept his eternal existence (John 1:1-5), his virgin birth (Luke 1:26-37), his divine authority (John 20:21), and his heavenly messiahship (Luke 2:11). A deep spiritual grasp of these doctrines is necessary to an effective evangelism.

2. *The saving efficacy of his blood.*—We must confidently trust in his saving atonement as a means of our salvation and cleansing. "He was wounded for our transgressions, he was bruised for our iniquities: the chastisement of our

peace was upon him; and with his stripes we are healed" (Isa. 53:5). ". . . who his own self bare our sins in his own body on the tree, that we, being dead to sins, should live unto righteousness: by whose stripes ye were healed" (1 Peter 2:24). "Neither by the blood of goats and calves, but by his own blood he entered in once into the holy place, having obtained eternal redemption for us" (Heb. 9:12). "In whom we have redemption through his blood, the forgiveness of sins, according to the riches of his grace" (Eph. 1:7). "Unto him that loved us, and washed us from our sins in his own blood, and hath made us kings and priests unto God and his Father; to him be glory and dominion for ever and ever" (Rev. 1:5-6). Paul's ringing testimonies should be those of every soul-winner: "God forbid that I should glory, save in the cross of our Lord Jesus Christ, by whom the world is crucified unto me, and I unto the world" (Gal. 6:14), and "I determined not to know any thing among you, save Jesus Christ, and him crucified" (1 Cor. 2:2).

3. *Salvation by grace, without works of any kind.*—The winner needs to be right on the plan of salvation. This is basic. Salvation is by grace through faith plus nothing. "For by grace are ye saved through faith; and that not of yourselves: it is the gift of God: not of works, lest any man should boast. For we are his workmanship, created in Christ Jesus" (Eph. 2:8-10). ". . . being justified freely by his grace through the redemption that is in Christ Jesus" (Rom. 3:24). "Not by works of righteousness which we have done, but according to his mercy he saved us, by the washing of regeneration, and renewing of the Holy Ghost" (Titus 3:5). The conditions of this grace are repentance (Acts 3:19; 17:30; 19:4; 20:21) and faith (John 1:12; 3:16-36; 5:24).

4. *The sinful nature of man, the peril of his lost condition, and the impending doom awaiting him.*—Men are by nature children of wrath (Eph. 2:3) and of Satan (John 8:44; Acts

13:10). They are conceived in sin and born in iniquity, and have all gone astray from the womb (Psalm 51:5; 58:3). Because of personal sin they are lost to God, hope, and righteousness, without Christ and without God, until they repent and believe (Luke 19:10; Eph. 2:12). They are under wrath (John 3:36), condemned (John 3:18), alien enemies of God (Rom. 5:10), and slaves of unrighteousness (Rom. 6:17-20). They are imperiled by eternal death and hell every hour after they come to the years of accountability until they are saved or die. They stand on "slippery ways in the darkness" (Jer. 23:12), with hell moving to meet them at their coming (Isa. 14:9). And God says, "Their foot shall slide in due time: for the day of their calamity is at hand, and the things that shall come upon them make haste" (Deut. 32:35).

That there is an eternal punishment waiting the impenitent and unbelieving is as sure as anything can be sure. To deny this is to traduce all revealed truth, repudiate God's Word, and deny the deity of Christ himself. Job said, "Do ye not know their tokens, that the wicked is reserved to the day of destruction? they shall be brought forth to the day of wrath" (Job 21:29-30). David said, "The wicked shall be turned into hell, and all the nations that forget God" (Psalm 9:17). Isaiah said, "Hell from beneath is moved for thee to meet thee at thy coming" (Isa. 14:9). Daniel said, "And many of them that sleep in the dust of the earth shall awake, some to everlasting life, and some to shame and everlasting contempt" (Dan. 12:2). Paul said that the Lord Jesus is coming, "in flaming fire taking vengeance on them that know not God, and that obey not the gospel of our Lord Jesus Christ: who shall be punished with everlasting destruction from the presence of the Lord, and from the glory of his power" (2 Thess. 1:8-9).

Peter said, "The Lord knoweth how to deliver the godly out of temptations, and to reserve the unjust unto the day of judgment to be punished" (2 Peter 2:9). John said, "But the fearful, and unbelieving, and the abominable, and murderers, and whoremongers, and sorcerers, and idolaters, and all liars, shall have their part in the lake which burneth with fire and brimstone: which is the second death" (Rev. 21:8). Jesus Christ, on his divine authority, says: "Depart from me, ye cursed, into everlasting fire, prepared for the devil and his angels," and "These shall go away into everlasting punishment: but the righteous into life eternal" (Matt. 25:41, 46). "He that believeth on the Son hath everlasting life: and he that believeth not the Son shall not see life; but the wrath of God abideth on him" (John 3:36). Christ tells the tragic story of the unsaved man's destiny in Luke 16:19-31.

5. *The inspiration of the Bible.*—The Bible is "God-breathed," the infallible Word of God concerning man, binding in its authority upon the conscience and conduct of every man. It will never fail, and on its truth alone the world is to be reconstructed. "All scripture is given by inspiration of God" (2 Tim. 3:16). "Holy men of God spake as they were moved by the Holy Ghost" (2 Peter 1:21). The proofs of the divine authorship and binding authority of God's Word are overwhelming, and should be accepted and believed by everyone desirous of winning souls. The Word of God is the sword of the Spirit (Eph. 6:17); and if you wish to have the power of the Spirit, you must accept his weapon.

6. *The obligation of Christ's command to go into all the world to win men.*—The soul-winner must feel in the depths of his soul Christ's call for time and talent (Matt. 28:18-20; John 20:21; Acts 1:8). Lack of conviction or obedience here will limit power in winning men to Christ.

7. *Our Lord's second advent.*—The soul-winner need not worry over the times and seasons of Christ's second coming, for Christ says no man or angel, nor the Son himself, knows when he will come again (Mark 13:32; Acts 1:7; 2 Thess. 2:1-2). But we should pray for, watch for, and love his appearing, and ever be ready ourselves, and get everybody

else we possibly can ready for his coming (Matt. 24:42-46; Luke 21:34-36; 2 Tim. 4:8).

8. *The Holy Spirit.*—In the power of the Holy Spirit alone can we hope to win.

These doctrines—of the deity of Christ, the saving efficacy of his blood, salvation by grace, the sinful nature of man and his lost condition, the divine inspiration of the Bible, the obligation of the Great Commission, the second coming of Christ, and the Holy Spirit—ought to be most heartily believed by everyone wishing to be a winner of men.

4.

The Winner's Compassion

PSALM 106:23. Therefore he said that he would destroy them, had not Moses his chosen stood before him in the breach, to turn away his wrath, lest he should destroy them.

PSALM 126:5-6. They that sow in tears shall reap in joy. He that goeth forth and weepeth, bearing precious seed, shall doubtless come again with rejoicing, bringing his sheaves with him.

ISAIAH 58:10. And if thou draw out thy soul to the hungry, and satisfy the afflicted soul; then shall thy light rise in obscurity, and thy darkness be as the noon day.

ISAIAH 66:8. Who hath heard such a thing? who hath seen such things? Shall the earth be made to bring forth in one day? or shall a nation be born at once? for as soon as Zion travailed, she brought forth her children.

EZEKIEL 22:30-31. And I sought for a man among them, that should make up the hedge, and stand in the gap before me for the land, that I should not destroy it: but I found none. Therefore have I poured out mine indignation upon them; I have consumed them with the fire of my wrath: their own way have I recompensed upon their heads, saith the Lord God.

MATTHEW 9:36. But when he saw the multitudes, he was moved with compassion on them, because they fainted, and were scattered abroad, as sheep having no shepherd.

MATTHEW 14:14. And Jesus went forth, and saw a great multitude, and was moved with compassion toward them, and he healed their sick.

LUKE 15:20. And he arose, and came to his father. But when he was yet a great way off, his father saw him, and had compassion, and ran, and fell on his neck, and kissed him.

LUKE 19:41. And when he was come near, he beheld the city, and wept over it.

JOHN 3:16. For God so loved the world, that he gave his only begotten Son, that whosoever believeth in him should not perish, but have everlasting life.

Acts 20:31. Therefore watch, and remember, that by the space of three years I ceased not to warn every one night and day with tears.

Romans 9:1-3. I say the truth in Christ, I lie not, my conscience also bearing me witness in the Holy Ghost, that I have great heaviness and continual sorrow in my heart. For I could wish that myself were accursed from Christ for my brethren, my kinsmen according to the flesh.

The Need for Compassion

The preceding verses reveal to us the heart of the Three in the Godhead. The Father loves us and gave us his best, his only Son. The Saviour wept with longing compassion and died a cruel death on the cross for us. The Spirit intercedes for us through unutterable groanings. The psalmist said we must weep if we would win. The prophet Isaiah said we will rise out of obscurity and be watered gardens if we draw out our souls to the lost and needy. The apostle Paul, weeping over a lost city for three years, said he had great heaviness and continual sorrow in his heart and was willing to be accursed that his brethren might be saved. Moses, the lawgiver and leader, stood in the breach between the people and God's wrath, and saved them from the consequences of their sins. In Ezekiel 22:30, God searched for someone to stand in the gap before him lest he should destroy the land. But he failed to find any; so he poured out his indignation and the fires of his wrath. No prophet or priest with compassion!

In Ezekiel 34:1-19, God made awful charges against the shepherds of his people: "Ye eat the fat, and ye clothe you with the wool, ye kill them that are fed: but ye feed not the flock. The diseased have ye not strengthened, neither have ye healed that which was sick, neither have ye bound up that which was broken, neither have ye brought again that which was driven away, neither have ye sought that which was lost" (vv. 3-4). Then he said, "Behold, I am against the shepherds; and I will require my flock at their hand, and cause them to cease from feeding the flock" (v. 10). He added with burning words, "I will seek that which was lost" (v. 16). He sought the lost through the life, death, and ministry of Jesus Christ, and through the centuries he has continued to seek them by the persistent calls of the Holy Spirit and by the efforts of his people.

A compassionless Christianity drifts into ceremonialism and formalism. Our greatest need now is for a compassionate leadership in the Christian movements of the world. Every niche of this lost world needs the ministry of a fired soul, burning and shining with the zeal and conviction of a conquering gospel. Spiritual dry rot is worse for the churches of Jesus Christ than the plagues were for Egypt and the simooms are for the Sahara. Many a minister is on a treadmill, marking time, drying up, not earning his salt, because he has no passion for souls and no power for effective service. May our God kindle holy fires of evangelism in all churches and pulpits where such is needed!

The Food for Compassion

How can our hearts be stirred and aroused with a heavenly enthusiasm for God and souls? The answer is found in certain heart foods.

1. *An insight into the inner and spiritual meaning of the Word of God.*—Study God's Word. Delve into the riches of grace, the manna of the soul. Somehow you must go to the juicy roots of revelation. You must go in for the sweets and fats of the Word.

2. *A constant contemplation of God and his mercies.*— Seek God's face and favor in quiet hours.

3. *A constant companionship with Christ and the Holy Spirit.*—Travel the "Emmaus road" with Christ, continually seeking the power of the Holy Spirit.

4. *Secret prayer.*—Develop a life-habit of prayer. Passion for souls grows in the heart in hours of communion with God.

5. *A persistent effort in soul-winning.*—Nothing grows spiritual muscle and consequent motive like "winning work." Winning one person creates the hunger for more, and on it goes, until the soul-winner is consumed with a burning passion to win others to Jesus Christ.

6. *Contact with great soul-winners.*—Association with great soul-winners, in person or through books, will stimulate your own compassion of heart. Eternity alone will tell the full story of the influence of Paul, of Spurgeon, of Moody, in creating the soul-winning hunger in others.

7. *A constant realization of the meaning of spiritual ambassadorship.*—We hold a trusteeship, are under a holy debtorship, and carry from our God a spiritual guardianship for lost souls (Ezek. 33:7-11; Rom. 1:14; 2 Cor. 5:20). Realize that your neglect may cause some soul to lose heaven and bring you to judgment with his blood on your hands. Do not be unfaithful to such a responsibility and duty. Does not the grace of God in your own heart now send out an inexpressible longing of soul to see others come to Christ? Cultivate this hunger.

8. *A true evaluation of the worth and destiny of the soul out of Christ.*—We must see the unsaved in the light in which Christ saw them when he died for them. The knowledge of their doom ought to speed in our hearts the flow of spiritual passion for them. The saving of one soul is worth more than the making of a Magna Charta for a thousand worlds. Put Christ's value on men, and you will long to see them right with God.

The Results of Compassion

If there flow into our beings the tides of compassion, we will soon and constantly see some meaningful results.

We will grow in the knowledge and grace of God. We will rapidly make for the mark of the high calling in Christ Jesus, and more and more approach the stature of the perfect man. We will see and apprehend the boundless dimensions of the love of God and come more and more to possess the power of the resurrection life (Eph. 3:16-20).

We will have an abundance of the "overflow life." We will no longer be "bottle Christians," but "flowing river Christians." From within us will flow rivers of living water (John 7:37-39). Christ came to give us life more abundantly (John 10:10).

A restfulness of spirit will characterize our service for Christ. The peace of God which passeth all understanding, the "perfect peace" which comes from the "mind stayed on" him, will bring its joys and cast out all the fret and worry (Isa. 26:3; Phil. 4:7).

Compassion will deepen the desire and appreciation for the happy, sacrificial life. Calvaries and Gethsemanes will be wings instead of weights, and we will joy to "suffer with him" and to give our best and most priceless to his service— whether it be ourselves, our money, our talents, or our children.

Compassion will generate power. The soul that knows the passion of Calvary is sure to experience a Pentecost (Isa. 58:10-14).

This inner longing for the lost will drive us out into fruitful service. The heart that yearns and burns to see men come to Christ will know no idleness in the kingdom. This compassion will surely fruit in successful soul-winning.

5

The Winner's Heavenly Unction

MICAH 3:8. But truly I am full of power by the spirit of the Lord, and of judgment, and of might, to declare unto Jacob his transgression, and to Israel his sin.

ZECHARIAH 4:6. Then he answered and spake unto me, saying, This is the word of the Lord unto Zerubbabel, saying, Not by might, nor by power, but by my spirit, saith the Lord of hosts.

LUKE 11:13. If ye then, being evil, know how to give good gifts unto your children: how much more shall your heavenly Father give the Holy Spirit to them that ask him?

LUKE 24:49. And, behold, I send the promise of my Father upon you: but tarry ye in the city of Jerusalem, until ye be endued with power from on high.

JOHN 7:38-39. He that believeth on me, as the scripture hath said, out of his belly shall flow rivers of living water. (But this spake he of the Spirit, which they that believe on him should receive: for the Holy Ghost was not yet given; because that Jesus was not yet glorified.)

JOHN 14:16-17. And I will pray the Father, and he shall give you another Comforter, that he may abide with you for ever; even the Spirit of truth; whom the world cannot receive, because it seeth him not, neither knoweth him: but ye know him; for he dwelleth with you, and shall be in you.

JOHN 20:22. And when he had said this, he breathed on them, and saith unto them, Receive ye the Holy Ghost.

ACTS 1:8. But ye shall receive power, after that the Holy Ghost is come upon you: and ye shall be witnesses unto me both in Jerusalem, and in all Judaea, and in Samaria, and unto the uttermost part of the earth.

ACTS 2:38-39. Then Peter said unto them, Repent, and be baptized every one of you in the name of Jesus Christ for the remission of sins, and ye shall receive the gift of the Holy Ghost. For the promise is unto you, and to your children, and to all that are afar off, even as many as the Lord our God shall call.

Acts 5:32. And we are his witnesses of these things; and so is also the Holy Ghost, whom God hath given to them that obey him.

Ephesians 5:18. And be not drunk with wine, wherein is excess; but be filled with the Spirit.

1 Thessalonians 5:19. Quench not the Spirit.

1 John 2:20. But ye have an unction from the Holy One, and ye know all things.

Work of the Holy Spirit

In every move we make toward and for Christ we are dependent on the operation of the Holy Spirit. If we are to win men to Jesus, we must get in with, and keep up with, the divine Paraclete.

1. He calls us to eternal life. "The Spirit and the bride say, Come" (Rev. 22:17).

2. He convinces and convicts of sin, righteousness, judgment, and unbelief (John 16:8-11).

3. It is evidently he that draws us to the Father (John 6:44).

4. He teaches and guides into truth (John 14:26; 16:13). He testifies of Christ (John 15:26) and shows us the things of Christ (John 16:14).

5. He makes alive the dead but penitent soul through the grace of God (Eph. 2:1, 5).

6. He is the divine agent (John 3:5-7; Titus 3:5), and Christ the divine substance (Rom. 5:10), of eternal life.

7. He sheds abroad in our hearts the love of God (Rom. 5:5).

8. He is God's agent in our justification and sanctification (1 Cor. 6:11; 2 Thess. 2:13; 1 Peter 1:2).

9. He puts the divine seal on our spiritual sonship (Eph. 4:30) and gives the constant witness of our acceptance with God (Rom. 8:16). It is by the marks of his leadership that we are to demonstrate to the world that we are Christ's (Rom. 8:14).

10. Our daily victories over the flesh and the devil are to be won through his power (Rom. 8:13), and we are to look to him for strength in the inner man (Eph. 3:16).

11. He is the heavenly instrumentality through whom our mortal bodies are to be made alive and brought back from the grave (Rom. 8:11).

12. It is he who intercedes for us in our prayers and tasks (Rom. 8:26).

13. He is our comforter in sorrow (John 14:16-18).

14. He is our power in praying, testifying, preaching, teaching, and otherwise winning men to Christ (Zech. 4:6; Matt. 28:18-20; Luke 24:49; Acts 1:8; Eph. 6:18).

Our dependence on the Holy Spirit is absolute and complete.

Manifestation of the Holy Spirit

He has promised to go before us (Isa. 45:2), behind us (Isa. 58:8), beneath us (Deut. 33:27), with us (Matt. 28:20), within us (John 14:17), upon us (Acts 1:8), and all around us (Matt. 3:11). The word "Paraclete" means one standing beside us. He has promised to hold us with the right hand of his righteousness (Isa. 41:10) and never to let us fall (John 10:27-28; Jude 24).

Conditions for Receiving the Holy Spirit

The Spirit's power is an absolute necessity in winning men to Christ. "Not by might, nor by power, but by my spirit, saith the Lord of hosts" (Zech. 4:6)—this law is written in large letters in all the history of evangelism. There are no substitutes for the power of the Spirit. Personality—stirring, attractive, winsome personality—is of much value in influencing men, but it is no substitute for the Spirit's power. Eloquence and charm of voice in song or speech may sweep men off their feet temporarily, but it takes the power of God to win them from their sins and regenerate them. Profound learning and great scholarship are of great value in intelligently bringing men to Christ and building up his glorious kingdom on earth; yet these are not substitutes for the power of God. "The Spirit of God has an affinity for a trained mind." Culture and a graciousness of manner can greatly aid us in our heavenly task of bringing men to a full knowledge of Christ, but these must not be regarded as sufficient in themselves. They must be vitalized and breathed through and through with the dynamic of the Third Person of the Trinity.

Certain spiritual conditions must be met if we are to be endued with this power. They constitute the price we must pay for this divine infilling.

1. *A spiritual apprehension, an intellectual comprehension, and an inner appropriation, of the Word of God.*—We must have more than a scholarly knowledge of the Word of God. It is possible to know what it says, understand its original languages, be familiar with its history, its philosophy, and its prophecies, and yet not have a spiritual concept of its inner dynamic. We must feed on it. We should know just what it says and means, and possess a spiritual grip upon its glories. God's Word burns, hammers, penetrates, cuts, divides, makes alive, and lives (Jer. 23:29; Hos. 6:5; Heb. 4:12). We should be familiar with all the truth of God if we would have the Spirit of God and use the sword of the Spirit in service for men.

2. *An obedience to the whole will of God.*—God's redemptive program must be adopted by our souls, and our part in that plan cheerfully accepted (Acts 5:32). We must go further than an obedience to his will. We must know in our deepest spiritual natures a divine mastery. "The Spirit of God clothed itself with Gideon" (Judg. 6:34 ASV marg.), preceding and conditioning his great victory with the immortal three hundred.

3. *An inner, psychic enthronement of Jesus Christ as Lord and Master.*—Christ must sit on his rightful throne in our hearts, and self must be daily crucified, if we would see

his power in our service. Christ delights to give power in the heart where he has been glorified.

4. *A compassion for men out of Christ.*—The soul that longs for men's salvation will, by that very fact, be clothed with the power from God with which to win them to Christ (Isa. 58:10-12). In the proportion that we care for men's souls we will cry for God's power to win them.

5. *Earnest and persistent prayer and supplication for this power of the Spirit* (Luke 11:13).—We are not only to receive the Holy Ghost, but we are to pray for his enduing power (Luke 24:49; Acts 1:14; 2:1, 42). Prayer opens our hearts, submits us to God's will, and fixes our souls so that the Spirit can fill us with power. God's anxiety to give us his Spirit (Luke 11:13) does not do away with the necessity for our prayers for this power. God has definitely promised a Pentecost of soul-winning power to Christ's disciples, but the promise does not abolish, or make unnecessary, spiritual tarrying in prayer precedent to this Pentecost. We must pray in order to have the fulfilment of the Father's promise of power. Pentecosts do not come to prayerless Christians.

6. *A willingness to partake of the afflictions and sacrifices of the gospel.*—We must be willing to endure all the hardships and sacrifices incident to the will and way of God for our lives.

Power of the Holy Spirit

When we possess the unction of the Holy Ghost, it makes a difference in everything about us. It lubricates all the inner machinery of life. It removes much of the friction, worry, fret, and fear. It increases tenfold our spiritual efficiency, our opportunities, and the results of our labor. It multiplies our joy in service. Preaching, teaching, and testifying are easier and sweeter. Waiting crowds will fill the vacant pews, the lost will flock to our ministry, and a thousand opportunities will open to us. Unction is a necessity in Christ's cause. Let us pay heaven's price for this great power.

Filled with the Holy Spirit

"Be filled with the Spirit," is the command of the risen Saviour, whose Father is far more willing to give the Spirit to us than we are to give good gifts to our children (Luke 11:13). This imperative is—

1. A prayer to be offered (Luke 11:13; Acts 4:31).
2. A command to be obeyed (Eph. 5:18).
3. A promise to be claimed (John 16:7; Acts 1:8).
4. A gift to be received (John 20:22; Acts 2:38).
5. A life to be volunteered (Psalm 110:3).
6. A Christ to be enthroned (John 7:39).

Pray, obey, claim, receive, volunteer, enthrone Christ, go forth to win in his power; and Pentecost will mark your way.

Part Two

SOME INSPIRING EXAMPLES

6

The Matchless Winner

Christ Jesus

> LUKE 19:10. For the Son of man is come to seek and to save that which was lost.

Jesus Christ is distinctly the world's chief soul-winner and evangelist. He came "to seek and save that which was lost" (Luke 19:10). His example will be the standard for all time for all who seek to bring men to God: "Follow me, and I will make you fishers of men" (Matt. 4:19). Our guarantee of success is found in our appropriation of his methods. To all evangelists he says, "Follow me."

A brief study of this peerless evangelist will be profitable.

1. Prophecy set him out as one who would win souls (Isa. 59:20; 62:11; Zech. 9:9; 13:1; Matt. 1:21).

2. An early group witnessed to his messiahship: (1) Mary and Elizabeth, (2) the angels and shepherds, (3) Anna and Simeon, and (4) the Wise Men of the East.

3. The forerunner introduced him as the evangelist of the new day.

4. All hell put forth its utmost to prevent his successful entrance on his campaign.

5. His first public act—baptism at John's hands—announced him as one approving this new ordinance, the evangelist's sign of a soul-winning victory.

6. He began his role of evangelist by starting out Andrew as a soul-winner, and by himself winning Philip and sending him out to win Nathanael.

7. Then for three years in public sermon, quiet teaching, and in personal, face-to-face dealing with men about their

souls, Jesus set all the world an example in evangelism. Philip, Nicodemus, Zaccheus, Bartimeus, the Samaritan woman, Pharisees, scribes, priests, soldiers, publicans, men and women, children and young people, testified to his power to win and save. He sought and saved the lost everywhere, day and night. He sought out men and women of all classes and conditions until a world's sin crucified him.

His Ideal Marks of Evangelism

Jesus' evangelism was characterized by—
1. A holy, sinless life.
2. Knowledge of God and complete surrender to his will.
3. A realization of man's condition, need, helplessness, and impending doom.
4. Limitless compassion for a ruined race, as shown by (1) his words of love and mercy, (2) his life of unselfish service, (3) his tireless and unremitting ministry, (4) his broken heart over the sinning, and (5) his sacrificial death.
5. Intercessory and importunate prayer.
6. An artful, tactful method in reaching men.
7. Enduement without measure by the Spirit of God.

His Preaching

Some of the winning characteristics of Jesus' preaching were:
1. Simplicity.—He utilized everyday illustrations, spoke in simple but pungent words.
2. Positiveness and divine authority.
3. Heart-searching, conviction-bringing power.
4. Abundance of fundamental doctrine and principle.
5. Supreme tenderness and love, often mingled with scathing, blistering denunciation for the hypocrite.
6. Direct and personal reach.
7. Unfailing appeal to the highest in man.

His Personal Work

1. Jesus used both direct and indirect methods of reaching men with the truth.

2. He was always tender with those who recognized themselves as being sinners. His scathing denunciations were turned loose on hypocrites.

3. Instead of directly accusing the unsaved, he usually led them to a confession of their sins, as in the case of the Samaritan woman in John 4.

4. He always refused to be sidetracked from the main matters of the soul by discussion of difficult theological matters, as seen when he dealt with Nicodemus in John 3 and with the Samaritan woman in John 4.

5. His method of illustration and impartation of truth was from the natural to the spiritual, from the simple to the complex. This is shown in his dealings with Nicodemus, the cultured moralist, and with the Samaritan woman, the fallen outcast.

6. Both to the wise, cultured, and scholarly, and to the ignorant and desperately wicked, he taught the profoundest and most complex doctrine and principle, as shown in the case of Nichodemus, to whom he first taught the doctrine of the new birth, and of the Samaritan woman, to whom he revealed the necessity of a spiritual conception of his kingdom.

7. He was never vague or indefinite about the nature, guilt, and direful consequences of sin, and the necessity of a divine regeneration, a deep work of grace, in the heart. There was no veneer or whitewash in his teachings on man's moral condition before God. He had one gospel for all—repentance and faith, the sure and only way to eternal life.

8. He put baptism and church membership in their proper places, as the simple duty of every disciple, immediately following regeneration and public profession (Matt. 28:18-20).

9. He put teaching and instruction in spiritual and kingdom matters in an important place in all evangelism, as a

necessity for growth in grace, for development of character, and for usefulness in his service.

10. The methods he would have us use were strongly demonstrated in his earthly ministry. To large and small audiences he preached sweeping sermons, bringing men into his kingdom. In private and personal approach he faced men and women one by one with the holy truths of life and death. Blind Bartimeus by the roadside, curious Zaccheus up a tree, scholarly Nicodemus in the quietness of night in an upper room, the scarlet woman by the well curb —these and many others can testify to Christ's marvelous tact as a personal soul-winner. He was a "highway and hedges" preacher; he was a quiet seeker after souls.

11. He was a tremendously sincere and compassionate evangelist. His tears and sorrowing for the lost have come down to us, not his jokes and wit and humor. He rightly valued souls in all their eternal relations and went straight after them with Gethsemanes of agony and Calvaries of blood. His soul ached to the dying for lost men. He spared not himself; he emptied himself and brought men to God by his own blood on the cross. His tears on Olivet and in the garden are the insignia of his broken heart for a ruined world. The ministry needs to follow his example. "They that sow in tears shall reap in joy."

7

The Apostle of Holy Fires

John the Baptist

JOHN 5:35. He was a burning and a shining light: and ye were willing for a season to rejoice in his light.

The writers of the Gospels picture John the Baptist as a country preacher of strange birth, a mountain man raised in the Judean hills, fed on locusts and wild honey.

John was a preacher, evangelist, and prophet. In denunciation of hypocrisy his voice was the thunder of God's dynamics, yet it was soft and tender when in love he called the sorrowing sinner to faith in the coming Christ. He was God-sent and Spirit-filled. His pulpit was the mountains of Judea; his auditorium was the valleys and vaulted sky; his audiences were the crowds of all sorts—publicans, sinners, Pharisees, scribes, Sadducees, soldiers, and people from city, plain, and mountains. Kings and governors came to listen and went away to fear. He was great in tenderness; lionlike in boldness; simple, pungent, convincing in speech; powerful like a storm from Lebanon's snowy summits. He was no sissy, no compromiser, no apologist. He was God's big preacher and prophet of a new day and of a coming kingdom of heaven.

His was a strange and new message—sin, repentance, faith, confession; God's Messiah-Lamb ready for the sacrifice; and baptism as a demonstration of one's purpose to live a new life, carrying a new doctrine of redemption by death, arched with resurrection hope and Holy Ghost power. He brought in a new day for dying men. That day has grown brighter ever since.

His ministry was a short one—six or twenty-four months—but, oh, how meaningful to the world's destiny! He overturned the traditions of centuries. He brought multitudes to the Light of life and introduced the Light of the ages to men everywhere. One of the saddest tragedies in all spiritual history was his death at the hands of a drunken king to gratify the desires of an enraged, adulterous woman.

His Heavenly Commission

He was a Spirit-filled soul-winner, sent by God—
1. To make ready a people to receive the Redeemer.
2. To turn the hearts of the fathers to the children and of the children to the fathers.
3. To introduce the world's Saviour.

His Evangelistic Characteristics

As an evangelist, he was characterized by—
1. Simplicity in dress, manner, life, method, thought, and words.
2. Honesty in life and truth to self, men, and God.
3. Humility.—He was willing to decrease that Christ might increase. He was in humility unworthy to unlatch Christ's shoes, but powerful enough in personality and ministry to empty the cities when he preached in the wilderness of Judea.
4. Spiritual courage.—He feared only God's disapproval. He told kings of their sins and faced soldiers and high ecclesiastics with their wrongdoings.
5. Burning and shining messages.—His sermons were hot with holy fires.

His Doctrines

His preaching was filled with the vital doctrines afterward so wonderfully brought out in the Gospels:
1. Sin—deep-dyed, hell-deserving sin.
2. Repentance—genuine, soul-moving, heart-cleansing,

life-purifying repentance, carrying with it fruit in life and conduct.

3. Faith in Christ as the only hope—trustful, reliant, confident faith.

4. The deity of Jesus.—To John he was God.

5. Baptism in water as a public proclamation of repentance from sin and the initial step in a new life of service for God.

6. The atonement.—He called Christ God's Lamb.

7. A holy infilling and enduement of the Spirit for world-conquering service.

His Greatness

These elements made him a great evangelist:

1. God's call and the Spirit's leadership.
2. A life of separation from sin and of supplication to, and communion with, God.
3. An unselfish humility and a fearless courage.
4. A mighty spiritual grip upon the vital truth of God.
5. A faithful proclamation of the gospel.
6. An unchanging, soulful yearning for lost men, which made him face any peril and endure any sacrifice in order to win them to God.
7. A life filled with, and used by, the Spirit of God.—He had yielded to God's leadership in earliest childhood, and he stayed in the Father's mastery until his head was carried to the sinning queen on a platter.

John taught that life, in its eternal bearings and meanings, does not consist in meat, drink, clothes, place, earthly honor, or space of years. It consists in doing God's will in God's place and through God's power. A life wholly given to God in soul-winning in the hills of Judea in a remote age has cast a golden glory and given a radiant hope to all subsequent history. Jesus said that John, the simple, country Baptist preacher, was the greatest born of women. By God's assize, a country preacher leads humanity's greatness. He introduced the Saviour to a ruined world and pointed men to him. The first man among men, thank God, is the soul-winner. Introduce the same Saviour, point sinners to him, preach the same gospel in the power of the divine Spirit, and you will walk the way of divine favor and glory.

8

The Pentecostal Preacher

Simon Peter

Acts 2:38. Then Peter said unto them, Repent, and be baptized every one of you in the name of Jesus Christ for the remission of sins, and ye shall receive the gift of the Holy Ghost.

Simon Peter is world-famed as an evangelist. His fame was made eternal and secure by one sermon and one day's evangelism. He was the head spokesman for the most wonderful group of men who ever lived—the apostles of Jesus Christ.

Elements of character were mixed strangely in Peter. He was simple and yet complex in his make-up. No one ever knew when he would break out in a new place. He cowered before a Jewish lass in his denial of Christ, and yet faced without a tremor an angry mob of ecclesiastics when his soul was set in the power of the Holy Spirit. He faced an infuriated gang of crucifiers with his single sword at one moment, and a little later played the coward when facing his duty to the deserted Saviour. He was a commoner in Christian discipleship. His thinking and life were close to the common needs of men.

He was an uncouth, untrained, untutored fisherman of the waters of Galilee until his brother Andrew showed him the Christ. He trusted and committed himself to Jesus on the spot the first time he saw him. He was called, and he yielded as one of the very first apostles. He was with Christ as a privileged disciple unto the end. He was a witness to his miracles and an auditor of his sermons, teachings, and parables. He was present at Lazarus' resurrection, the transfiguration, the Gethsemane tragedy, and the crucifixion, and was one of the first witnesses of the resurrection. He was present at nearly all of Christ's postresurrection appearances. He witnessed Christ's ascension and heard the last commission, and got the last word of the angels in white after the Saviour had gone. He was at the election of Judas' successor as an apostle and at the ordination of the seven deacons. He led Cornelius to Christ and brought in a Gentile dispensation. He was the friend and helper of the great apostle to the Gentiles.

But Peter's greatest distinction is that he was the evangelist of Pentecost. God chose him as the central human figure in the most momentous day in Christ's churches after Christ's own resurrection. He preached the first sermon in the world under the vicegerency of the divine Spirit. John the Baptist introduced Jesus, and Peter introduced the Holy Spirit, to a lost world.

His Life's Crises

1. His conversion and call—the evangelist saved and sent (John 1:35-42; Matt. 4:18-22; Mark 3:13-16).

2. His vision of Christ's messiahship—the evangelist instructed and humbled (Matt. 16:13-23; John 6:66-69).

3. His unsuccessful effort to walk on the sea—the evangelist tested (Matt. 14:28-31).

4. Christ's transfiguration—the evangelist seeing the Redeemer's glory (Matt. 17:1-13; Mark 9:2-13; Luke 9:28-36; 2 Peter 1:16-18).

5. His fall and backsliding—the evangelist realizing his weakness (Matt. 26:58-75; Mark 14:54-72; Luke 22:54-62; John 18:15-27).

6. His restoration to Christ's favor—the evangelist appropriating his only hope of usefulness (Luke 24:34; John 21:1-23).

7. Pentecost—the evangelist endued for service (Acts 2:14-41).

8. His persecutions—the evangelist strengthened for further battles (Acts 4:1-22; 5:17-20; 12:1-9).

9. His experience at Joppa and with Cornelius—the evangelist getting a vision of the world's need and Christ's commission (Acts 10:1-48).

10. Crossing swords with Paul—the evangelist indoctrinated (Gal. 2:11-21).

11. His death—the evangelist sent home (John 21:18-19).

His Winning Power

His power was enhanced by his simple straightforwardness of character and of manner. He was unconventional. He had no dignity to bother him. He was hampered by no sacred traditions. He struck straight. Peter went after lost men as he sought the finny tribe in stormy Galilee—cast his net in where the fish were and pulled them into his boat.

He preached plain, unvarnished truth right out, without apology or compromise. He saw men as sinners, realized that their need was Christ, and knew that the gospel revealed Christ to them. His sermon on the day of Pentecost was packed with doctrine. Study that sermon (Acts 2:14-40), and you will find that he preached the deity of Christ, the rejection of Jesus Christ as the darkest sin, the resurrection, hell, the enduement of the Holy Ghost, the final victory of Christ's gospel over sin, Christ's second advent, repentance, faith, baptism. He did not mince matters. He dodged nothing. Such preaching accompanies all evangelistic victories.

He faced all dangers for Christ and, filled with the Holy Spirit, feared no man or group of men and was willing to die for the truth. Difficulties did not bother Peter. He went through them all to do his duty. He did not have influence enough to keep out of jail, but he had power enough to break out. He did not take his orders from man, but from

God alone. A Petrine boldness is needed in evangelism today.

Peter was a master at organization for evangelism. He must have put every member of the Jerusalem church to doing personal work on the day of Pentecost and afterward. Pentecost was a victory of personal evangelism. It took organization to carry through the divine program on that day.

Peter did his work in the power of the Holy Spirit. His gospel was irresistible because spoken in heaven's power, Here lies the worth of Peter's example to the world: God was with him. His whole being was yielded to heaven's will and way.

9

The Topmost Evangelist

Paul

Acts 20:24, 26-27. But none of these things move me, neither count I my life dear unto myself, so that I might finish my course with joy, and the ministry, which I have received of the Lord Jesus, to testify the gospel of the grace of God. . . . Wherefore I take you to record this day, that I am pure from the blood of all men. For I have not shunned to declare unto you all the counsel of God.

Acts 22:12-15. And one Ananias, a devout man according to the law, having a good report of all the Jews which dwelt there, came unto me, and stood, and said unto me, Brother Saul, receive thy sight. And the same hour I looked upon him. And he said, The God of our fathers hath chosen thee, that thou shouldest know his will, and see that Just One, and shouldest hear the voice of his mouth. For thou shalt be his witness unto all men of what thou hast seen and heard.

Romans 1:14-16. I am debtor both to the Greeks, and to the Barbarians; both to the wise, and to the unwise. So, as much as in me is, I am ready to preach the gospel to you that are at Rome also. For I am not ashamed of the gospel of Christ: for it is the power of God unto salvation to every one that believeth; to the Jew first, and also to the Greek.

Romans 9:1-3. I say the truth in Christ, I lie not, my conscience also bearing me witness in the Holy Ghost, that I have great heaviness and continual sorrow in my heart. For I could wish that myself were accursed from Christ for my brethren, my kinsmen according to the flesh.

1 Corinthians 9:22. To the weak became I as weak, that I might gain the weak: I am made all things to all men, that I might by all means save some.

The apostle Paul is, by universal consent, the finest product of the gospel and the greatest man yet made by the creative and re-creative power of God. He tops all others in character and as a spiritual philosopher, Christian statesman, mission leader, church-builder, religious writer, theologian, preacher of the gospel, religious teacher, and soul-winning evangelist. He was Christ's master soul-winner. His influence in the world today, after twenty centuries, is next to Christ's. He is God's most powerful human advocate and exponent. He is Christ's noblest witness. He ranks first in the world's long list of evangelists. He said he was the chief of sinners, but the world says he is the chief of saints.

Factors in His Conversion

1. First among the hidden forces which operated in his, and every other man's, salvation was God's predestinating love. He said, "But when it pleased God, who separated me from my mother's womb, and called me by his grace, to reveal his Son in me, that I might preach him among the heathen; immediately I conferred not with flesh and blood" (Gal. 1:15-16). The effective grace of God's election operated in him and thus fulfilled God's eternal purpose (Rom. 8:28-29).

2. God's Spirit worked in his soul with convicting power and voiced God's call for his soul and service (Rom. 8:30; John 16:8-11).

3. Apostolic preaching and testimony contributed to his salvation, and Stephen's sermon and dying testimony broke his heart (Acts 7:58-60). He was welcomed into the hospitable home of one Judas. Ananias, devout Christian, came to remove the scales from the eyes of the blind, convicted sinner.

4. His own supplication in the hour of sorrow for sin was a factor in his conversion. "And the Lord said unto him [Ananias], Arise, and go into the street which is called Straight, and enquire in the house of Judas for one called Saul, of Tarsus: for, behold, he prayeth" (Acts 9:11).

5. Also, there was the personal impact of the risen and ascended Christ. Paul's redemption was a victory for and by the personal, present Christ. He appeared to the archpersecutor and overwhelmed him with his glorious, redeeming love. Paul got a vision of the Crucified, and with a complete inward yielding of all, he said, "Lord, what wilt thou have me to do?" The gospel embodied in the Redeemer won, re-created, mastered, and took complete control of, the greatest personality yet found among men, filled him with the Holy Spirit (Acts 9:17), and sent him forth to bear witness to all men.

His Soul-winning Success

Some of the elements of his success were:

1. A fourfold vision.

(1) He saw himself a lost, ruined sinner, dead in trespasses and sin, without God, without Christ, and without hope.

(2) He saw Christ and his gospel as God's dynamic power to save to the uttermost (Rom. 1:16).

(3) He realized the lordship and mastery of the conquering Christ, whose every order must be obeyed and every purpose fulfilled.

(4) He saw the world ruined by sin and heard its inmost and deepest soul-cry for spiritual help. He yielded his life to such a service. He said, "I was not disobedient unto the heavenly vision" (Acts 26:19).

2. A holy courage.—He feared only God's disfavor. His courage ran in the following lines:

(1) A courage to die to self and the world.

(2) A courage to live for Christ only.

(3) A courage to suffer for Christ's sake.

(4) A courage to face any danger or to undertake any task for Christ.

(5) A courage to persevere in perilous ways and against overwhelming difficulties.

(6) A courage to preach plain truth and to stand for Christ's doctrines against all the world.

3. A victorious, reliant, restful faith, which made him sing while bleeding in chains behind prison bars.

4. A holy optimism, based on God's predestination and Christ's unfailing promises.

5. A consuming love for Jesus Christ and a deathless compassion for lost men (2 Cor. 5:14; Rom. 9:1-3).

6. A mighty, relentless grip on the vitals of the truth.—The inspiration and authority of God's Word; sin, deep and ingrained in the souls of all men; the deity of Christ; the saving efficacy of Christ's blood; the reality of heaven and hell; the resurrection; the eternal keeping power of Christ; his second advent—all these and other vital truths were a part of his soul. They were the substance of his faith, and they filled his preaching.

7. A versatility and adaptability of method.—He never got in ruts. He was all things to all men that by all means he might win some. He believed in winning men by public preaching, by private teaching, and by personal appeal, at all times and everywhere.

8. A holy and consecrated life.—He was a pure man. In Romans 12, 2 Corinthians 6, Galatians 5, and Ephesians 4:11 to 5:11, he laid out the pattern of character and conduct of a Christian which he himself followed.

Paul was a man full of the Holy Spirit, who built all his ministry around the crucified, risen Christ. His preaching, his teaching, and his life were in the power of the Spirit.

Part Three

THE WAY TO WIN

•

Section A
Perennial Evangelism

10

The Evangelistic Church

THE NEW TESTAMENT CHURCH WAS EVANGELISTIC

That Christ established his church with evangelism as its primary and supreme motive is shown by its history.

Its genesis (John 1:35-51).—Christ took John's baptized followers as a nucleus, and led them in a soul-winning campaign in which Peter, Philip, and Nathanael were the first fruits.

Its first preachers (Matt. 4:19).—He called its early leaders to be fishers of men, thus laying the foundation for an evangelistic leadership for his churches for all time to come.

Its law of life (Matt. 5-7).—The Sermon on the Mount is the very heart of militant, aggressive conquest in winning men to God's way.

Its basic foundation (Matt. 16:18).—The church is shown as a militant army against the walled, entrenched powers of evil, conquering even the gates of hell.

Its marching orders (Matt. 28:18-20).—The Great Commission, to churches, preachers, and individual Christians, is purely and simply a command to win men everywhere to Christ and eternal life.

Its first great revival (Acts 2).—At Pentecost Christ put his church to work in prayer and in soul-winning. Pentecost is Christ's ideal for his church.

Its lay leaders (Acts 6).—Christ put unmistakable soul-winning qualifications on the diaconate. Pure character, good reputation, bold faith, and enduement by the Holy Spirit are qualities which would equip every deacon for soul-winning.

Its other leaders (including Peter and Paul) *and its victories* in the Acts of the Apostles and the Epistles.—For a hundred years these leaders went out to win souls and build soul-winning churches in all the earth.

Christ's program for every church is an evangelistic program. The churches which do not constantly seek to win men to a saving knowledge of the truth and enlist them in Christ's service have missed the mark of the divine purpose and requirement. Soul-winning is the main task of every organization claiming to be a church of Jesus Christ.

The Importance of the Evangelistic Church

The need for an evangelistic church in every community is very great, and the value of such churches is beyond human computation. Their importance is seen from several standpoints. The world can never be won to Christ by revivals only. The churches need to work at this task seven days in the week, every month and every year until Jesus comes again. But it is in evangelistic churches that revivals are most easily held and have the most far-reaching results. These churches are ready for Pentecostal movements and can best conserve the results of evangelism.

It is in evangelistic churches that the ripest Christian character grows and the richest spiritual leadership develops and comes to usefulness. Great laymen cannot be enriched and led out into service in unevangelistic churches. In evangelistic churches the fellowship of God's people finds its ripest fruitage; the devil cannot grow dissension and discord in a soul-winning church. The soul-winning atmosphere is the best place for scriptural indoctrination; the sinew and bone of spiritual life grow strong on God's basic truths in evangelistic churches. Liberality abounds in such churches, and men most easily part with their possessions for the extension of Christ's kingdom. A man cannot keep his soul hot after lost men and be covetous. Evangelism opens hearts and purses. It is in evangelistic churches that the young hear most easily the call of God to service and most easily surrender to his will. Evangelistic churches are the main supply houses for leaders in the ministry and in missions.

The permanent advancement of Christ's kingdom depends more on the labors, leadership, and liberality of evangelistic churches than upon any other group of forces in the world. They are the salt of the earth, and the King needs them to carry out his will. All of these things are illustrated and exemplified in the first church at Jerusalem, from Pentecost on for years. The explanation is that they prayed until they were filled with power; and they continued to win in that power, and "the Lord added unto them daily such as were being saved" (Acts 2:47 ASV marg.).

The Essentials of an Evangelistic Church

Without certain essential factors a perennially evangelistic church cannot be maintained. The starting point is reliance upon the Holy Spirit. In all our labor of love for men and for God, there should be an unfailing reliance upon the indwelling Holy Spirit. The entire soul-saving movement must center in Jesus, our Lord and Master, and must be carried on in the strength and wisdom of the Holy Spirit.

Every opportunity to win men to the Saviour should be utilized. The entire program of the church should be aimed at winning souls to Christ and at building up souls in him. Personal work bands should be used, and the church membership organized for witnessing in crowded centers and neglected quarters. This witnessing will carry the gospel to hospitals, parks, jails, street corners—to every place where needy men are found.

The fires of soul-winning power must be kindled and fed in the life of the entire church membership. In the homes of the people, in the prayer meetings, and in all religious gatherings there should burn a spiritual yearning for lost souls. Prayer groups should meet constantly to pray for souls and for spiritual power.

The officers and the organizations of the church must be trained to win. Detailed study of the essentials of an evangelistic church follows.

A Soul-winning Diaconate

A pattern for deacons.—"For they that have used the office of a deacon well purchase to themselves a good degree, and great boldness in the faith which is in Christ Jesus" (1 Tim. 3:13). Every deacon ought to be a soul-winner, and he can if he tries. Out of the seven deacons of the first church at Jerusalem, two became great unordained evangelists. Stephen's dying testimony started conviction in the heart of Saul of Tarsus and doubtless led to his conversion. Philip held a great meeting in Samaria, led the treasurer of an African kingdom to Christ, and won the lost in the coast cities of the Mediterranean Sea for many years.

Qualifications of deacons.—From the pertinent Scripture passages, the following qualifications of deacons are selected:

1. "Honest report" (Acts 6:3); "blameless" (1 Tim. 3:10) —the right sort of reputation, which will enable their influence to count in winning men.

2. "Full of the Holy Ghost" (Acts 6:3)—the enduement of divine power for the winning task.

3. "Full of . . . wisdom" (Acts 6:3)—the right approach and sound judgment in drawing the net.

4. "Full of faith" (Acts 6:5)—the inner attitude which enables the deacons to be conquerors in the field of soul-winning.

5. "Grave, not doubletongued, not given to much wine, not greedy of filthy lucre" (1 Tim. 3:8)—qualities essential for success in any spiritual endeavor.

6. "Holding the mystery of the faith in a pure conscience" (1 Tim. 3:9)—the knowledge of God's doctrines and teachings, so that they are qualified to lead souls aright.

7. "Husbands of one wife, ruling their children and their own houses well" (1 Tim. 3:12)—the domestic relations conducive to the best evangelism.

All of these qualifications indicate that there is more required of deacons than the mere handling of the finances of the church. Christ meant that the deacons should be the spiritual cabinet of the pastor and the recruiting officers of the church. A deacon should know how to handle men, as well as money, for Christ.

Much should be expected of deacons. They should have a conscience against worldliness and against compromise. A deaconship whose lives do not differ from the lives of the worldlings will never win the lost about them to Christ, but will be a positive hindrance to all evangelizing. Deacons must be good, pure, clean, consecrated men.

Men should be selected as deacons who are of a spiritual turn of mind, who love the cause in a marked way and possess a compassion for lost men. The unspiritual and unevangelistic should not be put in as deacons, and those who are already deacons and refuse to attend to the vital matter of soul-winning should be wisely but firmly eliminated and others elected in their places. Prayerful wisdom should be shown in the selection of deacons. As far as possible follow the requirements of the Word of God in Acts 6 and 1 Timothy 3.

Developing soul-winning deacons.—The pastor will cultivate a soul-winning psychology among the deacons. He is the spiritual pivot on which this whole matter turns, and his leadership will count for much. If he fails, the deacons will fail. Peter and the other apostles were mighty factors in determining the evangelistic fervor of the deacons of the early church. Philip and Stephen would hardly have been such great evangelists if they had not been touched by the fires of Peter's Pentecostal leadership.

Ever so often the pastor should see that his deacons make a careful study of the best methods of winning men to Christ—the methods of Christ, of the apostles, and of the best modern soul-winners—looking to the end of their becoming experts in their main task. Getting money and administering the affairs of a church are only means to the great end of winning men from sin and death to life and Christ.

The pastor should organize his deacons for soul-winning and actually lead them out into it in his own church and Sunday school and in near-by communities. Regular, perennial evangelism in the church; meetings of a week or so in downtown missions and neglected communities; and soul-winning services on streets, in jails or parks will provide opportunities for training and channels of service for the deaconship in this fundamental matter. He should have a committee on soul-winning, and let them get information and direct in a search for souls. He should keep before the deacons a list of the lost and encourage them to visit the unsaved in their places of business and homes. In meetings for soul-winning he should use the deacons in song, prayer, testimony, personal work, and should help them to memorize pointed Scripture passages for this purpose.

There followed David a "band whose heart God had touched." If such a band of deacons, whose hearts God had touched with his soul-winning power, should follow every pastor in city, town, or country, the kingdom would come in a new and greater fashion in all the world.

A Soul-winning Sunday School

MATTHEW 28:18-20. And Jesus came and spake unto them, saying, All power is given unto me in heaven and in earth. Go ye therefore, and teach all nations, baptizing them in the name of the Father, and of the Son, and of the Holy Ghost: teaching them to observe all things whatsoever I have commanded you: and, lo, I am with you alway, even unto the end of the world. Amen.

1 CORINTHIANS 12:28. And God hath set some in the church, first apostles, secondarily prophets, thirdly teachers, after that

miracles, then gifts of healings, helps, governments, diversities of tongues.

EPHESIANS 4:11-12. And he gave some, apostles; and some, prophets; and some, evangelists; and some, pastors and teachers; for the perfecting of the saints, for the work of the ministry, for the edifying of the body of Christ.

The Sunday school's task.—In Christ's commission he commanded two kinds of teaching. One is the teaching that wins men to Christ—evangelistic, soul-saving instruction. The other is soul-building, character-constructing teaching. The one wins the faith, the affections, and the spiritual loyalty to Christ as Redeemer and Lord. The other wins the whole man to Christ's doctrines, program, and world plans, and grows the soul up into the stature of Christ Jesus. The task of the church school is to perform this double duty for the entire community. The instruction should be both evangelistic and constructive.

An evangelistic Sunday school cannot be built with uncompassionate, unspiritual officers and teachers.

The leaders in a soul-winning Sunday school.—The superintendent ought to be chosen in part because of his ability to lead in constructing a soul-winning agency. He must not only love lost men, but must know something of the way to create an evangelistic atmosphere and an evangelistic organization. The teacher, likewise, should be a winner. Christ and Paul, the world's two greatest teachers, were winners of the highest type. Their example should call every teacher to highest endeavor in soul-winning.

The pastor of a soul-winning Sunday school.—The pastor is the evangelist of the Sunday school in his church. He stands as one who "watcheth for souls," and should realize that his Sunday school force is his best aid in soul-winning and that the school is his greatest, most constant, and most fruitful field of opportunity in winning the lost to Christ. He should keep up with the unsaved in all the classes, constantly encourage the teachers and the Christian pupils to look out for and to bring in other unsaved ones and ever to be praying for and seeking to win them to Christ. He should teach his teachers the art and method of soul-winning and seek constantly to create in his school the atmosphere of evangelism. Never should a month pass that he does not conduct an evangelistic service in the Sunday school.

Suggestions for a soul-winning Sunday school.—All the teaching force should have a clear conception of the scriptural teaching regarding the spiritual condition of the unsaved before God, the perils of postponing salvation, and the certain doom awaiting their impenitence and unbelief.

David said: "Behold, I was shapen in iniquity; and in sin did my mother conceive me" (Psalm 51:5). "The wicked are estranged from the womb: they go astray as soon as they be born, speaking lies. Their poison is like the poison of a serpent" (Psalm 58:3-4). "The wicked shall be turned into hell, and all the nations that forget God" (Psalm 9:17).

Isaiah said man was "called a transgressor from the womb" (Isa. 48:8).

Paul said: "For we have before proved both Jews and Gentiles, that they are all under sin" (Rom. 3:9). "And you hath he quickened, who were dead in trespasses and sins" (Eph. 2:1).

Christ said: "Except a man be born again, he cannot see the kingdom of God" (John 3:3). "He that believeth not is condemned already" (John 3:18) and "shall not see life; but the wrath of God abideth on him" (John 3:36). "And these shall go away into everlasting punishment: but the righteous into life eternal" (Matt. 25:46).

These sad and tragic truths should be known and pondered by the Sunday school forces in order that they may do their best to win the pupils to Christ.

The Sunday school leaders should have a deep-laid purpose and plan to make soul-winning one of the main matters in the life of the school. As they value the life of the immortal soul, so should they give first place to this high calling. The praying, the thinking, the teaching—all should be pitched to this soul-winning note, and the leaders should ever be on the watch to win someone to Jesus.

At least once a month there should be an evangelistic service in some department of the Sunday school, led by the pastor or someone else who can do it well. The gospel should be presented in a plain, earnest fashion, and the net should be drawn, each teacher and Christian pupil doing personal work and giving all the lost a pressing call to come to Christ. The definite decision day is good if held often enough.

During the revival periods in the church all the Sunday school forces should rally to the meetings, doing their best to win every unsaved one in the school. Every teacher in a Sunday school ought to be an active soul-winner in the church revival. However, great care should be exercised that none be allowed to come into the church without a genuine work of grace in their hearts.

When someone has made a profession of faith in Christ, the pastor, the teacher, and the parents (in the case of a child) should calmly and carefully talk over with the convert the plan of salvation, the meaning of church membership, the ordinances of the church, and the high requirements made by God's Word. Try to save the life as well as the soul. Someone has said that 85 per cent of the converts today come into the churches from the Sunday schools and that 45 per cent of the unsaved in the Sunday schools are never saved at all. If this be true, there is a tremendous responsibility on the Sunday school leaders.

Every year or so all the officers, teachers, and many of the Christian pupils in the Sunday school should be trained by the pastor, or some other person competent to do it, in personal soul-winning. Scripture on this subject should be studied, and the methods of soul-winners should be gone over in class. It is doubtful whether one who will not learn to be a winner ought to be allowed to teach in a Sunday school. If the pastor does not know how to lead his teaching forces in this primary matter, he ought either to learn or to resign. Nothing is more important or needed in the life of a church than a trained soul-winning force in the Sunday school. Any pastor with the grace of God in his heart and the love of lost men in his soul can learn to win men to Christ and to teach others how to do it. If he does not do this, has he not missed the main thing in his ministry? Christ says to all preachers: "Follow me, and I will make you fishers of men" (Matt. 4:19).

A Soul-winning Training Union

The purpose of the Training Union, to train Christians for service, is ideal for an evangelistic church. In the Training Union definite instruction may be given in the methods of personal soul-winning. Perhaps no other organization is better adopted naturally to that end.

Training Union members should lead in soul-winning.

1. For their own sake.—The young people of a church need to be organized into lines of Christian activity in order to give expression to their enthusiasm and exuberance and to keep them from going into the world's way and amusements and thus becoming entangled in sinful practices. They also need to have spiritual exercise in order to grow up in the knowledge of God. To interest them in spiritual victories in bringing others to Christ is to do them the best possible service. It frees them from doubt and brings them true happiness.

2. For others' sake.—The young people have a mighty influence with each other. Their arm is one of great strength in all the life of a community. When this strength of influence is directed toward winning the unsaved to Christ and his holy cause, it brings glorious results.

3. For the church's sake.—Often the only way a pastor and a church can ever get out of old, deep-laid ruts and into a new, aggressive life for Christ is to organize the young people into bands of winners and lead them out into the

work of bringing to Christ their friends and comrades. It is one sure way to build a great evangelistic church. The young people become great factors in the regular evangelism of the church and in the revival seasons, and thus from the young people's organizations the church is constantly receiving new life.

4. For the kingdom's sake.—John, the beloved apostle, said: "I have written unto you, young men, because ye are strong, and the word of God abideth in you, and ye have overcome the wicked one" (1 John 2:14). God means that the young people saved by his grace shall aid him in bringing this world to Christ. If they fail, many will never have the opportunity of knowing Christ as Saviour.

How young people can be trained in soul-winning.—To initiate, promote, and maintain an organization among the young people for soul-winning is a worthy, meaningful, far-reaching, and difficult task.

There must be a wise, persistent, patient, consecrated person to lead the young. Many pastors can do it. Some teachers in the educational institutions of the community can do it. Some trained young businessmen or professional men and some cultured young ladies who prefer Christ's cause to the world's ways can do it. In many cases the pastor and church may have to find and train the leader in the beginning.

A spiritual atmosphere must be generated in the young people's organization. Overstress on the social side or the pleasure-loving side or even the intellectual side will make it difficult to create a soul-winning atmosphere. It will take time and patience to cultivate a state of mind for evangelism, but persistent effort will be rewarded.

There should be a personal workers' or an evangelistic committee to stress evangelism in the organization. Meetings where the unsaved are present should be arranged. Special prayer should be had for this meeting, a short evangelistic talk should be made, and the net should be drawn and personal work done with the unsaved. Care should be exercised to see that the unsaved are not driven away by unwise or improper approach.

The members of the young people's organizations should have a prayer list of the unsaved, for whom they constantly pray and to whom they may write letters and send tracts. When a person is saved, the young people should help him follow up his experience by bringing him into the church and the young people's organizations.

Some of the meetings of the young people should be devoted to a study of soul-winning methods. The pastor or some other person who knows how to do it should instruct them in this finest of the fine arts, winning the lost to Christ.

11

The Soul-winning Pastor—Priest, Preacher, Evangelist

PSALM 126:5-6. They that sow in tears shall reap in joy. He that goeth forth and weepeth, bearing precious seed, shall doubtless come again with rejoicing, bringing his sheaves with him.

ISAIAH 58:10. And if thou draw out thy soul to the hungry, and satisfy the afflicted soul; then shall thy light rise in obscurity, and thy darkness be as the noon day.

EZEKIEL 33:7. So thou, O son of man, I have set thee a watchman unto the house of Israel; therefore thou shalt hear the word at my mouth, and warn them from me.

EZEKIEL 34:1-4. And the word of the Lord came unto me, saying, Son of man, prophesy against the shepherds of Israel, prophesy, and say unto them, Thus saith the Lord God unto the shepherds; Woe be to the shepherds of Israel that do feed themselves! should not the shepherds feed the flocks? Ye eat the fat, and ye clothe you with the wool, ye kill them that are fed: but ye feed not the flock. The diseased have ye not strengthened, neither have ye healed that which was sick, neither have ye bound up that which was broken, neither have ye brought again that which was driven away, neither have ye sought that which was lost; but with force and with cruelty have ye ruled them.

MATTHEW 4:19. And he saith unto them, Follow me, and I will make you fishers of men.

LUKE 5:10. And so was also James, and John, the sons of Zebedee, which were partners with Simon. And Jesus said unto Simon, Fear not; from henceforth thou shalt catch men.

LUKE 15:4, 8. What man of you, having an hundred sheep, if he lose one of them, doth not leave the ninety and nine in the wilderness, and go after that which is lost, until he find it? ... Either what woman having ten pieces of silver, if she lose one piece, doth not light a candle, and sweep the house, and seek diligently till she find it?

1 Corinthians 1:17-18, 21, 23.   For Christ sent me not to baptize, but to preach the gospel: not with wisdom of words, lest the cross of Christ should be made of none effect. For the preaching of the cross is to them that perish foolishness; but unto us which are saved it is the power of God. . . . For after that in the wisdom of God the world by wisdom knew not God, it pleased God by the foolishness of preaching to save them that believe. . . . But we preach Christ crucified, unto the Jews a stumblingblock, and unto the Greeks foolishness.

1 Corinthians 9:22.   To the weak became I as weak, that I might gain the weak: I am made all things to all men, that I might by all means save some.

2 Corinthians 2:14-16.   Now thanks be unto God, which always causeth us to triumph in Christ, and maketh manifest the savour of his knowledge by us in every place. For we are unto God a sweet savour of Christ, in them that are saved, and in them that perish: to the one we are the savour of death unto death; and to the other the savour of life unto life. And who is sufficient for these things?

2 Corinthians 5:20.   Now then we are ambassadors for Christ, as though God did beseech you by us: we pray you in Christ's stead, be ye reconciled to God.

Colossians 1:25-29.   Whereof I am made a minister, according to the dispensation of God which is given to me for you, to fulfil the word of God; even the mystery which hath been hid from ages and from generations, but now is made manifest to his saints: to whom God would make known what is the riches of the glory of this mystery among the Gentiles; which is Christ in you, the hope of glory: whom we preach, warning every man, and teaching every man in all wisdom; that we may present every man perfect in Christ Jesus: whereunto I also labour, striving according to his working, which worketh in me mightily.

1 Thessalonians 1:5.   For our gospel came not unto you in word only, but also in power, and in the Holy Ghost, and in much assurance; as ye know what manner of men we were among you for your sake.

1 Timothy 6:20-21.   O Timothy, keep that which is committed to thy trust, avoiding profane and vain babblings, and oppositions of science falsely so called: which some professing have **erred concerning the faith. Grace be with thee. Amen.**

2 Timothy 2:15. Study to shew thyself approved unto God, a workman that needeth not to be ashamed, rightly dividing the word of truth.

Hebrews 13:17. Obey them that have the rule over you, and submit yourselves: for they watch for your souls, as they that must give account, that they may do it with joy, and not with grief: for that is unprofitable for you.

The Pastor as Priest

His responsibility.—In God's Word the pastor is described, both in plain teaching and by example, as a spiritual priest, representing God to men and men to God, seeking to bring them into a saving relation. The spiritual function of the priesthood in the Old Testament is brought over into the preaching and teaching ministry of the New Testament pastor. He is a soul-winning daysman, a go-between for God and man, the human representative of Christ to man and the intercessory priest for man with God.

His ministry.—The care for souls must show itself masterfully everywhere in the pastor's ministry.

His doctrinal system will be based on the fundamental involved in ministerial priesthood: "Men are lost; I am Christ's priest to them; I hold a holy trusteeship, a spiritual debtorship to all lost men."

A care for souls will frame his sermons and saturate his prayers. His passion for lost men will show itself in his choice of sermons. He will pray much or little in proportion as he longs for lost men, and his sermons will gauge his distance from God.

His conception of his soul-winning responsibility will shape his world mission program. If he tenderly shares Christ's call of the cross, he will see in his ministerial tasks a chance to carry the gospel to a ruined world. Because missions will mean to him an opportunity to get men to Christ and Christ to men, he will lead God's people in giving their money and their sons and daughters to missionary endeavors, showing them that it is their privilege in winning men to Christ.

A passion for the lost will fire his soul and direct his energies in every prayer meeting, conference, and pastoral visit, and in all his contacts with men. He will ever remember that he is God's priest for soul-winning purposes and that heaven has called him to, and separated him for, the task of bringing lost men and a saving Christ together.

The Pastor as Preacher

His responsibility.—Preaching has a high place in the Word of God and in all the history of Christianity. The preacher and his gospel message are the primary human factors in redemption. Nothing in human civilization can compare with the gospel ministry as a constructive force. The God-called, Spirit-ordained, consecrated preacher with a scriptural message and a burning zeal for lost men is God's "big man." He occupies a central place among the makers of civilization and among the builders of the kingdom of God. His life and service are vital to the world's progress. Without him and his message the world would turn back to savagery and death.

Not only have the sermons of great, world-famed preachers been powerful and constructive, but the sermons and ministry of the thousands of obscure but faithful preachers in small and out-of-the-way places, the great crowd of unsung evangels, have also turned men to God.

His preaching.—All preaching, whether didactic, apologetic, hortatory, or expository, should be in the evangelistic spirit. The objective, whether direct or indirect, should be to bring men to Christ in salvation and service and to train them in the art of soul-saving and life-serving. The Sermon on the Mount by God's Son, the Pentecostal message by Simon Peter, the doctrinal deliverance of the apostle Paul in the eighth chapter of Romans—all had the same objectives: the saving of souls, the construction of character, and the building of Christ's kingdom among men. All three of these messages breathe with the saving Spirit of God. They are all evangelistic.

Below are listed some of the distinguishing features of evangelistic preaching. All of these marks can be found in the spiritual ministrations of Jesus Christ, John the Baptist, Simon Peter, and the apostle Paul—God's holy quartet and his prime ministers in the history of grace and glory.

It is *positive*. The lost sinner wants certainty, and the preacher must preach with conviction if he is to win by his message.

It is *direct* and *pointed*. "Thou art the man" preaching brings sinners to their knees. Peter's sermon at Pentecost brought personal conviction and made men feel guilty before God then and there.

It is *bold, plain,* and *simple*. The preacher should speak fearlessly, in terms clear and uncompromising. His preaching should shield not and give no covert for sinners, high or low. It should bring to light the hidden secrets of the heart and be so clear that the simplest can comprehend.

It is *tender*, full of love and tears. There is enough in human life and destiny to break the preacher's heart. His gospel message, if it is to win, must come with compassion. He must love men and show it in his tone, his spirit, and his speech. He must himself know Calvary and Gethsemane if he is to bring men to their knees. "They that sow in tears shall reap in joy." He that weepeth in his seed-sowing is the one who returns joyful with his harvest (Psalm 126:5-6).

It is *scriptural*. "Preach the word" is heaven's command. Evangelistic preaching is saturated with God's Word. It sticks close to God's truth. "The gospel . . . is the power of God unto salvation" (Rom. 1:16). The Word of God is the sword of the Spirit. It cuts, breaks, burns, cleanses, revives, inspires, and gives life to souls astray from God.

It is *doctrinal*. Though not always consciously doctrinal, it is always latently and potently so. Present in every sermon to point men to God should be the fundamentals or divine truth: Christ's deity; his efficacious and life-giving death; his resurrection; his power now to save; sin, grace, sanctification; the inspiration and authority of God's Word. They will give bone, sinew, meat, and vitality to his message.

It is *constructive.* A newborn soul needs vital connections for its protection, sustenance, and growth in usefulness. Christ has made his churches responsible for the spiritual nurture of each newborn soul. Evangelistic preaching should turn these babes to the arms, the love, the protection, and the inspiration of the church, tying up the new-found life with life-fountains and foods.

It is *Spirit-inspired.* Dry, cold, lifeless preaching will get nowhere in soul-winning. Evangelistic preaching is dynamic and in the power of God's Holy Spirit—this is one of its chief characteristics. Pentecosts come only when God's Spirit comes. "Not by might, nor by power, but by my Spirit, saith the Lord" is true of winning preaching.

It is *expectant.* The preacher who largely and widely wins men to Christ will put God's dynamics in the present tense and confidently expect to "bring his sheaves with him." The evangelist should believe in a "today gospel" as well as a "tomorrow gospel." He will "cash in" on his preaching now and give the sinner a chance to trust, confess, and obey Christ on the spot.

It is *Christocentric.* The crucified Lord should be central in every prayer, every sermon, and every song. The preacher will preach only Christ crucified, glory only in the cross of Christ, and faithfully trust that he will overcome Satan in the blood of the Lamb (Rev. 12:11). Christ will be the Alpha and Omega, the first and the last, in preaching that is evangelistic.

The Pastor as Evangelist

The first preachers Christ called in his earthly ministry met the challenge, "Follow me, and I will make you fishers of men." The last command of the ascending Saviour was, "Ye shall be witnesses unto me . . . unto the uttermost part of the earth" (Acts 1:8). Whatever else Christ calls his preachers to do, he does not call them away from the high duty of soul-winning. To this one end Christ came, "to seek and to save that which was lost." And he said, "As my Father hath sent me, even so send I you."

His temptations.—There are certain things, deadly in their poisonous effect on the preacher's life, which he needs to guard against. They produce professionalism, spiritual inertia, and formality, and bring death to his vital powers.

A worldly spirit.—"Love not the world, neither the things that are in the world. If any man love the world, the love of the Father is not in him" (1 John 2:15). This is especially true of the ministry. World-lust and love eat spiritual power out of the minister's heart.

Indiscretion.—The preacher who flirts with women will ruin his influence and help destroy souls. His character is as delicate as a woman's and needs a safeguard about it.

Dishonesty, in either commercial or intellectual life.— If he fails to pay his debts or if he preaches other men's sermons, he is on the road to the scrap heap.

The money-heart.—The preacher whose heart is on money-making and who goes into speculations and commercial life is on the toboggan slide. "Ye cannot serve God and mammon," is God's message to the ministry as well as to the laity.

Ambition for place and promotion.—"And whosoever would be first among you, shall be servant of all" (Mark 10: 44 ASV), Christ said to all ambition in the ministry. If your place is not great enough to suit you, make it so. The minister who is unable to make a place great is too weak to hold a great one. All seeking of higher positions on the part of preachers is the effort of the devil to compass their ruin.

Ministerial jealousy.—Like the poisonous gases of modern battle fronts, jealousy destroys life. The envious or jealous preacher can have neither favor with men nor power from God. Jealousy is a trait of little spirits.

Unspiritual and irreverent scholarship.—Great learning, high and profound scholarship, strong and charming intellectualism—these are a prize worth while and should be sought by many. But if they are sought as an end rather than as a means, if the warmth of the soul and the spiritual power of the ministry are imperiled and neglected, then all these attainments in scholarship are a curse. "The Spirit of God has an affinity for a trained mind." But the mind must keep in with the Spirit of God while securing its training. The need of a lost world should constantly be on the heart of every preacher seeking scholarship.

His rewards.—The pastor's rewards in this holy endeavor are priceless and without number:

Heart-growth.—He feeds on God's sweetened manna. Eshcol grapes ripen for him on many vines.

A heavenly peace of soul.—Soul-winning irons out a thousand frets in the soul and smooths the way for grace and glory.

The opening of heaven's windows in answer to prayers.—It is the soul-winning preacher who tells of marvelous answers to prayers.

Endless and unspeakable joys.—Pessimism dies an unwept death in the heart of the soul-winning preacher. Floods of joy fill his soul day by day as he sees men living in and for Jesus Christ as a result of his efforts and prayer.

Opportunities for service.—The great soul-winner never has to ask for a task or a place to serve. The calls outnumber his days and overtax his strength.

Spiritual power.—Divine unction rests on, and abides in, him who longs to see men saved. Peter's Pentecost was born in a compassionate longing and praying for lost men on the part of Christ's church.

12

Visitation Evangelism

PSALM 126:5-6. They that sow in tears shall reap in joy. He that goeth forth and weepeth, bearing precious seed, shall doubtless come again with rejoicing, bringing his sheaves with him.

MATTHEW 4:19. And he saith unto them, Follow me, and I will make you fishers of men.

MATTHEW 9:37-38. Then saith he unto his disciples, The harvest truly is plenteous, but the labourers are few; pray ye therefore the Lord of the harvest, that he will send forth labourers into his harvest.

MATTHEW 28:18-20. And Jesus came and spake unto them, saying, All power is given unto me in heaven and in earth. Go ye therefore, and teach all nations, baptizing them in the name of the Father, and of the Son, and of the Holy Ghost: teaching them to observe all things whatsoever I have commanded you: and, lo, I am with you alway, even unto the end of the world. Amen.

JOHN 15:16. Ye have not chosen me, but I have chosen you, and ordained you, that ye should go and bring forth fruit, and that your fruit should remain: that whatsoever ye shall ask of the Father in my name, he may give it you.

ACTS 1:8. But ye shall receive power, after that the Holy Ghost is come upon you: and ye shall be witnesses unto me both in Jerusalem, and in all Judaea, and in Samaria, and unto the uttermost part of the earth.

2 CORINTHIANS 5:20. Now then we are ambassadors for Christ, as though God did beseech you by us: we pray you in Christ's stead, be ye reconciled to God.

PHILIPPIANS 4:13. I can do all things through Christ which strengtheneth me.

Soul-winning should not be left to the pastor and a handpicked group of trained workers. It is the responsibility of every Christian to win others to Christ. It is the business of the whole church—not of a church group or groups—to seek and to save the lost. Only when the church constantly maintains an all-inclusive program of evangelism will Christ's commission be carried out and his commendation won.

The term "visitation evangelism" might properly be used to designate this church program, since visitation is the heart of a definitely planned program of evangelism. The ideal is every church member visiting the lost in Christ's name and for his glory.

It Should Be Planned

An all-church program requires an over-all planning source. This source is the evangelistic committee, or if the church does not have such a committee, the church council. The latter would probably be composed of the pastor as chairman and the heads of the church agencies, namely, Sunday school superintendent, Training Union director, Woman's Missionary Union president, Brotherhood president, and the chairman of the deacons. If there is a paid church staff, the members of the staff should be included in the council.

It Should Be Regular

The church council should plan a weekly visitation program of evangelism that is as regular as teaching the Sunday school lesson on Sundays. A monthly visitation program is better than none, but long intervals between periods of action tend to destroy interest, inspiration, and effectiveness. We attend church each week; we pray, or should pray, daily; we read the Bible daily; we pay our tithes weekly. Why should we visit for lost souls only once a month? Why should we wait for a revival to do the visiting? The main thing, the first thing, in the program of the New Testament church was soul-winning. Why do we give it the last place in our program of service?

It is suggested that the church council might well schedule a calendar of visitation that would rotate week by week, as follows: The Sunday school might visit the first week in each month; the Training Union, the second week in each month; the W.M.U., the third week; and the Brotherhood, the fourth.

It Should Be Worked

In a church visitation program, there are three "musts," as follows: locate the prospect, keep up-to-date records, visit the prospect.

Locate the prospect.—There are many methods to be used in locating unsaved people and unattached Baptists. Visitors' cards may be kept on the back of the church pews or passed to visitors in the congregation at the worship services. A religious census should be taken regularly. In a church program of visitation evangelism, some organization, perhaps the W.M.U., should take a weekly census of the territory served by the church. This territory should be divided into blocks in the cities, into sections or districts in rural communities. A circle or group should be responsible for definite and permanent sections and visit all newcomers each week, securing the regular census information from them. This perpetuating census should be kept up week by week as the population changes. All prospects found through any method should be turned over to the one keeping the records.

Keep the records accurately.—The key person in a church visitation program of evangelism is the secretary of visitation. In larger churches this person should be one of the paid staff of workers. If this is not practical, then the very best qualified person to be found in the church membership should be selected for the task.

The secretary of visitation should keep the name of each prospect on a visitation card. This card has a threefold purpose: It serves as an assignment card for the personal worker, supplying him with information about the prospect; it is used to give a complete report after the contact is made; it indicates the church agency that is to receive credit for the visit. Every card should be returned to the secretary after the personal worker has made the contact.

Records of names, addresses, and work done must be kept accurately, and credit for contacts must be properly given if the work is to be effective. A separate tabulated list should be kept for each of the agencies: Sunday school, Training Union, W.M.U., and Brotherhood.

Visit the prospects.—It is not so difficult to locate prospects. Unattached Baptists and lost souls are everywhere. Statistics reveal that there are seventy million persons in the United States who have never confessed Christ as Saviour and who have no church affiliation. Today the evangelistic problem is not seeking the one lost sheep while ninety-nine lie safely in the fold. Forty-nine who once were in the fold are now drifting on the misty flats between the shelter and the wilderness. If you live in an average neighborhood, 47 per cent of those around you are unchurched. We must win them to Christ and his church, but we cannot do it without effort. We cannot wish people into the kingdom of God. We must follow Jesus' example and go out after them. This will never be done to any extent unless we plan to do it. Over-organization is not our greatest danger. Failure to work the organization we have is our greatest weakness. All of our church agencies can engage in a program of perennial soul-winning and can do it without overlapping in effort and without conflict in periods of visitation.

Usually the most effective visitation will be done by two visiting together. Do not become discouraged or impatient if a prospect does not respond immediately. Regular, persistent, effective visitation will keep people constantly walking the aisles seeking membership in the church or making a public confession of Christ.

It Should Be Strictly Evangelistic

This visiting program must be held strictly to evangelism if it is to succeed. Visits to the sick, the absentees, and the unenlisted church members should be made at another time. It is much easier for the average Christian to visit them than to try to win a lost soul to Christ. Human nature follows the course of least resistance. Make this program strictly visitation evangelism.

It Should Be Supported

Soul-winning classes should be taught. There are many splendid study course books on the subject of soul-winning. Have the entire church studying how to win the lost.

Challenging sermons should be preached. The pastor should by all means preach sermons on personal soul-winning, giving emphasis to the church program of visitation evangelism and making clear the plan.

Prayer should be magnified. Follow the instructions of our Saviour. Pray for "labourers into his harvest." It would be profitable occasionally to devote the entire midweek prayer meeting to praying for workers in the vineyard.

Reports should be emphasized. Give much emphasis to reports on work done, and at every possible occasion give opportunity for workers to testify concerning experiences they have had in visitation. When Jesus sent out the seventy, they returned testifying and rejoicing as they told the good news of their unusual experiences.

Evangelism should be stressed in every church organization. The leadership of all agencies should give soul-winning its proper place in their plans and programs. Any church will be evangelistic if the leadership is rightly concerned about lost souls. God will look upon the church with favor, and an atmosphere conducive to progress in all phases of kingdom work will be created.

13

Music in Evangelism

2 KINGS 3:15. But now bring me a minstrel. And it came to pass, when the minstrel played, that the hand of the Lord came upon him.

PSALM 98:4-9. Make a joyful noise unto the Lord, all the earth: make a loud noise, and rejoice, and sing praise. Sing unto the Lord with the harp; with the harp, and the voice of a psalm. With trumpets and sound of cornet make a joyful noise before the Lord, the King. Let the sea roar, and the fulness thereof; the world, and they that dwell therein. Let the floods clap their hands: let the hills be joyful together before the Lord; for he cometh to judge the earth: with righteousness shall he judge the world, and the people with equity.

PSALM 100:1-2. Make a joyful noise unto the Lord, all ye lands. Serve the Lord with gladness: come before his presence with singing.

PSALM 104:33. I will sing unto the Lord as long as I live: I will sing praise to my God while I have my being.

ACTS 16:25. And at midnight Paul and Silas prayed, and sang praises unto God; and the prisoners heard them.

EPHESIANS 5:18-19. And be not drunk with wine, wherein is excess; but be filled with the Spirit; speaking to yourselves in psalms and hymns and spiritual songs, singing and making melody in your heart to the Lord.

THE PLACE OF MUSIC IN RELIGION

Music is older than sermons and has ever been inseparably connected with worship. All triumphant religions have made much of music. The ancient Jews were unique in their emphasis on and love of music. They had schools of music, both instrumental and vocal. Some of their greatest leaders were professors of music. The Temple choirs were world-famous. The longest and one of the most important books in God's inspired Word is a volume of spiritual hymns and songs, the Psalms. For nearly three thousand years it has lived unsurpassed as the hymnbook of the Jews and Christians.

The history of gospel songs since Christ's time is as thrilling as a romance. For twenty centuries the movement has been upward, until today the influence of gospel music in worship, in missionary inspiration, in the development of spiritual power, in the stimulation of evangelistc fervor, and in the moving of God's people to heroic deeds and sacrificial service, is unsurpassed. Gospel songs vie with gospel sermons in the triumphs of missions. By their gospel songs missionaries often quiet the rage of heathendom and open avenues to their preaching and teaching. Only heaven will be able to measure the value of songs in the lives, the worship, and the work of God's people through the centuries.

Spiritual song has ever been the inspirational handmaiden of gospel preaching and teaching. Sermons have been spoken to enraptured audiences, printed in tracts and books, and have gone out to bless the world. But what sermon has gone further, or reached as many souls and inspired and ennobled as many lives, as have many of the great songs of Zion? "Amazing Grace," "How Firm a Foundation," "Rock of Ages," and many others sound out today their gospel message to stir and inspire lives to noble deeds in a fashion never known by the sermons of even the world-famed preachers. Sermons, after they are delivered, move people one by one as they are read in books; but gospel songs move and sweep their souls, one by one and in great crowds, up to God in worship and out to man in noble, helpful service.

Hymnologists, singers, and players on instruments have ever been as popular and as much loved as great preachers. David, the sweet singer and time-honored psalmist, is loved and known as far as is Moses, the lawgiver and leader. Sankey is loved as much as Moody, Alexander as much as Torrey, Rodeheaver as much as Sunday, Coleman as much as Truett. Music of the right sort is the greatest aid to preaching. We sandwich our sermons in gospel songs, which enrich the heart of the preacher and prepare the soil of souls for the spiritual seed.

The Importance of Music in Evangelism

The records of soul-winning movements show the power of gospel music in bringing men to God. There have been no great revivals where song has not been regnant. The Welsh Revival was especially marked by its gospel singing. The people preached, prayed, testified in great fashion, but they sang till their songs searched out sinners in all of Wales and sent waves of singing redemption throughout many lands. Gospel songs are powerful not only during great sweeping revival movements, but also in local revivals. A songless revival is unknown among soul-winners. If the people will not sing, they will not hear or heed the gospel. Charles Wesley's songs did almost as much as John Wesley's sermons to stir all of England and put Methodism on the religious map of the world.

The importance of the right kind of gospel music in church and evangelistic work cannot be overemphasized. Some of the values of spiritual songs follow:

1. They create an evangelistic atmosphere, and tune and temper the heart as nothing else can do. They kindle the revival fires.

2. They enrich the lives of preacher and people and bring the power of God into the hearts of men. The prophet Elisha valued music as the instrument which brought on him the hand of God in order that he might prophesy aright (2 Kings 3:14-15).

3. They give a martial spirit to the people to advance against sin. They stir men to their best in the service of God.

4. They are a powerful evangel of the gospel. They preach and teach the truth of God. The basic doctrines of

grace are taught and applied to human hearts in a most effective way by gospel song.

5. They lift and elevate the people and give wings to their aspirations.

6. They win souls. Conviction is carried by song into hearts never otherwise open to the gospel. They melt and break down hard hearts.

7. They solidify fellowship and marshal the forces of Christ's kingdom. Gospel songs aid greatly in the unification of Christian people.

Essentials of Congregational Singing

Congregational singing is necessary for a great soul-winning movement and for regular church evangelism. For the best results in congregational singing there are certain essentials:

1. *A consecrated Christian song leader,* trained in gospel music.

2. *A trained accompanist.*—Much of the failure to have good gospel music is due to poor accompanists. In order to accompany gospel singing well, the accompanist should have special training in gospel hymn playing.

3. *A properly arranged choir platform,* not one put up as an ornament or placed in as an afterthought of the architect, but one put in the proper place so as to be an aid to the worship of the church.—Probably the best arrangement is to have the choir platform near and on a level with the pulpit, elevated and arranged to give proper emphasis to the music. It should be large enough for a great chorus.

4. *A good quality and sufficient quantity of hymnals and songbooks.*—Much of the life of the church will depend on the kind of songbooks used.

5. *The support and sympathy of the pastor and congregation.*—Interest, time, and money should be given to this important phase of the Lord's work.

The Gospel Singer

The gospel singer ought to be deeply spiritual and consecrated in his Christian life, a man full of the Holy Ghost and of faith.

He should have an abundance of patience, tact, common sense, and adaptability.

He must know music. He should have a thorough knowledge of voice, piano, notation, sight-reading, conducting, harmony, composition, history of music, and the history of hymns and tunes and their proper use.

His usefulness will be greatly enhanced by a thorough literary and seminary education. He should know much about the Word of God and how to win men to Christ.

More care should be given to the training of gospel singers. All denominational schools, especially theological seminaries, should give well-prepared courses in gospel music. Courses in classical music in college mean far less in the extension of Christianity and the growth of Christ's kingdom than properly conducted instruction in gospel music. Religious schools should give attention to gospel music in their courses of study. The neglect of gospel music, both instrumental and vocal, in Christian schools is greatly injurious to music in church worship and evangelistic effort.

14

Evangelism in the Home

DEUTERONOMY 11:18-21. Therefore shall ye lay up these my words in your heart and in your soul, and bind them for a sign upon your hand, that they may be as frontlets between your eyes. And ye shall teach them your children, speaking of them when thou sittest in thine house, and when thou walkest by the way, when thou liest down, and when thou risest up. And thou shalt write them upon the door posts of thine house, and upon thy gates: that your days may be multiplied, and the days of your children, in the land which the Lord sware unto your fathers to give them, as the days of heaven upon the earth.

LUKE 17:2. It were better for him that a millstone were hanged about his neck, and he cast into the sea, than that he should offend one of these little ones.

LUKE 18:15-17. And they brought unto him also infants, that he would touch them: but when his disciples saw it, they rebuked them. But Jesus called them unto him, and said, Suffer little children to come unto me, and forbid them not: for of such is the kingdom of God. Verily I say unto you, Whosoever shall not receive the kingdom of God as a little child shall in no wise enter therein.

PARENTAL RESPONSIBILITY FOR THE CHILD

Soul-winning should begin in the home. The parent is responsible to God for the spiritual welfare of the child. Especially is the father commanded to make known God's truth to the child: "The father to the children shall make known thy truth" (Isa. 38:19). "Bring him hither to me" (Matt. 17:17) is Christ's command to every father who has a child possessed of the devil. "Have mercy on me, O Lord, thou son of David; my daughter is grievously vexed with a devil" (Matt. 15:22) should be the constant heart-cry of every mother whose child is out of Christ. Timothy's grandmother and mother taught him the Word of God from his childhood (2 Tim. 1:5; 3:15). Moses commanded the people to teach God's Word unto their children, speaking of them when they sat in their homes (Deut. 11:19-20). Christ said: "Suffer little children to come unto me, and forbid them not" (Luke 18:16). He was not talking primarily about bringing them into the church as some interpret, but about their coming to him early for light and salvation.

The parents' obligation for the temporal well-being of the child is no stronger than their obligation for the child's eternal welfare. If we must clothe, feed, house, protect our children and educate them for earthly citizenship, we should also give them the preparation needed for a heavenly citizenship. Elisha's burning question to the Shunammite mother, "Is it well with the child?" (2 Kings 4:26), is a question which should constantly bear down on the conscience of every parent. "Is the young man Absalom safe?" (2 Sam. 18:29) is a question which every parent should raise concerning his son long before he comes to the hour of his death. David's lament, "O my son Absalom, my son, my son Absalom! would God I had died for thee" (2 Sam. 18:33), would not have been necessary if he had given attention to his boy earlier in life. Many a father has neglected his boy's eternal welfare while his son was young, and as a consequence the boy brought sorrow on his father by his sinful life and hopeless death. The saddest of neglects is the neglect of the soul.

Parental Obligation to Win the Child

The parent should seek to win the child at an early age:

Because of the great influence exercised by the parent over the child.—The child's confidence in his parents is sincere, simple, and reliant. This makes fertile soil for Christian instruction.

Because of the ease with which the children can be turned toward Christ.—Their hearts are responsive to religious truth and have not been hardened by sin's indulgences. They are sinners by nature, but practice in outstanding sin has not calloused their souls. They yield easily to God's call.

Because the parent has the best opportunity to know the children's disposition and needs.—Parents can most easily observe the rise of a consciousness of sin in their children and their coming to the hour of accountability to God. The parent has such an abundant opportunity to plant saving truth in their little hearts.

Because of the possibility of death and disease among childen.—There are many short graves in our cemeteries, and there should be many converts among children. Parents run an awful risk when they give death a chance to carry their children to hell. That parent prays a great prayer and works toward a glorious purpose who prays: "O God, let me so live before my children, teach them the way of life so clearly and simply in their early years, so pray for them day by day, that they may give their hearts to Christ the very hour they pass from under his atoning blood into accountability to God, and thus may there never be a time when sin can claim them for hell."

Because their lives and characters are thus won to Christ for service.—To save a life for Christ's service approaches in importance the saving of a soul from eternal death. The parent has no moral right to be a party, by neglect or indifference, to either the unspeakable tragedy of the damnation of his child's soul or the eternal waste of his life.

Some Words of Caution

Parents should be exceedingly careful not to overpersuade their children in this vital matter. Teach them as earnestly and yet as sensibly and calmly as you do in other matters. Because they are young and cannot understand all of God's plan, we should not therefore turn them over to the devil.

Give them the "milk of the Word." Accepting Christ is the simplest thing a soul can do. Be careful to teach the children right, but teach them.

Parents should make a distinction to the child between the commands of Christ and their obligations to their parents. Coming to Christ and joining the church are duties to God and not to the parent. We must make this clear and let the child act on his own initiative and volition after he has been plainly instructed in God's Word concerning salvation, profession of faith, church membership, baptism, and other doctrines.

Parents ought to exercise the most gracious care in encouraging the child in every move toward Christ, his church, and his service. The tender plant can be easily bruised and set back. I know a mother who will carry a heartache to her grave because she prevented her little nine-year-old daughter from joining the church after she had made an intelligent acceptance of Christ and public profession of him on her own initiative. The child died in thirty days. The mother grieves until yet after many bitter years. The child's destiny was not altered by a failure to join the church, but the mother can never get over her part in preventing the child from doing her duty to God.

Parents should be careful to see that their lives and conduct influence the children in the right way. "It were better for him," says Christ, "that a millstone were hanged about his neck, and he cast into the sea, than that he should offend one of these little ones" (Luke 17:2).

Examples of Parental Love

Take the Shunammite mother and her dead child (2 Kings 4:8-37). The son came to bless the home in answer to prayer. He grew to strength, suddenly became ill, and died in his mother's arms. The father, like many modern fathers, was too busy about the harvest to bring the sick son home from the field himself, or to saddle the ass and go after

Elisha. The mother had it all to do. Her anxiety was shown in her going after the man of God, clinging to his feet, and bringing him to her home. Her burdened heart, her persistence and tireless effort in securing God's power in behalf of her child, and her unstaggering faith make up one of the most beautiful stories in all history. She got her child back from death because she brought God's power into requisition.

The dead son in the Shunammite home is a picture of the spiritually dead children in our homes. Oh, that all mothers were as anxious to bring to life eternal their children, "dead in trespasses and sins," as was this great mother to bring her boy back to life again!

Take the Syrophenician mother and her demon-possessed daughter (Matt. 15:21-28). Notice how she realized her daughter's condition; how she went to Jesus in all humility; how she overcame his silence, the disciples' rebuff, and the doctrinal difficulties Christ presented; and how with simple faith she pressed her suit until Christ said: "O woman, great is thy faith: be it unto thee as thou wilt."

Here was a mother standing in the breach for a daughter in the devil's hands. She won over difficulties. Her faith conquered; Jesus did her bidding. If only all mothers would carry their daughters thus to Christ!

Look at the case of the father pleading for his sin-mastered boy (Luke 9:37-42). The father, in despair at sin's ravages with his boy, brought him to Jesus and said: "Look upon my son." He learned the lesson of fasting, prayer, and faith, and carried his son home in his right mind, delivered from the power of Satan.

Prayer and faith will deliver the hardest cases if only parental love will do its duty.

15

Educational Evangelism

Denominational Schools

Denominational schools are a necessity of life to a militant Christianity. Christian education is inseparably connected with missions and evangelism. Christ put the two, education and evangelism, at the heart of his world program. His commission to his people is to preach and teach so as to win men to discipleship, and then to preach and teach so as to build them up into forces of spiritual power. Teaching is not less important than preaching.

The teacher in a denominational school is an evangelist in an important sense. His work organizes, trains, and utilizes the results of the evangelist's victories in soul-winning. Those Christian people who do not educate will not be able long to evangelize. They will die for lack of trained leadership. Denominational schools should be supported by the prayers and money of Christian people and attended by their children. They should be the equal of the best anywhere in endowment, libraries, laboratories, and other equipment.

Value of denominational schools.—These schools are recruiting stations for leaders in all lines of church and kingdom activity. They call out the called. Many a young man has answered the call of God to preach, and many young men and women have given their lives for missionary service, while studying in denominational schools.

Not only in the line of furnishing preachers, missionaries, church educational and music workers, church secretaries, and so forth, is the value of a Christian school found, but also in sending trained laymen back to the churches. They give the churches a militant leadership, loyal to Christ, with a knowledge of his truth and with training that will insure the triumph of Christianity throughout the world.

Imperatives for denominational schools.—If the denominational school is to fulfil its mission, certain imperatives must be given careful consideration.

1. In administration.—Great care should be exercised in the matter of ownership of denominational schools and in regard to their control by managing boards. The safest principle is to keep these institutions within easy reach of the people. The trustees should not be a perpetual, closed corporation but should be responsible to the people. Self-perpetuity of trusteeships and independent endowments are dangerous to the best interests of denominational schools. The people can be trusted.

2. In faculty.—Care should also be exercised in the selection of teachers, to the end that all shall be loyal, devoted, active Christians. The ideal is for all the teachers in a denominational school to be faithful members of that particular denomination. Thus the best results will be obtained for the students, the churches, and the denomination as a whole. Certainly no one has a right to teach in a Christian school who is unfaithful to the fundamentals of Christianity. Such a person as teacher will hinder the faith and usefulness of the students.

3. In scholarship.—The highest standards of scholarship should be maintained. There should be no lowering of scholastic ideals just because a school is a Christian school. The church is entitled to the best.

4. In curriculum.—A Christian school should seek to make trained Christians out of its students, and this cannot be done without teaching the Bible. Every student should have a comprehensive course in it. Practical courses in church activities should also occupy central places in the curriculum; and the history of missions, with its rich stores

of biography and achievement, should be taught. Sunday school methods should have a place. All these courses provide spiritual and intellectual backing for evangelism.

5. In atmosphere.—The spiritual life and atmosphere of Christian schools should be kept distinctly and continuously evangelistic. This can be accomplished through chapel addresses, school prayer meetings, mission bands, personal workers' groups, and local church activities. There should be frequent college revivals, wherein the administration, faculty, and student body are called to prayer and to personal soul-winning under the leadership of some competent evangelist. Efforts should be made to win to Christ all the unsaved and to enlist all the saved in active service.

While the Baptist Student Union is not limited to denominational schools, its place in evangelism should be noted here. It is the purpose of this body to relate the college student to the local church. It has served, however, in many other valuable ways. One of these has come to be an emphasis on soul-winning. As students have met together to pray for their college friends, they have become burdened for those who are lost. This burden has caused them to go out under the leadership of the Holy Spirit to witness personally to the lost and to lead them to the Lord. The next step has been organized efforts on the part of the students to win the lost. Out of this has grown a refreshing emphasis on youth-led revivals. This work has been marvelously blessed as consecrated youth has given its best in song, witnessing, and preaching. It should be encouraged and used wisely.

Since 1940 there has been an increasing emphasis on Religious Focus Weeks in our Baptist schools. This new but effective approach takes the message of Christianity to every student, every faculty member, and every servant of the college family. Each is led to face frankly the status of his spiritual life and the possibilities for growth and greater effectiveness as the idea of maximum Christianity is presented. The unique features of the Religious Focus

Week are the use of a team of efficient workers, specialists in various Christian emphases, rather than one speaker, and the throwing open of all classes for visitation by team members for a discussion of Christianity in connection with the subject being studied. The conducting of seminars on vital problems, group discussions, chapel exercises, forums, and interviews with individuals and groups of students afford an emphasis which was previously unknown.

A denominational school should certainly be loyal to the denomination. Its leaders and representatives should always have access to the students for the promotion of their work, and the entire student body should be encouraged by example and by instruction to wholeheartedly support the denominational program.

Religious Literature

Value of religious literature.—The printing press is one of God's mightiest agencies in evangelism and missions. "The pen is mightier than the sword." Many Christian workers have not yet rightly valued and utilized the power of the printed page, which in civilized lands is next to omnipresent. The preaching of the gospel is indispensable to the world's salvation; the teaching of the gospel is essential to the cause of righteousness and intelligence. And the preacher and teacher alike are dependent on the printer and his art.

The triumphs of printing fill the world in many lines, but the chief crown of the printer is his service in sending out God's Word. The Bible in the hands of the people has probably done more for civilization and man's redemption than any other human agency. The heart of man can never pay its debt for the blessing it has received from the "leaves of life" sent out from the printer's hands. The printing press is God's light-carrier and vehicle of intelligence.

The devil is greatly advancing his cause by the wrong use of this handmaiden of light. Heresy, the aggressive cults of error, and every agent of sin have utilized the printing press. God's people should learn a lesson from this and put the printed page in its proper place of transcendent power. The maintenance in Christian schools and theological seminaries of departments of journalism, where preachers and other religious workers would have opportunity to study the art of journalism, would mean much to the kingdom of God.

Media of religious literature.—Among the media of religious literature are the Bible, religious and other good books, denominational literature, tracts, and letters.

1. Holy Scriptures.—There should be an increased circulation of the Bible, either in whole or in part, in the homes of the people of all lands. In the best and most religious communities there are many homes without Bibles. What can be said of the heathen and Catholic lands?

2. Religious and other good books.—God's preachers and missionaries should write more. The denominational boards and church organizations should support publishing houses in the endeavor to furnish the people with good books. Colporteurs should be sent out by religious organizations into every corner of the earth, and missionary compounds should be centers for the distribution of good literature.

3. Sunday School Board literature.—The denominational literature used in the Sunday school and other educational organizations of the church should contribute its part in the emphasis on evangelism. Sunday school and Training Union lesson materials should seek at all times an opportunity to aid in the instruction and training of soul-winners. Helps for teachers and leaders should be planned to enable them to use an approach which will be positively evangelistic.

4. Denominational papers.—Religious and denominational papers and magazines should be fully supported. Every church member should feel that it is his duty and his privilege to take and read the periodicals put out by his denomination. Every pastor should consider himself, as in truth he really is, an agent of his denomination's publications. He

should promote their interest in every home in his church. These magazines and papers throb with the soul and spirit of evangelism. They carry God's enlightening grace and power into the hearts, homes, and churches of God's people. Nothing is more important to the constructive life and spiritual conquests of God's churches than the denominational press.

5. Tracts.—One of the effective uses of the press is found in the publication and circulation of tracts. They are valuable for soul-winning, soul-building, indoctrination, and for teaching the truths of God's Word. Brief, pointed, and well-printed tracts will often attract attention and carry the Christian message home to the heart in a way nothing else will. Churches with their Sunday school and Training Union forces could be made centers for the distribution of tracts. Pastors, missionaries, and evangelists should keep a supply of well-selected tracts on hand all the time. They can be mailed out, handed out in making visits, given to passers-by on the streets, and distributed at church doors as congregations gather and disperse. The tract given should be chosen to suit the need of the one receiving it and should be handed out with a prayer for God's blessing on the message. It is often good to follow up the tract with a conference, another tract, or a personal letter.

6. Letters.—Personal letter writing is a very effective way of reaching men and women for Christ. Paul, Peter, James, John, and Jude set a noble example for us in this medium of soul-winning. Their letters, inspired by the Holy Spirit, have thrilled, enriched, and saved multitudes through nearly twenty centuries. Mothers' and fathers' letters to sons and daughters have wrought wonders in the kingdom. Sisters' and sweethearts' letters have brought many a brother and many a lover to Christ. A letter from an esteemed friend will often reach a person when a sermon will not be heard or heeded. A widowed mother, joined by pastor and friends, did her utmost to win her son before he left for army duty

in the Philippine Islands. All efforts failed, and he went away lost, but with a marked Bible as his mother's gift. Three years later a letter, with his mother's tears marking every line, reached the boy, and the word came back: "After reading your letter, telling of your tears and prayers, I read Revelation 3:20; and by some strange but holy presence I opened my heart and let Jesus come in, and I am happy in his peace and love."

Such letters as a means of grace and salvation should not be neglected in the face of such large returns and so little expenditure of time and energy.

16

The Spiritual Value of Money

PROVERBS 11:24-25. There is that scattereth, and yet increaseth; and there is that withholdeth more than is meet, but it tendeth to poverty. The liberal soul shall be made fat: and he that watereth shall be watered also himself.

MALACHI 3:10. Bring ye all the tithes into the storehouse, that there may be meat in mine house, and prove me now herewith, saith the Lord of hosts, if I will not open you the windows of heaven, and pour you out a blessing, that there shall not be room enough to receive it.

LUKE 16:9. And I say unto you, Make to yourselves friends of the mammon of unrighteousness; that, when ye fail, they may receive you into everlasting habitations.

2 CORINTHIANS 9:6-7. But this I say, He which soweth sparingly shall reap also sparingly; and he which soweth bountifully shall reap also bountifully. Every man according as he purposeth in his heart, so let him give: not grudgingly, or of necessity: for God loveth a cheerful giver.

3 JOHN 1-2. The elder unto the well-beloved Gaius, whom I love in the truth. Beloved, I wish above all things that thou mayest prosper and be in health, even as thy soul prospereth.

Here are five meaningful Scripture passages on the Christian and his money. How shall we interpret them?

Proverbs 11:24-25.—God says a man can scatter his money in helping the poor, caring for the orphans, educating the young, and winning people to Christ, and yet increase his own wealth, both of pocket and soul. He says a man can withhold from others and save for himself and yet be a pauper. Covetousness may fatten the purse, but it will starve the soul. "The liberal soul shall be made fat."

Malachi 3:10.—God owns all we have but asks us to recognize his right to the immediate use of one tenth of our income. He says that heaven's windows swing open to us on the hinges of our liberality. Even a tithe rightly used for Christ will swing back God's granary windows and let fall from his bounteous storehouse his richest blessings—sometimes financial, sometimes spiritual—so full and plentiful that our poor hearts cannot receive them all.

Luke 16:9.—Christ is speaking. A man was called to give an account of his stewardship of money entrusted to him. Because of his misuse of the money and his unfaithfulness in financial affairs, he was about to lose his place as steward. He resolved to so use the money as to buy friends who would receive him into their homes when he should be without means.

Here Christ commands his people and his churches to so use their money for spiritual purposes, in soul-saving and kingdom-building institutions, that when it is gone, those helped and won to Christ, who have gone on to glory, may receive them into their eternal reward.

Dr. Jesse Mercer, of Georgia, in 1838 gave $2,500 to the Home Mission Society of Northern Baptists to send two Baptist preachers to evangelize Texas. In 1949 as a result of this investment, there were 3,334 churches co-operating with the Baptist General Convention of Texas, with more than a million members; 4,210 Baptist preachers; twelve great schools; six hospitals; the largest theological seminary in the world; and the largest orphanage in the United States. The 3,334 churches reported 50,855 baptisms in 1949 and total gifts of more than $34,000,000. The Sunday school attendance for the year averaged 367,353; the Training Union attendance, 128,754. Surely millions of souls won to Christ as a result of Jesse Mercer's gift are constantly thanking him as they meet him on the streets of glory.

2 Corinthians 9:6-7.—Here is God's law of harvest in financial and spiritual matters. The soul that sows to itself will gather a selfish, scanty harvest. The soul that sows bountifully shall reap bountifully. Paul says, "God loveth a cheerful giver." Our attitude toward our money will either gain or lose the favor of God for us. If mammon masters the man, God refuses to live in him and love him.

3 John 1-2.—John is writing to a rich layman, Gaius. He wishes him health of body and prosperity in proportion to his spiritual prosperity. John here sets up the true standard of prosperity, which keeps the purse and the soul on the same level. If the pocket prospers and the soul remains in spiritual poverty, the man has lost. Every Christian needs a liberal heart to take care of a prosperous purse.

A Case of Bad Company

PSALM 10:3. For the wicked boasteth of his heart's desire, and blesseth the covetous, whom the Lord abborreth.

1 CORINTHIANS 5:11. But now I have written unto you not to keep company, if any man that is called a brother be a fornicator, or covetous, or an idolater, or a railer, or a drunkard, or an extortioner, with such an one no not to eat.

1 CORINTHIANS 6:10. . . . nor thieves, nor covetous, nor drunkards, nor revilers, nor extortioners, shall inherit the kingdom of God.

EPHESIANS 5:5. For this ye know, that no whoremonger, nor unclean person, nor covetous man, who is an idolater, hath any inheritance in the kingdom of Christ and of God.

God considers the selfish lover of money an idolater and puts him in the same company with whoremongers, drunkards, thieves, extortioners, and the like. He shuts heaven's door on all who pretentiously claim Christ as their Saviour and yet love money better than him. No man's money brings him salvation, but his attitude toward money proves whether or not he has salvation.

Inspiring Examples

Thirteen dollars liberally given started Buckner Orphans Home. In seventy years this orphanage grew to a plant worth $1,500,000, and in that time had housed, mothered, fed, clothed, and educated approximately ten thousand homeless children, and sent them out as trained Christians to serve God and humanity. The Buckner Home Baptist Benevolences now include a welfare mission "for girls who need refuge and care," a ranch-school "for boys who need and want a chance," and a haven for the aged.

A little dying girl in Philadelphia, six-year-old Hattie May Wiatt, gave fifty-seven cents to start a new meeting-house for her church. Her pastor, Dr. Russell H. Conwell, took this small sum and, with her dying testimony and example as an inspiration, built the Baptist Temple, with an auditorium seating 3,135; built Temple University, where 100,000 were enrolled during his lifetime; built the Philadelphia Orphans Home; built three hospitals—the Good Samaritan, the Garretson, and the Greatheart; and built the Samaritan Rescue Mission. He delivered one lecture, "Acres of Diamonds," more than six thousand times, and with the proceeds helped almost ten thousand young men secure an education. The little girl's money failed to buy her life back, but, dying, she gave it to Christ; and her investment is bringing in a measureless harvest to Christ.

A man of wealth, Dr. James P. Boyce, was led to make possible the establishment of the Southern Baptist Theological Seminary. Through the years he replenished its scant treasury and supplied its needs. That seminary, now ninety years old, recently enrolled its ten-thousandth student. Its graduates have gone out to bless the world, win souls, and preach and teach a saving gospel to a lost world. Its record of immortal service has just begun. His investment is bringing eternal dividends; and the souls which these trained preachers have won and will win will receive Dr. Boyce's wealthy, liberal, fat soul into everlasting habitations.

"The liberal soul shall be made fat." Make investments of money, time, and talent for Christ, and God's granaries will fill your lap and heart with riches.

17

Conserving Results

MATTHEW 28:19-20. Go ye therefore, and teach all nations, baptizing them in the name of the Father, and of the Son, and of the Holy Ghost: teaching them to observe all things whatsoever I have commanded you: and, lo, I am with you alway, even unto the end of the world. Amen.

JOHN 15:16. Ye have not chosen me, but I have chosen you, and ordained you, that ye should go and bring forth fruit, and that your fruit should remain: that whatsoever ye shall ask of the Father in my name, he may give it you.

ACTS 2:42. And they continued stedfastly in the apostles' doctrine and fellowship, and in breaking of bread, and in prayers.

NEED FOR SPIRITUAL CONSERVATION

Christ's program for souls, as outlined in the New Testament, is salvation, confession, baptism, church membership, instruction, and service. We cannot break or disregard this order and have permanent, constructive evangelism.

True evangelism is more than winning souls to accept Christ as Saviour. This is one of its tasks, its first great one. But there follows an important and far-reaching task of conserving this victory and utilizing the newly-saved soul in effective service in Christ's kingdom. Men are not saved so that they may keep out of hell or gain heaven. They are saved to serve. The evangelism that stops at conversion and public profession is lopsided, wasteful, incomplete. It should go on to teach, to train, and to develop, and utilize the talents and powers of the new convert. This educational phase of evangelism is transcendently important and should receive the careful attention of all the forces engaged in the promotion of Christ's kingdom.

Modern evangelism finds here its greatest leakage and waste. Much of modern evangelism leaves its spiritual children orphans, homeless and motherless. Churches often let the new "babes in Christ" go without a mother's protecting arms, warm heart, love, and food, until they become backsliders and spiritual driftwood. Such neglect of spiritual children is unpardonable and sinful. Here lies, also, the unspeakable weakness of great "union meetings." The evangelists of such meetings usually do not stress these important duties to the new convert; to be baptized and follow Christ in church membership, to join up in Christ's service and go to work for him. A new convert is entitled to knowledge of all that Christ wants him to do, and to training for his service.

Imperatives for Spiritual Conservation

In order to care for and train the new converts, there are several important matters which should receive the constant attention of the church leaders.

Positive message.—A positive note of truth and conviction should be sounded at all times. Flabby, lopsided preaching will fruit in spineless and convictionless converts. Just as there must be a vital food element in the milk children drink if they are to grow bone and muscle, so in Christian life, there must be indoctrination of vital truth.

Adequate organization.—The church is the home of the new convert. He should be shown the way to this home, with its warmth, love, food, and protection. But the church must be organized to care for and train its spiritual children. The local church with its Sunday school, Training Union, W.M.U., Brotherhood, and church music program, can provide a place for every new convert; and it sins against God and against man if it does not go vigorously and at once after these spiritual possibilities as soon as they are saved.

schools, Training Unions, Christian colleges, and seminaries

Active leadership.—It is the business of churches, Sunday

to furnish an alert, active, and tactful leadership, ready to take hold of every new convert. The deadest thing on earth is a dead church with a dead pastor, dead deacons, a dead Sunday school superintendent. The greatest thing on earth is a live, spiritual, wide-awake, evangelistic church with an aggressive leadership.

Aggressive spirit.—Spiritual aggressiveness is needed to care properly for the new currents of life coming into a church from evangelism. Ice houses, refrigerators, and cold storage vaults are out of place in a church of Jesus Christ. A dry, stiff, cold, ministerial refrigerator in the pulpit is "an abomination of desolation . . . standing where it ought not." An uninspirational, unevangelistic, and unaggressive ministry in the churches is a curse to humanity. Divine currents of power, God's dynamics in life streams, should flow through our churches if they are to draw, hold, and develop a strong and virile constituency and send them out to take this world for Christ.

Persistent effort.—Furloughs and vacations should not be permitted in this work. The devil is never off the job in his task of damning men. Christ's people should be as constant, faithful, and tireless in saving and conserving the souls of men.

Adequate social life.—A new convert must have a place to develop his social life. He must have new companions to take the place of the old ones. He must have joy and pleasure. The church should direct in much of the social life of its people, or the devil will.

Worldwide vision.—The entire program of the church and the denomination should be put into the thinking and life of every new convert. The institutional, benevolent, educational, and missionary program should be brought to his attention, so that he may know, love, and support it. Great undertakings should be put before him to challenge his faith, his liberality, and his powers of soul. Great Christian character cannot be grown on little tasks.

Practical Steps in Spiritual Conservation

Magnify the reception of the new member, either at the time he joins or soon after. This can be done in various ways: a prayer service where he is given special attention, a special introduction to the congregation at some opportune time, a social event in his honor.

Provide each new member with material pertinent to his new relation to the church, perhaps in a kit handed him when he joins or mailed to him shortly thereafter. Such a kit would include a letter of welcome from the pastor, a copy of the church covenant, a pledge card, church envelopes, information about the denominational literature, and perhaps a card on which to check his preference as to type of service.

New members, especially those joining by baptism, should be urged to attend a class of instruction in denominational beliefs and ordinances, church membership, the duties of a Christian. Occasionally a study course on doctrine, stewardship, missions, or a kindred subject might be provided for the new members.

The new member should be enlisted immediately in the organizations of the church—Sunday school, Training Union, Woman's Missionary Union, Brotherhood, choir. Delay at this point can be fatal.

Some specific task, suited to the talent and ability of the new convert, should be assigned. Some may teach, some do charity or hospital work, some distribute tracts, some visit. There are manifold opportunities waiting for willing minds and ready hands.

Each new member should be assigned to an older and mature Christian for encouragement and guidance. This may be done through a Watchmen's or Brothers' Club. The older Christian is to visit the new member in his home, help him with any problems that may arise, encourage him in Bible study, prayer, church attendance, tithing, and witnessing. In time the "babe in Christ" will himself become a member of this group and have the blessing of helping new converts grow to maturity in their spiritual lives.

Section B
Seasonal Evangelism

18

Revivals—How to Promote Them

Psalm 85:6-7. Wilt thou not revive us again: that thy people may rejoice in thee? Shew us thy mercy, O Lord, and grant us thy salvation.

Habakkuk 3:2. O Lord, I have heard thy speech, and was afraid: O Lord, revive thy work in the midst of the years, in the midst of the years make known; in wrath remember mercy.

Acts 1:8. But ye shall receive power, after that the Holy Ghost is come upon you: and ye shall be witnesses unto me both in Jerusalem, and in all Judaea, and in Samaria, and unto the uttermost part of the earth.

Acts 247. . . . praising God, and having favour with all the people. And the Lord added to the church daily such as should be saved.

Revivals in the Bible[1]

1. A revival by the brook, Genesis 32:24-30
2. A revival by a lawyer, Exodus 33
3. A revival by a judge, 1 Samuel 7:1-14
4. A revival by a prophet, 1 Kings 18:21-39
5. A revival by a king, 2 Kings 23:1-27
6. A revival of Bible reading, Nehemiah 8:1-12
7. A revival of sabbath keeping, Nehemiah 13:15-22
8. A Baptist's revival, Matthew 3:1-12
9. A revival in the streets, Matthew 21:1-17
10. A personal work revival, John 1:35-51
11. A woman's revival, John 4:28-42
12. A revival in a graveyard, John 11:30-45
13. A revival in a city, Acts 2:1-4, 14-47
14. A revival in the church, Acts 4:23-37

---

[1]Cf. E. D. Head, *Revivals in the Bible*, (Fort Worth: Seminary Book Store, 1951).

15. A revival growing out of fear, Acts 5:1-14
16. A revival growing out of persecution, Acts 7:54 to 8:4
17. A layman's revival, Acts 8:5-25
18. A revival in a carriage, Acts 8:26-40
19. An unlawful revival, Acts 10:23-48
20. A sabbath day revival, Acts 13:44-52
21. A revival by the riverside, Acts 16:9-15
22. A revival in a jail, Acts 16:23-34
23. A Holy Ghost revival, Acts 19:1-20
24. A revival in Rome, Acts 28:30-31; Philippians 1:12-14

Value of Revivals

The importance and spiritual value of revivals of religion to the cause of Christ cannot possibly be set down in human language or calculated by human mathematics. From the day of Pentecost, when Christ's little church in Jerusalem won three thousand souls in one day to eternal life and obedience to the Saviour, down to the great revivals of our own day wherein hundreds of thousands of people have professed Christ and their renewal of faith and restoration to the joys of salvation, revivals have blessed humanity, saved souls, inaugurated great movements for God's kingdom, set forward the cause of Christ, and brought glory unmeasured to his holy name.

The value of these spiritual awakenings may be somewhat estimated from the following statements:

They reap a harvest of souls. A majority of believers are won to Christ in revivals. Millions of souls now in heaven or in Christ's service on earth would have been in hell or on their way there if it had not been for revivals of soul-saving power.

They result in lives being volunteered and dedicated to God's work.

They lift churches and communities out of lethargy and spiritual dearth, up to the higher planes of spiritual power. They quicken religious zeal, strengthen faith, brighten hopes, arouse energies, enlist forces, call out new agencies for God, and breathe into the souls of the people the breath of God.

They are the very breath and life of missions. Revival fires light up the mission fields and guide God's people to worldwide proclamation of the gospel. Spiritual passion to save one's neighbor kindles a longing to reach the lost beyond the seas. Thus revivals reach around the world. Pentecost sent out waves of spiritual power which yet encircle the world, and promoted enterprises which yet uplift humanity.

They are fruitful in initiating new movements for God and humanity and in organizing new agencies for the promotion of Christ's kingdom. Many educational institutions and benevolent enterprises have found their inspiration and beginnings in revivals.

They are the richest means of church extension. Most churches in home lands and foreign fields were started as a result of a season of gospel revival.

They have brought out and developed some of the world's greatest leaders, including preachers, singers, and lay workers of all kinds. The Wesley brothers, Dwight L. Moody, Sankey, and Sunday are examples. John the Baptist and the apostle Peter found their chance and way to fame through revivals.

They open up the fountains of liberality in the hearts and purses of the people. Visions of Christ's kingdom and the value of life, talent, and money put into his cause have been found in revival times.

Factors in Promoting Revivals

Revivals result from the harmonious co-operation of two great forces: a redeeming Saviour and a compassionate, consecrated people. The presence of God is an absolute necessity. His divine Spirit is the primary factor. He is the true and only source of revival power. "Not by might, nor by power, but by my Spirit, saith the Lord of hosts" (Zech.

4:6). Yet even God needs, and must have, men in promoting a revival.

As these two forces work together to promote a revival, there are certain factors which are essential.

Foremost among the human factors is *prayer*. Prayer brings God's energy and wisdom to man's tasks. All spiritual history proves that prayer is vital and essential in revivals. Pentecost's soul-saving conquests came after the continuous prayers of the Jerusalem church. All of Christ's earthly movements were marked by prayer. The successful ministry of all evangelists has been immersed in soulful supplication.

In promoting a revival great emphasis must be put on prayer. The preacher must lead the people in much praying. It should be planned and organized. Cottage prayer meetings should be held, family and group prayers should be encouraged, and individual praying should be stimulated. Prayer generates power, creates spiritual atmosphere, and makes preaching, singing, and personal work easy. It lubricates all the wheels of the church machinery and guarantees evangelistic victory.

Equal in importance with prayer is the *preaching* of the gospel of Christ as laid down in God's inspired Book. There is no substitute for gospel preaching in the promotion of Christ's kingdom. The presentation of Christ crucified is still God's means for enlightening the souls of lost men, turning them away from their sins, and causing them to seek relief from the awful malady of sin and escape from its doom. The right sort of preaching in revivals of religion is tremendously important.

Revival preaching should be filled with the real gospel of Christ. It must present Christ as Priest, Lord, and King of the soul, telling of his deity, his death, his vicarious atonement for sin, his unmistakable resurrection to life, his present reign at God's right hand, and his personal return in the consummation of the purpose of God. Christ's mission, from his birth through his ascension to the throne of God, should be presented with soul-breaking passion in the power of the Spirit of God to the hearts of men, if revivals do what they ought. No shams, substitutes, camouflages, spiritual narcotics, or philosophies of men can, in God's sight, be put in the place of the gospel of a crucified Christ. Songs, homilies, testimonies, and exhortations are good and helpful, but they cannot take the place of virile gospel preaching.

This gospel preaching should be spiritual, heartful, compassionate, enthusiastic, intelligent, sane, and plain. It should set out, but not in a controversial spirit, the vital and fundamental doctrines of God's Word. Every lost soul is entitled to know the truth and just the true steps to God, and every saved man can justly claim his right to know all that God commands him to do. A doctrineless preaching is a spineless and powerless preaching.

The great truths of the gospel and about sin should be proclaimed to men seeking Christ: sin, hell, the cross, the blood, repentance, faith, confession, obedience, baptism, and service. Men should be told of all these by the preacher, their spiritual leader. The preacher who stands as an ambassador for Christ between God's mercy, love, and wrath and man's doomed, dying, sinning soul, and minces, dodges, dallies with, evades, or fails to preach, the gospel is a traitor and sinner of the worst sort. If he plays with lost souls on the way to hell, he joins the devil's Judases and deserves the frown of God and the execrations of outraged Christianity.

Brother preacher, when you deal with dying, immortal souls, show them God's light, God's Son, God's truth. Your words will meet you at the judgment. Souls may depend on them and lose all that is dear in eternity.

After an awful, head-on collision, the engineer, pinned under his burning engine and bleeding at mouth, nose, and ear, with his dying strength waved a little piece of yellow paper, and said, "Somebody gave me the wrong orders." Some doomed man may stand at God's last great day and point his finger at you and say, "You gave the wrong orders." If you give him anything but the gospel, you will not be guiltless in that awful hour. "Preach the word," for "the gospel . . . is the power of God unto salvation"; preach "Christ and him crucified"—these are God's orders to preachers.

Another essential factor in evangelism is *personal work*. Results will largely depend on the amount and character of the personal work done.

The pastor should lead his people in personal work, organizing and training them for this important service. The church officers and the Sunday school teachers and officers are the main ones in the church to go out in personal soul-winning. They are the pastor's cabinet in evangelism.

Personal work can be done with some in the congregation at the close of the sermon; it is better to see others privately in their homes or in some other quiet place. In either case, great wisdom and tact are needed in approaching and winning people. Only "they that be wise" will win souls.

It is usually best for women to deal with women and men with men, though often splendid results are obtained otherwise.

Nothing is more powerful than the use of Scripture in personal work. The worker must know the Scripture passages to use and be able to turn to them and quote them without looking at the Bible.

The worker should pray for the Spirit's power before and during the approach to the unsaved.

The worker should never be sidetracked by an argument on any doctrinal controversy, but should keep on the main line of sin and the Saviour.

Essential to effective evangelism is church *co-operation*. Pentecost teaches us that the best revivals come from a prepared church with a co-operating membership. The 120 in the Jerusalem church were all together and of one accord in prayer and personal work. The men of a church, as well as the women, should put their strength back of every revival movement. The miracle of healing recorded in the second chapter of Mark proves what co-operation will do in evangelizing. The four men made their plans, then pushed those plans with faith and effort, and persistent over every difficulty, won through Christ's power. Every evangelistic effort should be backed by a co-operating church.

Nothing is more important in a revival than the spiritual attitude of *compassion* on the part of the people of God. "They that sow in tears shall reap in joy" is God's law of the harvest. "As soon as Zion travailed, she brought forth her children" (Isa. 66:8). This is as true today as ever in the history of the world. If God's people do not weep over sinners, sinners will not weep over their sins. The true atmosphere and psychology of a revival stems from burdened and brokenhearted discipleship.

Publicity is essential to a successful revival, but it should be marked by sanity and judgment. Newspapers, billboards, handbills, large signs, personal letters, public announcements, personal approach—all these can be used. The people ought to be informed in an impressive way about the meetings.

Thorough *organization* should be made, including place of meeting, time of services, ushers to handle and seat the crowds. Special attention should be given to the organization of personal workers. They should be inspired, instructed, given definite tasks, given opportunity for reporting results. Proper care should be taken to follow up converts, securing their enlistment in church membership and in the service of God. Revivals do not go off by spontaneous combustion. If they are to be properly conducted and their results conserved, they must be organized. Half of Billy Sunday's and Dwight L. Moody's success was due to their organization. Revivals of smaller proportions should be organized to get larger results.

Music is an important factor in revivals. The singing should be led by a trained, consecrated, spiritual man of God. The accompanist should know gospel music and have enthusiasm and fire in her touch. All sorts of instruments can be used to great effect in revivals. The songs should be gospel songs, true in their teaching, soul-moving in their sentiment and power. Much of the singing should be congregational. All the people should be induced to sing. The choir is to lead, but the people must sing for the best results.

An *after-meeting* can be an instrument of great effectiveness in a revival, but wisdom is needed in managing it. It is best to have the personal workers distributed throughout the congregation before the dismission. Cordial appeal should be made for all who feel the need of help to remain. Much prayer and personal work should be used in the after-meeting. Propositions to the unsaved should be plain and clear. Opportunity for church membership should be given to all who profess faith in Christ at the close of every service. Obedience and church membership should be plainly pressed on all who trust the Saviour.

Following up the revival in *conservation* is an important matter. The impressed who do not surrender to the Saviour should be seen and urged to settle the matter. Those who have not joined the church should be urged to join. Great meetings are often lost at this point. The new members should be enlisted, trained, and given a place of service; the pastor and officers should put this high in their program. The called should be called out; volunteers for special service should be encouraged and helped to secure the necessary training.

Remember: "There isn't any easy way to have a good revival. If you would have a great revival in your church, you must make great plans for it."

19

Simultaneous Crusades

MATTHEW 9:36. But when he saw the multitudes, he was moved with compassion on them, because they fainted, and were scattered abroad, as sheep having no shepherd.

MARK 16:15. And he said unto them, Go ye into all the world, and preach the gospel to every creature.

ACTS 2:1. And when the day of Pentecost was fully come, they were all with one accord in one place.

1 CORINTHIANS 9:22. To the weak became I as weak, that I might gain the weak: I am made all things to all men, that I might by all means save some.

THE VALUE OF A SIMULTANEOUS CRUSADE

A method of evangelism that has developed largely from the tremendous undertakings and mass movements of this day is the simultaneous revival, a crusade in which all of the churches of like faith and convictions within a given territory enter into a revival, beginning and closing at the same time. Simultaneous campaigns are gaining in popularity and power, and God has singularly blessed them in recent years under the mighty leadership of some of our outstanding preachers.

The simultaneous crusade is effective in groups of small town and country churches as well as among the churches in metropolitan centers, and is an integral part of a great nation-wide and worldwide effort to bring men to Christ and to establish his kingdom upon the earth.

Below are listed a few of the obvious advantages of such a united effort:

1. It engenders a Pentecostal condition, conducive to Pentecostal results.

2. It is church-centered, thus strengthening the local churches and making possible the conservation of results in each church.

3. It gives every church in the territory, large or small, the same assistance and direction in leadership.

4. It enlists every church in prayer and promotion.

5. It makes possible more, and a higher type of, publicity.

6. It greatly strengthens the fellowship among the churches.

7. It leads to the more effective promotion of extension work.

8. It wins the lost, puts hell to mourning and heaven to rejoicing, and adds stars to the crown of the Redeemer.

Dangers to Be Avoided in a Simultaneous Crusade

In his *Handbook for Southern Baptist Revival*,[1] Dr. Roland Q. Leavell mentions eight dangers of mass evangelism:

1. Publicity without prayer
2. Preaching without personal work
3. Sensationalism without spirituality
4. Emotion without instruction
5. Exhortation without indoctrination
6. Criticism without construction
7. Campaigns without continuity
8. Ingathering without enlistment

As one writer has put it, "there is the danger of depending upon publicity, visiting evangelists, good music, and a community interest rather than upon God and his Holy Spirit. Churches that would promote such a co-operative meeting must be reminded often that it is 'not by might, nor by power, but by my Spirit' that such meetings are helpful."[2]

---

[1] Atlanta: Home Mission Board, 1939.

[2] W. L. Muncy, Jr., *New Testament Evangelism for Today* (Kansas City: Central Seminary Press, 1941), p. 252.

Preceding a Simultaneous Crusade

As is true of any endeavor, the results will very largely depend upon the amount of wise preparation and work that has gone before.

Prayer.—Prayer should initiate, precede, and undergird the campaign as a whole, as well as the effort in each participating church.

Organization.—The organization should be carefully set up well in advance, with a sufficient number of leaders and committees to insure the maximum results. A steering committee might be composed of a general chairman and the chairman of each of the following committees: financial, publicity, radio, fellowship, extension, census, special rallies, and prayer. Each association should have one or more officers charged with the responsibility of promoting evangelism within that association, just as it has officers who are actively engaged in promoting Sunday school, Training Union, W.M.U., and Brotherhood work. These men will naturally have the direction of the simultaneous crusade, seeing in it each year the climax of their perennial efforts to lead every church in the association to have at least one revival annually and to assume the initiative in sponsoring revivals in weak churches and unchurched communities.

Preparatory meetings.—Frequent meetings of the leaders and committee members and rallies of various interested groups should precede the revival period. One who has pioneered in this field feels that the special rallies are the most effective element in preparing for the crusade. These may include Sunday school rallies, Brotherhood rallies, W.M.U. rallies, youth rallies, musicians' rallies, cottage prayer meetings, all-church prayer meetings, and others.

During the Crusade

Many effective plans have developed as a natural outgrowth of methods used in simultaneous crusades. These include—

Fellowship meetings.—The pastors, evangelists, and song leaders meet regularly—perhaps daily except for Sundays—to report on the revivals, to enjoy the fellowship of others engaged in a common effort, to receive information as to plans which have proved successful in other churches and inspiration for the tasks ahead, and to engage in prayer for a great outpouring of God's Spirit.

High attendance day.—High attendance day in Sunday school is one of the most effective methods of meeting the perplexing problem of getting lost people and unattached Baptists to attend preaching services. All of the Sunday schools should strive to reach attendance goals on the middle Sunday of the crusade. Success depends upon the cooperation of every department and class and the untiring efforts of every teacher and pupil. The Sunday school and preaching services may be combined into an integrated service, with a simple evangelistic message and an invitation that will draw into the net those who should respond to the claims of Christ and who are present because of the challenge of the day.

Dr. C. E. Matthews, secretary of evangelism for the Home Mission Board, offers the following suggestions for promoting attendance for this Sunday:

> The pastor and Sunday school superintendent should agree on an attendance objective for the Sunday school. . . . The objective should be to break all records. . . . People respond to a challenge, but they will not respond to something easy. . . . After a tentative attendance goal is set, have a meeting with the departmental superintendents of the Sunday school and obtain their consent and cooperation in the effort. This should be done at least one week before the revival begins.
>
> Preceding the evening preaching service of the Monday after the first Sunday of the revival have a meeting for all teachers, officers, and organized class officers of the Sunday school. Serve a dinner for the occasion at 6:30 P.M. At this meeting break the attendance goal down by departments. Then allow time before the preaching service for a meeting by departments of at least twenty minutes in which each department will break the attendance goal down by classes.

In this precessional meeting make plans to contact every person enrolled in the Sunday school by Saturday night of that week. The best incentive for making these contacts that we have ever used is the chain method. The Baptist book store in each state has in stock chain links made of gummed paper. . . . Be sure to have them on hand at this meeting. Order at least twice as many links as you have persons enrolled in the Sunday school. The slogan is: "Don't break the chain. Do not be a missing link." Have every person in the Sunday school, from the pastor to the youngest baby in the nursery, sign a link. Of course, where children are too young to sign their names, the parent will sign for them.

Have a placard made for each department, showing the name of the department and the attendance goal for it. Hang these placards on the wall of the church or in the church foyer where the people can see them. Have the links turned in to the superintendents each evening. [Recognition should be given the first department that has its attendance quota pledged.] Tabulate [the links] and form a chain . . . , fastening them to the departmental placard to which they belong. The plan is to have the number of links signed by Saturday night that will equal the total attendance objective. When this is done, make a complete chain of all department links and stretch the chain around the walls of the church. The fact that each link represents a life makes this chain the most interesting and attractive object one can imagine.

The signing of these links puts people to work. A record number of visits will be made and interest in the revival engendered. The chain method can be used over and over in the same church without losing its effectiveness. Of course, there are many other methods that can be used in visitation. The idea is to reach the goal.[3]

Another method is to use a card, to be signed by the one solicited, which reads as follows: "I promise to be one of _____ in Sunday school at the _____ Baptist Church next Sunday and help to break all attendance records." At the bottom of the card following the name and address of the individual allow space for the department and class which they attend or to which they are assigned.

Specially sponsored meetings.—Different groups may sponsor the evening services during the second week and en-

---

[3]C. E. Matthews, *The Southern Baptist Program of Evangelism* (Atlanta: Home Mission Board, 1949), pp. 94-96.

deavor to secure as large an attendance as possible. For instance, Monday night may be women's night, sponsored by the W.M.U.; Tuesday, men's night, sponsored by the Brotherhood; Wednesday, Sunday school night; Thursday, family night; Friday, Training Union night; and Saturday, youth night.

Sunday school at night.—Dr. C. Y. Dossey, assistant secretary of evangelism for the Home Mission Board, has pioneered in the promotion of "Sunday School at Night" during the second week of a revival as a means of securing attendance and enlisting the entire Sunday school in visitation.

The plan is for the Sunday school membership to assemble by departments at night, thirty minutes preceding the preaching service, just as they assemble on Sunday morning. The departments have a ten-minute worship period, with the departmental superintendents in charge. Then the classes assemble, with the teachers in charge. A report is made by each class, listing the number present, the number of visits and telephone calls made, the number of lost souls contacted, and the number of unsaved and unenlisted present. These reports are handled just as the reports each Sunday, with a departmental report being made from the class reports and then a general report summarizing the departmental reports. In this way the evangelist is enabled to see the work that has been done during the day and also the number of prospects present for the service that evening.

After the making of the reports the teacher will have an opportunity to speak to the unsaved and unenlisted present. If there are none, the time may be spent in assigning additional prospects for visitation the next day, and in prayer.

The reports of the elementary departments include only the number present for the children, but the teachers and other workers should make the same report as the others. It is suggested that stories be used in the elementary departments after the reports have been made.

Prayer meetings.—Each evening service when the "Sunday school at night" is not in progress should be preceded by prayer meetings for the revival, the men, the women, and the young people meeting in separate prayer groups.

AFTER THE CRUSADE

The results of a simultaneous crusade should be conserved in each participating church as wisely and thoroughly as they are after an individual church revival. It is on the point of conservation of results that the enemies of mass evangelism have made their most effective criticism, and all too many times we have had to admit that it was justified.

The period just after a revival is a very crucial time in the life of a church and in the lives of those who have just been saved and enlisted. It is no time for the pastor and members to take a vacation, but rather a time to show the new members that they are as interested in them after their acceptance of Christ as they were in getting them to attend the revival and to accept Christ.

The new members—

have a readiness for the responsibilities of church membership which must be capitalized upon immediately if they are to become useful members. They should be enlisted in the various organizations of the church; they should be instructed in their stewardship responsibilities; they should be taught the doctrines of their church; their talents should be discovered and put to work. . . .

A good revival is always a beginning, or initiating, activity, and is not concluded with the close of the special services. There will perhaps be many who have been reached but who have not surrendered to Christ.[4]

The churches should be organized to continue their evangelistic work.

---

[4]Bernard King, "Using Men in the Church Revival," *Southern Baptist Brotherhood Journal,* January-February-March, 1949, pp. 44-45.

20

Youth Revivals[1]

Youth is God's best time with the soul. Logic, common sense, and tables of statistics all combine to prove that statement. More than 80 per cent of all church members are converted before they reach the age of eighteen. Techniques of evangelism aimed specifically and primarily at the winning and enlisting of young people are therefore useful and, indeed, imperative as a part of the total ministry of a church.

The youth revival is not a new or revolutionary development in evangelism. In a very real sense, the ministry of Jesus was youth-centered. He himself was in his early thirties, and he went to his cross with "the dew of his youth" upon him. Most of his followers were young people; his original twelve disciples were drawn from the ranks of the young. Christianity began as a young people's movement, and it has always made its greatest advances with a challenge to their enthusiasm, fervor, and zeal.

The youth revival is, in its simplest definition, an evangelistic effort aimed at young people. It is based upon the belief that youth can best be reached by those of approximately the same age and through the use of certain special techniques and methods adapted for this purpose. In the body of this chapter, these basic principles and special techniques will be considered.

---

[1] This chapter was prepared by Charles Wellborn, pastor of Seventh and James Baptist Church, Waco, Texas. He has been identified with the youth revival movement in Texas from its beginning. At the time of this writing, he is also serving as the preacher for the Southern Baptist Radio Hour.

Basic Principles

The youth revival must be *youth-centered*.

If young people are to be most effectively reached through the medium of a youth revival, young people must be placed at the center of the evangelistic effort. The activities of the entire church are to be directed toward the conversion and enlistment of the community's young people. Ordinarily this should mean at least these things:

The revival leadership—preacher, singer, and other workers—should be young people or should have definite youth appeal.

Local young people should be enlisted to do the bulk of the work in preparation for and in carrying on the services. Committees of young people should be formed for specific jobs; and with competent adult counsel, young people should be responsible for every phase of work. The more individuals enlisted for work in preparation for the meeting, the better. Often, effective and gratifying results will be seen in the lives of the church young people as a result of their assumption of responsibility during the preparation period.

Insofar as possible, young people should be in the forefront in the public services. They should preside at the services, usher, fill the choir, play the musical instruments, and give testimonies. Once again, it is important to use as many different persons as is practical.

The music used and the messages preached should be definitely and specifically designed to appeal to young people and to meet their spiritual problems. The preacher should be able to speak in a language which young people understand. His subjects, his themes, and his illustrations can be effectively molded to the particular needs of his congregation.

The youth revival must be *church-centered*.

In the emphasis placed upon conversion and in the zeal for the reaching of large numbers, many workers neglect to place proper value on the place of the church as the instrument by which Christian character is nurtured and matured. Here is one of the great dangers of present-day youth evangelism. Young converts must be brought into the full program of the church, and they must learn at the very beginning the basic importance of that institution as the body of Christ and the fellowship of believers.

In specific application to the youth revival, the term "church-centered" means at least two things: First, it means that the position of the church is definitely explained and taught in the course of the public services. Second, it means that the church as a whole recognizes its responsibilities in the youth evangelistic effort. The entire membership, through every agency, should support, attend, pray for, and work in, a youth revival.

The youth revival must be *Christ-centered*.

It is a cardinal principle, not only of youth revivals, but of every sort of evangelistic effort, that the center of the message and the ministry must be the personality and the redemptive work of Jesus Christ. This goes almost without saying. Especially do the daring, the humility, and the selfless sacrifice of the Master have a challenging appeal to youth. They are at the period of life when it is easiest to forsake the ordinary and the commonplace for the higher planes of consecration and dedication. "All for Christ" can be made an effective reality in their lives.

Techniques

In the discussion of organizational techniques which follows it is not intended to suggest that in these mechanics lies the secret of successful youth evangelism. The source of power for a youth revival is exactly the same as for any other evangelistic effort: It lies in prayer and in consecrated service. Spiritual power can, however, be implemented by these techniques.

Types of revivals.—Generally, two types of evangelistic campaigns have been used: the city-wide meeting and the local church meeting. Each has its function. Both are intended for the general purpose of evangelization, but the approach differs. The church revival is ideal for the winning of the largest number of lost young people, while the city-wide meeting serves to make a distinctive impact for God on the community and, at the same time, to reach people who would not attend a local church meeting. In the city-wide campaign special care must be taken to emphasize properly the role of the church.

Organization.—In both the city-wide and the local church campaigns, it has been found advisable to set up a committee system as a basis of organization. Each committee should be provided with a chairman and an adult adviser. The committee chairmen, along with the general chairman and the pastor or pastors, usually make up the steering committee. In the city-wide campaign, each participating church provides at least one member for each committee and then duplicates the committee setup within its own group of young people. It is absolutely imperative that each committee function effectively in its own area and that the members not be mere figureheads while the pastor or some other leader actually does the work.

The following committee plan is only suggestive and must be modified to fit the need of any individual situation:

1. Finances.—Many groups have preferred to raise all necessary money before the meeting began and to take no collections in the services themselves. This has proved especially effective in city-wide efforts. It is important that the young people themselves take an active part, not only in the raising of money, but in the actual giving from their own resources.

2. Publicity.—Publicity is an extremely important area of work. Youth groups have successfully used dozens of unique methods for publicity purposes. It is safe to say that any method of publicity which is in good taste and which does

not smack of cheap commercialism is valid for use. In addition to full employment of such important mediums as newspapers, radio, posters, and public announcements in churches and schools, various revivals have been advertised in school and college newspapers, by the dropping of leaflets or handbills from a circling airplane, by banners stretched across street intersections and placards attached to the backs or sides of automobiles, by bumper cards, milk bottle tops, doorknob hangers, sidewalk stencils, billboards, and even by parades. No publicity method should be used which cannot be well done and efficiently handled. For instance, it is not wise to schedule a parade unless it can be well organized and large enough to draw attention and secure a favorable reaction from the public.

When all is said and done, no method of publicity is more effective than personal contact. Many revivals have used as their chief publicity method a system by which the town or city is marked off into areas and every home in the city is contacted by a personal visit. In addition, every telephone number is called.

3. Arrangements. — The committee on arrangements handles the physical facilities for the services. Ordinarily its responsibilities include such matters as the ushering, the platform decorations, and flowers. In case the meeting is held outside or in a tent, the committee's work is increased, for its members will aid in securing attendance—getting people to go inside the meeting instead of loitering on the outside.

4. Music.—The music committee is responsible for working with the song leader in organizing the youth choir, in providing the best in special music, and in all other matters pertaining to the musical program of the meeting. The importance of the right kind of evangelistic music, especially in a youth campaign, cannot be overemphasized. The wise use of choruses will add much to the services. Almost all young people like to sing if they are given a chance and the kind of music they enjoy.

5. Spiritual Preparation.—In many ways, the spiritual preparation committee is the most important of all committees. It is charged with organizing the prayer efforts of the church or churches and with using every method possible to prepare spiritually for the meeting. Often this committee also handles the securing of individuals to give short, meaningful personal testimonies in the services. If this is carefully and prayerfully handled, it can be one of the most powerful instruments of the Holy Spirit. In the great Waco youth revival of 1946 on the campus of Baylor University, testimonies were given by college and high school athletic stars, social leaders, returned veterans, faculty members, popular campus girls, and others. Prayer groups should be organized; and an organized program for the visitation of prospects, both before and during the revival, should be set up.

6. Seminars and fellowship activities.—In the effort to appeal to young people from every possible angle, it has been found that seminars, or discussion groups, as well as social fellowship activities, can be effectively combined with the regular evangelistic services for the week. Discussion groups on problems of Christian living may be held before the services, and fellowship periods afterward; or they may be held on alternate nights after the services. In any case, they should be as carefully prepared as any other part of the service. Both seminars and fellowship periods should keep as their fundamental aim the leading of young people to a consecrated and dedicated relationship to Christ.

Seminar groups will discuss such subjects as the problems of Christian recreation, methods of witnessing, prayer, finding the will of God, and courtship problems. Clever and provocative titles can be used to inspire interest in these periods. One seminar leader uses these titles:

> How to Win Friends and Marry One
> I Have My Doubts
> On the Witness Stand

Getting Through to God
One Life—What to Do with It
What's Wrong with This—If Anything?
I'm a Baptist—So What?

Fellowship periods provide wholesome Christian recreation and generally end with refreshments, followed by a brief and impressive devotional period. Care should be taken that the games or other entertainment used does not descend to the childish level and so fail to interest the high school or college group for which the revival is primarily planned.

7. Follow through.—The work of the follow-through committee cannot be stressed too much. The eventual effect of a youth revival will very largely be determined by the way in which this committee functions. It should provide for a system of personal work in which mature Christians, especially prepared for the task, counsel and pray with each young person who comes in response to the invitation from night to night. This counseling work cannot end with the revival. It must go on for months afterward, until each new convert is led into a right relationship to the church, into prayer and Bible study, and into effective personal witnessing on his own. It is the function of this committee to preserve and conserve the spiritual results of the meeting.

Dangers

Because youth evangelism is particularly susceptible to certain dangers, it is wise to keep these weak points in mind and to guard against anything that will, in the long run, hurt the kingdom work.

There is a danger that the church will adopt the attitude that a youth revival is purely the concern of the young people and will take no active part in the preparation for the services. Such unconcern on the part of the church is one of the quickest ways to destroy the spiritual effectiveness of the meeting.

There is a danger that if the revival is successful, the young people of the church may feel that they have a "corner" on spirituality. Their enthusiasm and zeal must be effectively integrated into the total program of the church.

There is a danger that after a week or more of intensive youth revival activity, the regular youth program of the church may seem tame and unsatisfactory to many young people. The church has the responsibility of providing a program of activities which will supply their needs.

There is a danger that immature young Christians will go off on tangents and become radical or badly confused. This danger should be met by keeping wise and understanding adult leadership in constant touch with every phase of the youth revival.

Conclusion

This attempt at a summary of the information concerning youth revivals does not begin to cover the various phases of the subject. Each meeting will have its individual problems; these problems, in all cases, can be met and overcome by the use of prayerful common sense. The power of Christ has richly blessed in the transformation of countless young lives through the youth revival movement. At its best, the movement does not pretend to be that which will bring in the kingdom of God by itself. It is, however, being used of God. It should take its place as a valuable and important part of the total evangelistic program of every church.

21

Brotherhood Revivals[1]

1 SAMUEL 10:26. And Saul also went home to Gibeah; and there went with him a band of men, whose hearts God had touched.

MARK 16:15. And he said unto them, Go ye into all the world, and preach the gospel to every creature.

ACTS 6:8. And Stephen, full of faith and power, did great wonders and miracles among the people.

ACTS 8:5. Then Philip went down to the city of Samaria, and preached Christ unto them.

Although Jesus called men, taught men, and commissioned men to the essential task of soul-winning, his soul-winning program has, in a large measure, been left to the women of the churches. This is due to the unconcern of men as a result of many contributing causes; nevertheless, the kingdom task is primarily a job for men. This is so because the man is by divine right the head of the house, as Christ is head of the church. That being true, the responsibility for both the temporal and the spiritual welfare of the home and the church rests primarily upon the man.

As far as we are able to learn from the Scriptures, the Holy Spirit has his way of getting at the lost through the channel of them that are already saved. When the Holy Spirit sought to see that the Ethiopian eunuch was converted, he singled out Philip, a layman who was conducting a great revival in Samaria, and led him to a chariot that was returning to Ethiopia with the eunuch, who was reading Isaiah 53. Philip was used to lead the eunuch to faith in

---

[1]This chapter was prepared by Clifton Brannon, lay evangelist and president of the Baptist Brotherhood of Texas.

Jesus Christ, the Messiah. When Cornelius, the Roman centurion, was praying, he was told to send men to Joppa and to call for one Simon, whose surname was Peter, who should tell him things whereby he should be saved. The Holy Spirit today needs laymen and has used laymen to win the lost to Christ.

Revivals led by laymen are not a new thing. They date from Old Testament times. The pages of the Scriptures give several instances in which laymen led out in revivals. Just after the turn of the nineteenth century, the Lord spoke to Southern Baptist men, and there was organized what is now known as the Baptist Brotherhood of the South. Brotherhood revivals, sponsored by the Brotherhood and led by laymen, have been used by the Lord as one means of winning the lost. In this chapter, we shall endeavor to show the purposes, the methods, and the results of Brotherhood revivals, and how they can be employed in reaching the lost for Christ.

Purposes of Brotherhood Revivals

The purpose of the Brotherhood revival is the mobilization of the manpower of every community into a mighty army for God and righteousness. Such a program will normally challenge the latent powers of the men beyond the expectations of the church and the pastor. Through teamwork and the thrilling joy that follows in the course of winning the lost, soul-winning fires will be kindled, and the winner will be established in his Christian service. This was demonstrated in the experiences of the seventy sent forth by Jesus, as described in Luke 10. Once the satisfaction of winning a man to Christ is realized, with its full content of spiritual joy, the whole program of the church will be leavened by more Christlike living, witnessing, giving, and serving.

A Brotherhood revival will stir up men who are saved, showing them that the harvest fields are white, and causing them to come to a realization that the laborers are few. When men are stirred by the Spirit of the Lord for his cause and kingdom, the entire church will be moved for the Lord. When Joshua said, "As for me and my house, we will serve the Lord," the entire household was affected by the decision of the man. Today, when a father makes such a decision for Christ, it will affect the entire family.

The object of the Brotherhood is to discover, develop, and utilize men; and Brotherhood revivals have been used to implement, or effect, that object so that men find prospects, fetch them to the services, feed them the Word of God, and fold them in the church. It has been found that the program of men winning men is the best.

Methods

Church-authorization.—Every revival in a church should be authorized by church action; and if it is to be sponsored by or led by a particular group such as the Brotherhood, this should be clearly understood by the church.

Schedule.—Some Brotherhood revivals have been "week-end revivals," beginning Friday night and ending Sunday night. Others have begun on Sunday and ended Wednesday night or Friday night. All services except those on Sunday must of necessity be held at night because laymen are busy at their work during the day.

Organization.—All the organization set up for the revival should be with the fullest counsel and help of the pastor. Committees may be named for publicity, visitation, speakers, cottage prayer meetings, ushers, greeters, finding prospects, music, follow-up, and others as needed.

Preparation.—The results will depend upon many factors, such as vision, concern, organized effort, prayer, faith, and the going forth in the name of Christ. Careful preparation will include the following: (1) the dates set well in advance; (2) prayer meetings in homes or at the church, led by laymen; (3) generous publicity through printed matter, church bulletins, announcements, and letters or cards sent by mail to the church membership, to unaffiliated Baptists, and to nonchurch members; (4) the preparation of the laymen speakers, the men's choir, the personal workers, and also the laymen who are to preside over the services; (5) visitation to homes and to individuals to invite them to the service and to urge the claims of Christ; and (6) a conference of Brotherhood officers, the pastor, and all committees to make certain everything is ready.

The services.—All services should be characterized by a spirit of friendliness to all. Usually all the people are invited to attend all the services unless the pastor and church think it best to have some services "for men only." Laymen may be assigned definite areas of the church auditorium in which to sit and look for visitors and prospects for church membership.

A Brotherhood revival should be evangelistic in spirit, but evangelism is not its only purpose. It is also an agency of spiritual enlistment for church men. Messages may include topics on doctrine, stewardship, consecration, home life, church loyalty, the Bible, the plan of salvation, missions, and other themes closely related to Christian and church life.

Gideon was used of the Lord to bring a revival to Israel, and as a result of this revival, the nation was saved. "And he said unto them, Look on me, and do likewise; and, behold, when I come to the outside of the camp, it shall be that, as I do, so shall ye do" (Judges 7:17). "And they stood every man in his place round about the camp: and all the host ran, and cried, and fled" (Judges 7:21).

Results

The results of Brotherhood revivals have been enduring. Men who never tithed before have given the Lord what belongs to him. Men who were not faithful in their attendance upon the regular Sunday services of the church have become regular attendants, and at the prayer meetings as well. Men in horrible sin have been brought to Christ and gloriously saved in Brotherhood revivals.

Individual laymen have become concerned about their own households, with the result that whole families have been reached, enlisted, and established. Neighbors, friends, and fellow employees have received a faithful testimony and witness for Christ by the Christian layman at work for Christ.

New enterprises have been begun as the result of Brotherhood revivals, such as the establishing of a church mission station, the erection of a new church building, the adoption of a worthy stewardship or missionary program, and other movements that glorify Christ and honor his church.

The success of a genuine Brotherhood revival will be expressed, not only in the number won to Christ, but also in the deeper consecration of its members, in the enlistment of laymen and others for service, in the contribution it makes to the spiritual atmosphere of the church, its strengthening of family life, its elevation of the level of life in the community, and its projected influence leading to a perennial revival in the church.

22

Evangelism in the "Highways and Hedges"

MATTHEW 28:18-20. And Jesus came and spake unto them, saying, All power is given unto me in heaven and in earth. Go ye therefore, and teach all nations, baptizing them in the name of the Father, and of the Son, and of the Holy Ghost: teaching them to observe all things whatsoever I have commanded you: and, lo, I am with you alway, even unto the end of the world. Amen.

LUKE 14:21, 23. So that servant came, and shewed his lord these things. Then the master of the house being angry said to his servant, Go out quickly into the streets and lanes of the city, and bring in hither the poor, and the maimed, and the halt, and the blind. . . . And the lord said unto the servant, Go out into the highways and hedges, and compel them to come in, that my house may be filled.

LUKE 15:4. What man of you, having an hundred sheep, if he lose one of them, doth not leave the ninety and nine in the wilderness, and go after that which is lost, until he find it?

Christ's churches were not meant to be indoor institutions only, but outdoor agencies as well. His kingdom was inaugurated in its earthly expression on the hills of Judea and the banks of the Jordan, John the Baptist, the first gospel evangelist, never preached in a church house. Most of Christ's preaching and teaching was done out in the open. Pentecost was a big street meeting. Paul's evangelism was carried on, in the main, on the streets and in open places. The idea in most churches today seems to be, "If you will come to our meetinghouse, we will offer you the gospel." In New Testament times, the Christians worked on the theory of carrying the gospel to the people. Open air is good for the gospel. The reason for the consumptive condition of many churches is that they have kept their religion within the walls of their meetinghouses.

This chapter is a plea for an outdoor gospel, that God's servants will catch the spirit of the Saviour in his great parable: "Go out quickly into the streets and lanes of the city . . . out into the highways and hedges, and compel them to come in."

Possibilities for Witnessing in Highways and Hedges

The following list of possibilities for witnessing beyond the church building is directive in nature:

1. Tent and tabernacle meetings in the summer in unchurched country places and in neglected parts of cities.

2. Open air services in parks and on the streets in crowded centers and cities.

3. Gospel missions in rented buildings on the main streets of cities.—Carried on every night in the year and on Sunday afternoons, such missions have produced great results in many cities. They should be carried on by the downtown churches in every city where there is a large transient and wicked population.

4. Services on vacant lots near churches in the towns and cities.—The church could either put up a tabernacle or secure a tent, provide seats and lights, and have Sunday evening services, advertising them well, as a means of seeking to enlist the people who do not go to church. Such meetings should be exceedingly evangelistic.

5. Services in jails and other penal institutions, in sanitariums, old folks' homes—wherever there are people who cannot go to church to hear the gospel.

Essentials in Witnessing in Highways and Hedges

There are certain necessary factors in all this "outdoor" effort to win people to Christ.

There should be plenty of good *music,* with emphasis on the congregational part in it. There must be a good song leader, sane, sensible, and spiritual, who knows God and loves lost souls. A sufficient number of popular songbooks should be provided, and there should be frequent use of the old gospel songs. All this will do much to draw and hold and help the people.

The right sort of *preaching* is essential to the success of such meetings. The preaching should be: (1) spiritual and evangelistic; (2) brief, pointed, and positive; (3) personal, hortatory; (4) passionate, full of enthusiasm; (5) plain, simple, with frequent use of illustrations; (6) scriptural, packed with the vital fundamentals of the gospel—sin and its awful guilt, its consequences, its eternal punishment; the love, grace, and mercy of a crucified Christ; the judgment; the resurrection; the second advent of our Lord; hell and heaven; repentance and faith; obedience to the Word and confession of Christ; the duty to be baptized and join Christ's church; and the joy and power of a life of service.

Personal work is essential. Groups of workers should be organized, trained, and sent out in each service.

Much attention should be given to *prayer.* There is no success in winning the lost anywhere without much prayer. Prayer groups should be organized before every service. Cottage prayer meetings in connection with tent, tabernacle, or mission meetings, for days before and on each day of the meeting, will add largely to the results.

Special and wise attention should be given to the proper *advertisement* of meetings. Newspapers, billboards, handbills, and personal invitations can all be used with advantage.

Care should be given to *following up* the converts in every meeting. They should be visited, urged to join the church, enlisted in Sunday school, and assigned some definite task for the Master. We should remember that lives as well as souls are valuable in Christ's program.

The *expenses* of such meetings should be cared for promptly.

Value of Witnessing in Highways and Hedges

The value of open-air meetings is seen in the manifold results in the life of church and community.

They give a gospel, soul-saving atmosphere to a church and prevent spiritual dry rot. They bring a militant and martial spirit.

They deepen the evangelistic fervor and zeal of God's people and keep them ever after lost men. Thus they encourage spirituality, prayer, Bible study, and evangelism.

They constantly add to the church membership and Sunday school enrolment, and quicken all the life of the church. Fresh currents of life flow into the arteries of the church.

They stimulate the liberality of the people and open up their hearts and purses to the worldwide cries for help.

They reach people who could never be reached by meetinghouse services.

They call out, enlist, and develop new workers as nothing else ever does. They afford new channels for service. Great Christian workers come out of this sort of evangelism.

They take the chill, iciness, and stiffness out of the people, break down class walls and distinctions, and democratize the churches, causing them to have "favor with God and man."

They enrich in spiritual power the pastor who wisely leads his church thus to go out after the lost. Long and successful pastorates follow such a policy. Great preachers and laymen are developed in such a church program.

They establish and develop new churches and spiritual centers, and the "regions beyond and round about" are taken care of.

They glorify Christ in the streets, lanes, highways, and hedges, and fill his house.

23

Drawing the Net[1]

LUKE 5:4-5. Now when he had left speaking, he said unto Simon, Launch out into the deep, and let down your nets for a draught. And Simon answering said unto him, Master we have toiled all the night, and have taken nothing: nevertheless at thy word I will let down the net.

2 CORINTHIANS 5:11. Knowing therefore the terror of the Lord, we persuade men; but we are made manifest unto God; and I trust also are made manifest in your consciences.

2 CORINTHIANS 5:20. Now then we are ambassadors for Christ, as though God did beseech you by us: we pray you in Christ's stead, be ye reconciled to God.

REVELATION 22:17. And the Spirit and the bride say, Come. And let him that heareth say, Come. And let him that is athirst come. And whosoever will, let him take the water of life freely.

"Some will use only the rod and reel of personal evangelism. Others must throw out and haul in the gospel net in public evangelism."

The term "drawing the net" is applied to the preacher's invitation, at the close of his sermon, to the unchurched, the indifferent, and the unsaved to make a public response to the claims of Christ. It has reference to the destiny-determining action to be taken by those "fishing for men."

It has been said that in the matter of drawing the net probably lies the chief difference between a successful evangelist and an unsuccessful one. Therefore the most

---

[1]Acknowledgment is hereby made to Dr. C. E. Matthews and Dr. F. D. Whitesell for helpful material in their respective books: *The Southern Baptist Program of Evangelism* (Atlanta: Home Mission Board, 1949) and *Sixty-five Ways to Give Evangelistic Invitations* (Grand Rapids: Zondervan Publishing House, 1945).

earnest study humanly possible on the matter of net-drawing should be made by every preacher of the Word of God. "As the salesman studies how to persuade his prospective customer to sign on the dotted line, as the lawyer studies how to secure a verdict for his client, as the fisherman studies how to land his fish after he has a strike, even so must the gospel preacher study how to secure an adequate response to the evangelistic message."

The invitation is the logical climax of the evangelistic sermon. Without it the message is incomplete and its effect unknown. The gospel deserves a response. Christ's call to men expects an answer. What a pity it is to let anyone leave uncommitted who would have made a decision if the proper invitation had been given! When the gospel is preached faithfully and an urgent invitation given, the blood of the lost is no longer upon the preacher.

Scriptural Authority for Drawing the Net

The Bible is full of appeals, exhortations, entreaties, pleadings, and even commands to hear and heed the calls of God to men. Moses gave an invitation when, after the destruction of the golden calf, he stood in the gate of the camp and said, "Who is on the Lord's side? let him come unto me" (Ex. 32:26). Joshua appealed to Israel to make a definite decision when, near the close of his life, he gathered all the tribes to Shechem and said, "Choose you this day whom ye will serve; whether the gods which your fathers served that were on the other side of the flood, or the gods of the Amorites, in whose land ye dwell: but as for me and my house, we will serve the Lord" (Josh. 24:15).

Jesus gave invitations. He said to Peter and Andrew, "Follow me, and I will make you fishers of men" (Matt. 4:19). The apostles often used persuasion of an intense degree. On the day of Pentecost, Acts 2:40 tells us, Peter "with many . . . words did . . . testify and exhort, saying, Save yourselves from this untoward generation." On several occasions Paul "persuaded" people (Acts 19:8,26; 26:28; 28:23). If he did not use our methods of invitation, he must have used something akin to them. In 2 Corinthians 5, he says, "The love of Christ constraineth us" (v. 14), and "Now then we are ambassadors for Christ, as though God did beseech you by us: we pray you in Christ's stead, be ye reconciled to God" (v. 20). In an evangelistic invitation the preacher presents the constraining love of Christ and beseeches men to be reconciled to God by an immediate surrender and public manifestation of the same.

Definite Steps in Drawing the Net

Certain well-defined steps have been found most effective in drawing the net in an evangelistic meeting. We present them here in the order of their progression toward the objective of an abundant harvest.

In the first step, invite all present who have their church membership elsewhere to come forward to unite with the church by letter, on the promise of a letter, or by statement; and the unsaved in the congregation to come professing their faith in Christ as their personal Saviour. As long as there is response to this appeal, it is to be continued.

A second step is to be made when all have responded who will in answer to the first invitation. Ask all in the audience who know Christ as Saviour and are so grateful to him for saving them that they are members of the church where they live, to testify for him by raising their hands. Then press the appeal to those who could not raise their hands, urging them to accept Christ or to come by letter or statement or on the promise of a letter.

In making the third step, which comes, of course, when response to the second exhortation has ceased, ask the congregation to be seated and bow in prayer. The evangelist will, as a usual thing, lead this prayer himself. Following the prayer, while the audience is still seated, the evangelist will continue the appeal by quoting passages from the Word of God, such as: "Behold, now is the accepted time; behold, now is the day of salvation" (2 Cor. 6:2); "Boast not thyself of tomorrow; for thou knowest not what a day may bring forth" (Prov. 27:1); "He, that being often reproved hardeneth his neck, shall suddenly be destroyed, and that without remedy" (Prov. 29:1).

Now ask all who are saved and members of the church where they live, to stand. Press the appeal upon those who are seated, to make decisions for Christ as Saviour and for church membership. Encourage those who are church members to witness to one who is not saved. Give illustrations.

Thus we come to the final appeal in drawing the net. In these closing moments, remind those who have not responded that they are saying no to God, not to the preacher or the personal worker. Cite the following verse: "No man can come to me, except the Father which hath sent me draw him: and I will raise him up at the last day" (John 6:44). Tell them, further, that an impression to do God's will is the voice of the Spirit of God. Then state to the audience that one more verse of song will be sung, and if no one responds the service will be concluded, it being assumed that it is God's will. Of course, if there is response, the invitation will be extended while other verses are sung.

Powers Used in Drawing the Net

Drawing the net involves every power and every gift known to the Christian. Every faculty of our beings should be at the disposal of the Holy Spirit.

Use the power of persuasion. In an invitation we are persuading people to do right, not to do wrong. We are persuading them to break with the devil and come to God. We are persuading them to spend life on earth on the side of God instead of on the side of the devil. We are persuading them to spend eternity in heaven instead of hell. Our convictions and our hearts' concern will determine the earnestness with which we persuade.

Use the power of example. You have heard that one example is worth a thousand arguments. You have the opportunity of bringing to the attention of the Christians the fact that they may be used of the Holy Spirit in winning others. Be sure to call attention to any Sunday school teacher who leads a pupil to Christ, anyone who brings a friend to make a public confession, anyone who wins a classmate. A little child accepting Christ may be cited as an example of the faith God desires others to exercise.

Use the power of suggestion. If concrete examples of personal work are not available, resort to the power of suggestion. Suggest that a mother might speak to her daughter, a father to his son, a neighbor to a friend, a deacon to one for whom he has been praying. Numbers may wake up to the fact that they should do something and start trying to win others simply because the suggestion is made.

Use the power of psychology. Always begin with the easiest appeal and the kind that is least likely to be offensive to hearers. Make your appeal clear to the unaffiliated to come by letter, on the promise of a letter, or by statement, and to the sinner to come forward and confess Christ as Saviour. If the response is good, stay with it, but do not let the invitation drag. At every indication of lagging, change your appeal.

The music is a vital part of the invitation. It should be well planned, but free rein should be given to the Spirit's guidance if at any time during the invitation it seems wise to make changes.

Manner of Drawing the Net

Give the invitation clearly. Do not confuse people by mixing propositions.

Give the invitation confidently. Do your best under the leadership of the Holy Spirit, and expect God to bless your efforts and those of the others who are working with you.

Give the invitation earnestly. Plead as with dying men.

Give the invitation courteously. Do not embarrass your hearers or resort to tricks or deception.

Give the invitation naturally. Be yourself. The Holy Spirit respects our individuality and uses each of us differently.

Give the invitation prayerfully. It is important to maintain an atmosphere of prayer. We can pray as we plead for souls.

Give the invitation in entire dependence upon the Holy Spirit. You can do nothing apart from the presence and power of the Holy Spirit. Pray for his power, depend upon his guidance. Look for the Spirit's movements in the audience, try to discern his promptings regarding every step of the invitation, but do not try to do his work. He alone can convict men of sin and of righteousness and of judgment. He can reveal to sin-blinded minds the love of Christ and the efficacy of his atonement. Expect his presence, count upon him, and he will not disappoint you.

Part Four

PERSONAL WORK

24

Suggestions to Winners

Remember to pray. Your main chance to succeed in personal work is in your touch and fellowship with God. Jesus said: "No man can come to me, except the Father which hath sent me draw him" (John 6:44). God holds the reins that guide souls to him. It is absolutely necessary that you keep in and up with God. Prayer—constant, supplicating, importuning, soulful prayer—is God's key to his secret sources of power. Pray before, during, and after your efforts to win men. You cannot otherwise find your way successfully.

Pray that your own heart will be right, your motive heavenly, your words wise, your heart burdened, and that God's will may be done in and through you. Pray that you may be led to the right person, that your method of approach will be right. Pray that God will go before you as he has promised (Isa. 45:2), that he will mellow the heart of the lost and do his convincing and convicting work. Pray that you may easily find the key to the soul of the unsaved, that you will use the right Scripture passages, and that an abundant entrance may be given the gospel message. Pray for human tact and divine power. God promises you the Holy Spirit in this task (Luke 11:13; Acts 1:8). Pray that God will go behind you as he has promised (Isa. 58:8), that he will convert your mistakes into victories, override your errors, and bring to full fruition the seed sown and the work you sought to accomplish.

Remember that victory depends upon the Holy Spirit. Keep these verses before you: "Not by might, nor by power, but by my spirit, saith the Lord of hosts" (Zech. 4:6). "Without me ye can do nothing" (John 15:5). "Be filled with the Spirit" (Eph. 5:18).

Heaven bends low and longs unspeakably to endue you with resistless power (Luke 11:13). Seek it, obtain it. It is the reasonable claim of your spiritual birthright.

Remember that "faith is the victory." Conquering faith raises the dead, removes barriers, unlocks doors, accomplishes the impossible, and brings victory in personal soul-winning. "All things are possible to him that believeth" (Mark 9:23). "This is the victory that overcometh the world, even our faith" (1 John 5:4). "Concerning the work of my hands command ye me" (Isa. 45:11). "What things soever ye desire, when ye pray, believe that ye receive them, and ye shall have them" (Mark 11:24).

Remember to use the Bible. Make much use of God's Word—"it is the power of God unto salvation," the channel of life. It is "the sword of the Spirit," powerful in its discernment and incisiveness. It cuts, divides, separates, hammers, burns, and enters into the secret thoughts and intents of the heart. Put its most trenchant passages into your own heart and give them out to lost men, trusting in the Spirit to apply them in power.

Use the passages which tell about sin—its presence in the sinner's heart and life; its guilt, soiling and poisonous, pervading the entire spiritual and moral nature; its power; and its penalties and eternal punishment. Emphasize the passages on the way of life—repentance, confession of sin, faith, acknowledgment of Christ. Point out Jesus Christ as the only Saviour, stressing that he saves by his blood, by his grace, and by his wonderful risen life. "For there is none other name under heaven given among men, whereby we must be saved" (Acts 4:12).

Remember that your own life, motive, and conduct must be pure. Never seek a heavenly end with an earthly motive; never try to accomplish God's will with the devil's tools. "Be ye clean, that bear the vessels of the Lord" (Isa. 52:11).

Compromising with sin in your life will never bring you far on evangelism's road.

Remember that your attitude is of primary importance. If you are formal, purely intellectual, unemotional, and uncompassionate, you will fail. "They that sow in tears shall reap in joy" (Psalm 126:5).

Remember to be tactful and exhibit common sense. The matter of approach and of tactfulness in seeking an entrance for the gospel message is very important. Sometimes it is best to adopt indirect methods of approach, to come up on the "blind side"; sometimes the direct method is best. "Are you a Christian?" "Have you been born again?" "Are you saved or lost?" "Is your heart right with God?" These are some of the questions that may be used. Also, do not worry the unsaved with long, overpressed appeals. When you see they are irritated or bored, or restless or angered, leave them and seek to reach them at another time. Sometimes a brief, pointed, soul-stirring message will do more than any other to reach them. Watch the face, words, and tone of the sinner.

Remember that it is usually best to deal with your own sex and age. This is not always true, however.

Remember to talk with people alone, quietly. It is usually best to deal with the unsaved in a quiet place, some quiet room or office where, without embarrassment or a show of righteousness, you can pray and give the lost a chance to confess the Saviour.

Remember not to be sidetracked or led into an argument. Controversy will always divert attention and lead away from salvation. Keep to the main matter at hand.

Remember to be courteous. Always act in the most courteous way, never losing your temper no matter how severely tempted.

Remember not to be discouraged. Patience and persistence are virtues in soul-winning. The game is worth many failures. Christ seemed to fail in winning some. George Mueller, of Bristol, sought the soul of one man for more than sixty years before he won him. "In that day shall the Lord of hosts be . . . for strength to them that turn the battle to the gate" (Isa. 28:5-6) is one of God's promises to those who seek to win against odds.

Remember your own experience. The wise use of personal experience, one's own saving testimony, is often of great value in leading the lost to Christ, but care must be exercised for fear extravagant and extreme experiences will produce wrong impressions. Not all conversions are like Paul's. Many are like Philip's and Levi's. "They forsook all, and followed him."

25

How to Deal with Children

PROVERBS 8:17. I love them that love me; and those that seek me early shall find me.

MATTHEW 19:13-14. Then were there brought unto him little children, that he should put his hands on them, and pray: and the disciples rebuked them. But Jesus said, Suffer little children, and forbid them not, to come unto me: for of such is the kingdom of heaven.

DOCTRINAL QUESTIONS AND ANSWERS ABOUT CHILDREN

1. What is the condition of a child spiritually when it comes into the world? Let the Word of God answer:

PSALM 51:5. Behold, I was shapen in iniquity; and in sin did my mother conceive me.

PSALM 58:3. The wicked are estranged from the womb: they go astray as soon as they be born, speaking lies.

ROMANS 3:23. For all have sinned, and come short of the glory of God.

These and other verses speak of the place of sin in the experience of the human race. Adam was created in the spiritual likeness of God. When sin came into his life, that likeness was vitiated. Then Adam begat children in his own likeness, i.e., with a corrupt nature. This does not mean that they were born guilty of sin and under God's condemnation. It means that they were born with a nature predisposed to sin, a nature which would lead them to personal sin and guilt as soon as they should come face to face with personal, conscious choice between good and evil. Total depravity does not mean that a person is born guilty. It means that he **is** born with his tendency to choose evil stronger than his tendency to choose the good and that apart from the power of Christ he will continue to grow worse and worse in disobedience to God.

2. If a child dies before he comes to the time of accountability to God, what becomes of his soul?

He is covered by the atoning work of Christ and, not being responsible for any conscious act of sin, is saved by Christ's death.

3. When does a child become accountable to God for his soul?

There is no certain age—some are younger than others. When the child voluntarily chooses sin and is conscious of his wrong, then he becomes an active transgressor and comes under God's law. Home and church training and religious environment have much to do with the age at which he develops this consciousness. My own boy at five years of age said, "I am lost; I want you to show me the way to Jesus." He was converted at seven. Most children have a sense of sin between seven and ten years of age.

The Importance of Winning Children

The opportunity for soul-winning among children is almost universal. In almost every home there is a growing young life, with all of its possibilities.

Children are susceptible to gospel influences. Their hearts are tender and malleable, pliable to God's grace. They are easily reached, and hence it requires less time and energy to win them and start them off in Christian service than it does to win an older person. Test any large Christian group as to the time they became Christians. See the number who were saved when Juniors.

The saving of a child's soul offers a double opportunity to the worker in that there is also a chance to train and utilize the child's talents and powers for the service of God. A life is saved as well as a soul. Some of our most important and useful leaders and Christian workers come from those saved in youth. They give God a long life of delightful service and bring great glory to his name.

The prevalence of death among the young and the multiplied influences at work to lead them astray as they get older should urge us to win them "while the evil days come not."

Dangers in Seeking to Win Children

Parents and teachers should be very cautious, and yet zealous, in dealing with children. They can discourage them for life or they can overpersuade them and get them into the church unsaved, without an understanding of the way of life. Teach them; make the way plain; pray for them; give them favorable opportunity to find Christ. Do not overpersuade, but at the same time give them every opportunity to respond to the pleadings of the Saviour.

The devil will try to deceive you and to pacify your soul by saying that the child, even though conscious of sin, is not lost and does not need the saving efficacy of Christ's gospel as much as a fully grown sinner. "Ye must be born again" applies to children of tender years as well as to adults. They are not saved by culture, by Christian education and environment, or by the parents' consecration. Young Timothy, like Saul of Tarsus, though brought up in a devout home, had to come by the way of the cross to find salvation and peace.

The distinction between being saved and joining the church should be clearly made. If children seek the Saviour, encourage them and teach them the way of salvation. If they want to join the church, teach them the meaning and responsibilities of church membership.

Children must not be led to join the church in the hope that it will help them to find Christ. Regeneration is a necessary prerequisite to church membership. The church will not save, help save, or keep saved—it is the place for the saved to serve in helping to save others. Children should be taught and encouraged to join the church when they give evidence that they have fully and understandingly trusted Christ as their Saviour and Lord.

Opportunities for Winning Children

The best place to win children is in their *homes,* where the parents can teach the Word of God. Show them Christ by word and life. Pray with and for them. The mother should not be alone in this heavenly task. God says: "The father to the children shall make known thy truth" (Isa. 38:19). He should reinforce the mother every step of the way.

The next most fruitful place of soul-winning among children is in the *Sunday school,* where teacher, superintendent, and pastor can give them a winning gospel and urge them individually and by classes to accept Christ. The teacher may have to do some of the work by visits and prayers in the home in conjunction with the parents' efforts. Every teacher ought to be a soul-winner, and every Sunday school ought to have evangelistic services constantly.

Vacation Bible schools are becoming increasingly effective in the winning of children. Staffed by consecrated, trained workers, they give opportunities for concentrated, consistent effort seldom found elsewhere. The importance of special evangelistic services and personal work during these schools cannot be overemphasized.

Another glorious opportunity for child evangelism is in the *church services.* The Sunday school should occasionally be moved into the preaching service, and the pastor should preach so that the children will be interested and won. The teachers should give personal and careful aid to the pastor in this matter.

Special children's meetings during a revival offer a great chance for the evangelization of children. These can be held at a separate time and place, after school hours, on Saturday or on Sunday afternoons. Special attention should be given to advertising these meetings. Songs the children can sing should be used. The sermon should teach; it should be clear, plain, short, filled with the gospel, sparkling with illustrations. The plan of salvation, Christ as the Saviour, and the need for repentance and faith and for confession and obedience after salvation should be clearly put to the children.

An Effective Message

The following is a simple but effective method which has proved its value in children's evangelistic services many times. Call it "The ABC's of Salvation." Remind the children of their experience in school in learning to recognize and understand the use of the alphabet or their ABC's. Explain that there is an "ABC of salvation." Have the children repeat the Scripture verses, and teach them the plan of salvation by explaining the verses as they memorize them.

A   "*A*ll have sinned, and come short of the glory of God" (Rom. 3:23).
B   "*B*ehold the Lamb of God, which taketh away the sin of the world" (John 1:29).
C   "*C*ome now, and let us reason together, saith the Lord: though your sins be as scarlet, they shall be as white as snow; though they be red like crimson, they shall be as wool" (Isa. 1:18).

A good object lesson to illustrate will be helpful. Let a piece of red paper represent the soul that is "red like crimson." Let a piece of red glass represent the blood of the Lamb slain to cover our sins. Look through the red glass at the red paper; the paper will look white. Thus it is with our souls. God cannot see our sin when he looks through the blood of Christ. We can have our sins covered by his blood if we will trust him.

26

How to Win the Unconcerned

Convict Them of Sin

Most people are without spiritual interest in their own salvation. This is especially true in communities where the churches are lifeless and unevangelistic, where revivals are scarce, and where the tides of spiritual power run low. Vital, live, evangelistic churches and active, soul-winning Christians produce an abiding conviction in men's souls and keep the saving fires burning. Those who feel no conviction of sin, no need of a Saviour, are difficult to reach. The main, first task in dealing with the unconcerned is to bring conviction of sin to them.

The agencies for bringing this conviction about are—

Prayer.—Pray definitely for them, seeking the convicting power of God's Spirit on them (John 16:8-11).

Sermon.—Bring them under the influence of evangelistic and spiritual preaching or teaching.

God's Word.—Get them to study God's Word—in tracts, interesting books, in the Bible itself.

Fellowship.—Seek to bring them in contact with consecrated Christian leaders and workers.

Personal Appeal.—Strive to bring the work of these other agencies to fruition by a private appeal in some quiet place.

Use the Bible

God's Word should be used in showing them—

1. Their sin, its consequences, their eternal punishment.

Amos 4:12. Thus will I do unto thee, O Israel: and because I will do this unto thee, prepare to meet thy God, O Israel.

JOHN 3:18, 36. He that believeth on him is not condemned: but he that believeth not is condemned already, because he hath not believed in the name of the only begotten Son of God. . . . He that believeth on the Son hath everlasting life: and he that believeth not the Son shall not see life; but the wrath of God abideth on him.

JOHN 8:24. I said therefore unto you, that ye shall die in your sins: for if ye believe not that I am he, ye shall die in your sins.

ROMANS 6:23. For the wages of sin is death; but the gift of God is eternal life through Jesus Christ our Lord.

2 THESSALONIANS 1:7-10. . . . the Lord Jesus shall be revealed from heaven with his mighty angels, in flaming fire taking vengeance on them that know not God, and that obey not the gospel of our Lord Jesus Christ: who shall be punished with everlasting destruction from the presence of the Lord, and from the glory of his power; when he shall come to be glorified in his saints, and to be admired in all them that believe (because our testimony among you was believed) in that day.

HEBREWS 10:28-29. He that despised Moses' law died without mercy under two or three witnesses: of how much sorer punishment, suppose ye, shall he be thought worthy, who hath trodden under foot the Son of God, and hath counted the blood of the covenant, wherewith he was sanctified, an unholy thing, and hath done despite unto the Spirit of grace?

REVELATION 21:8. But the fearful, and unbelieving, and the abominable, and murderers, and whoremongers, and sorcerers, and idolaters, and all liars, shall have their part in the lake which burneth with fire and brimstone: which is the second death.

2. The love and mercy of God.

ISAIAH 38:17. Behold, for peace I had great bitterness: but thou hast in love to my soul delivered it from the pit of corruption: for thou hast cast all my sins behind thy back.

ISAIAH 55:3. Incline your ear, and come unto me: hear, and your soul shall live; and I will make an everlasting covenant with you, even the sure mercies of David.

JOHN 3:16. For God so loved the world, that he gave his only begotten Son, that whosoever believeth in him should not perish, but have everlasting life.

ROMANS 2:4-5. Or despisest thou the riches of his goodness

and forbearance and longsuffering; not knowing that the goodness of God leadeth thee to repentance? But after thy hardness and impenitent heart treasurest up unto thyself wrath against the day of wrath and revelation of the righteous judgment of God.

3. That Christ died for them.

ROMANS 5:8. But God commendeth his love toward us, in that, while we were yet sinners, Christ died for us.

GALATIANS 3:13. Christ hath redeemed us from the curse of the law, being made a curse for us: for it is written, Cursed is every one that hangeth on a tree.

1 PETER 2:24. . . . who his own self bare our sins in his own body on the tree, that we, being dead to sins, should live unto righteousness: by whose stripes ye were healed.

4. What they must do to be saved: repent of their sins and trust their souls to the keeping of Christ.

JOHN 3:16, 36. For God so loved the world, that he gave his only begotten Son, that whosoever believeth in him should not perish, but have everlasting life. . . . He that believeth on the Son hath everlasting life: and he that believeth not the Son shall not see life; but the wrath of God abideth on him.

JOHN 5:24. Verily, verily, I say unto you, He that heareth my word, and believeth on him that sent me, hath everlasting life, and shall not come into condemnation; but is passed from death unto life.

ACTS 3:19. Repent ye therefore, and be converted, that your sins may be blotted out, when the times of refreshing shall come from the presence of the Lord.

ACTS 4:12. Neither is there salvation in any other: for there is none other name under heaven given among men, whereby we must be saved.

ACTS 17:30. And the times of this ignorance God winked at; but now commandeth all men every where to repent.

ACTS 20:21. . . . testifying both to the Jews, and also to the Greeks, repentance toward God, and faith toward our Lord Jesus Christ.

5. How perilous it is to neglect or postpone the matter of the soul's salvation.

PROVERBS 1:23-31. Turn you at my reproof: behold, I will pour out my spirit unto you, I will make known my words unto you. Because I have called, and ye refused; I have stretched out my hand, and no man regarded: but ye have set at nought all my counsel, and would none of my reproof: I also will laugh at your calamity; I will mock when your fear cometh; when your fear cometh as desolation, and your destruction cometh as a whirlwind; when distress and anguish cometh upon you. Then shall they call upon me, but I will not answer; they shall seek me early, but they shall not find me: for that they hated knowledge, and did not choose the fear of the Lord: they would none of my counsel: they despised all my reproof. Therefore shall they eat of the fruit of their own way, and be filled with their own devices.

PROVERBS 27:1. Boast not thyself of to morrow; for thou knowest not what a day may bring forth.

PROVERBS 29:1. He, that being often reproved hardeneth his neck, shall suddenly be destroyed, and that without remedy.

LUKE 13:3. I tell you, Nay: but, except ye repent, ye shall all likewise perish.

HEBREWS 2:3. How shall we escape, if we neglect so great salvation; which at the first began to be spoken by the Lord, and was confirmed unto us by them that heard him.

LET THE HOLY SPIRIT LEAD

You cannot do much with a sinner ahead of God. The Holy Spirit is the main agency in stirring up his soul. Your work will be in vain unless the Spirit comes to your aid. You should seek his power (Luke 11:13). When the sinner begins to realize his need of Christ and becomes conscious of his sins and their pressure on his soul, then your task becomes easier rapidly.

27

How to Reach the Deceived and Deluded

In seeking to win men we are everywhere confronted with people who have been led astray from God's truth as it is in Christ Jesus. They are themselves usually very enthusiastic propagandists or personal workers. They seek by all means to make disciples for their cults. These errorists are not unknown to God's Word. They are spoken of, and we are warned against them.

See God's charge to his preachers and teachers in—

2 TIMOTHY 3:1-15. This know also, that in the last days perilous times shall come. For men shall be lovers of their own selves, covetous, boasters, proud, blasphemers, disobedient to parents, unthankful, unholy, without natural affection, trucebreakers, false accusers, incontinent, fierce, despisers of those that are good, traitors, heady, highminded, lovers of pleasures more than lovers of God; having a form of godliness, but denying the power thereof: from such turn away. For of this sort are they which creep into houses, and lead captive silly women laden with sins, led away with divers lusts, ever learning, and never able to come to the knowledge of the truth. Now as Jannes and Jambres withstood Moses, so do these also resist the truth: men of corrupt minds, reprobate concerning the faith. But they shall proceed no further: for their folly shall be manifest unto all men, as theirs also was. But thou hast fully known my doctrine, manner of life, purpose, faith, longsuffering, charity, patience, persecutions, afflictions, which came unto me at Antioch, at Iconium, at Lystra; what persecutions I endured: but out of them all the Lord delivered me. Yea, and all that will live godly in Christ Jesus shall suffer persecution. But evil men and seducers shall wax worse and worse, deceiving, and being deceived. But continue thou in the things which thou hast learned and hast been assured of, knowing of whom thou hast learned them; and that from a child thou hast known the holy scriptures, which are able to

make thee wise unto salvation through faith which is in Christ Jesus.

2 TIMOTHY 4:1-5. I charge thee therefore before God, and the Lord Jesus Christ, who shall judge the quick and the dead at his appearing and his kingdom; preach the word; be instant in season, out of season; reprove, rebuke, exhort with all long-suffering and doctrine. For the time will come when they will not endure sound doctrine; but after their own lusts shall they heap to themselves teachers, having itching ears; and they shall turn away their ears from the truth, and shall be turned into fables. But watch thou in all things, endure afflictions, do the work of an evangelist, make full proof of thy ministry.

We are not to share their errors but to do what we can to win them to Christ and his truth. Among these errorists we find Jews, Roman Catholics, Unitarians, Universalists, Spiritualists, Followers of Russell, Seventh-Day Adventists, and Christian Scientists.

All of these claim the Bible as their holy Book and profess to believe it and follow it. The Jews, however, reject the New Testament; the Catholics repudiate our Protestant version of the Bible; and the Christian Scientists put Mrs. Eddy's *Science and Health* above the Bible. The latter will deny this charge in the main, but practice it in their devotion to Mrs. Eddy's book. The other groups deny or misinterpret various parts of the Bible.

All of these people are hard to reach because Satan has blinded their eyes by the blind teachings of blind teachers, and they are usually well informed in their errors and set in their ways. It takes patience, kindness, gentleness, persistence, correct example, the Word of God, and the power of God to reach, reclaim, and instruct these errorists.

Many of them are really saved people. The truth of Christ in its dimmer rays has penetrated, pierced through their errors, found faith and repentance, and has done its saving work. Many of them are good people, living sincere, beautiful lives, honestly seeking the way to God.

If we would win them, our attitude should never be harsh, rarely controversial, always sincere and kindly. We should never allow an errorist to outstrip or surpass us in the Christian spirit and life. Their works of love and charity often put Christians to shame. Much prayer will aid in the task of winning these people who have gone astray from God and missed the way in sin's darkened paths. It takes consecrated tact, great spiritual power, an intimate and workable knowledge of God's Word, and an enduement of the Holy Spirit to do the best work with them.

The Jews

The Jews are the hard knot of Christian evangelism. Jesus and Paul failed in the main to break through their pride, traditions, self-righteousness, and previous conceptions. Christian effort has sadly failed since. Theirs is the outstanding national tragedy. "Their blindness and hardness of heart" seem still to prevail. The veil is yet over their eyes as a people. Thanks be to God, through the centuries some have come to know him whom to know aright is life eternal. Surely the tide will turn and God's unfolding cycles will see them coming home to him and Christ. We will yet see God's redemptive plan work out its details for the Jews. Till then let every Christian do his best to win every son of Abraham he can. The gospel can save him.

The fact that the Jews accept the Old Testament and worship God as Father does not make them Christians, for Christ says plainly: "I am the way, the truth, and the life: no man cometh unto the Father, but by me" (John 14:6). "He that entereth not by the door into the sheepfold, but climbeth up some other way, the same is a thief and a robber. . . . I am the door of the sheep. . . . By me if any man enter in, he shall be saved" (John 10:1,7,9). "Neither is there salvation in any other: for there is none other name under heaven given among men, whereby we must be saved" (Acts 4:12).

1. Help them to see Christ as God's Messiah, revealed in the Old Testament and fulfilled in the New Testament.

Use Psalm 22; Psalm 69; Isaiah 53; Daniel 9:26; Micah 5:2; Zechariah 12:10; Hebrews 7:25-28; Hebrews 9-10.

2. Show them the awful consequences of rejecting Christ.

JOHN 3:18, 36. He that believeth on him is not condemned: but he that believeth not is condemned already, because he hath not believed in the name of the only begotten Son of God. . . . He that believeth on the Son hath everlasting life: and he that believeth not the Son shall not see life; but the wrath of God abideth on him.

HEBREWS 10:26-29. For if we sin wilfully after that we have received the knowledge of the truth, there remaineth no more sacrifice for sins, but a certain fearful looking for of judgment and fiery indignation, which shall devour the adversaries. He that despised Moses' law died without mercy under two or three witnesses: of how much sorer punishment, suppose ye, shall he be thought worthy, who hath trodden under foot the Son of God, and hath counted the blood of the covenant, wherewith he was sanctified, an unholy thing, and hath done despite unto the Spirit of grace?

3. If they fear persecution when they turn to Christ, console them with God's promises.

MATTHEW 5:10-12. Blessed are they which are persecuted for righteousness' sake: for theirs is the kingdom of heaven. Blessed are ye, when men shall revile you, and persecute you, and shall say all manner of evil against you falsely, for my sake. Rejoice, and be exceeding glad: for great is your reward in heaven: for so persecuted they the prophets which were before you.

ACTS 5:40-41. And to him they agreed: and when they had called the apostles, and beaten them, they commanded that they should not speak in the name of Jesus, and let them go. And they departed from the presence of the council, rejoicing that they were counted worthy to suffer shame for his name.

2 TIMOTHY 2:12. If we suffer, we shall also reign with him: if we deny him, he also will deny us.

4. Assure them that through Christ is their only way to get to God the Father.

JOHN 14:6. Jesus saith unto him, I am the way, the truth, and the life: no man cometh unto the Father, but by me.

1 JOHN 2:23. Whosoever denieth the Son, the same hath not the Father: [but] he that acknowledgeth the Son hath the Father also.

ROMAN CATHOLICS

One who professes a false form of true religion is very hard to reach with the truth. In dealing with a Roman Catholic, plant an honest *doubt* in his mind. Then follow with the positive plan of salvation by grace through faith.

1. Ask him if he is assured of his salvation.

JOHN 5:24. Verily, verily, I say unto you, He that heareth my word, and believeth on him that sent me, hath everlasting life, and shall not come into condemnation; but is passed from death unto life.

ROMANS 8:14. For as many as are led by the Spirit of God, they are the sons of God.

1 JOHN 5:13. These things have I written unto you that believe on the name of the Son of God; that ye may know that ye have eternal life, and that ye may believe on the name of the Son of God.

2. Show him that to be really saved he must have a birth from above, a regeneration of soul.

JOHN 1:12. But as many as received him, to them gave he power to become the sons of God, even to them that believe on his name.

JOHN 3:1-5. There was a man of the Pharisees, named Nicodemus, a ruler of the Jews: the same came to Jesus by night, and said unto him, Rabbi, we know that thou art a teacher come from God: for no man can do these miracles that thou doest, except God be with him. Jesus answered and said unto him, Verily, verily, I say unto thee, Except a man be born again, he cannot see the kingdom of God. Nicodemus saith unto him, How can a man be born when he is old? Can he enter the second time into his mother's womb, and be born? Jesus answered, Verily, verily, I say unto thee, Except a man be born of the water and of the Spirit, he cannot enter into the kingdom of God.

ROMANS 10:9-10. . . . if thou shalt confess with thy mouth the Lord Jesus, and shalt believe in thine heart that God hath raised him from the dead, thou shalt be saved. For with the heart man believeth unto righteousness; and with the mouth confession is made unto salvation.

2 CORINTHIANS 5:17. Therefore if any man be in Christ, he is a new creature: old things are passed away; behold, all things are become new.

EPHESIANS 1:7. . . . in whom we have redemption through his blood, the forgiveness of sins, according to the riches of his grace.

2 PETER 1:4. . . . whereby are given unto us exceeding great and precious promises: that by these ye might be partakers of the divine nature, having escaped the corruption that is in the world through lust.

3. Show him that regeneration comes about by repentance and faith, not by doing penance.

LUKE 13:3. I tell you, Nay: but, except ye repent, ye shall all likewise perish.

JOHN 3:16. For God so loved the world, that he gave his only begotten Son, that whosoever believeth in him should not perish, but have everlasting life.

ACTS 3:19. Repent ye therefore, and be converted, that your sins may be blotted out, when the times of refreshing shall come from the presence of the Lord.

ACTS 10:43. To him give all the prophets witness, that through his name whosoever believeth in him shall receive remission of sins.

4. Show him that Christ is our only mediator.

1 TIMOTHY 2:5. "For there is one God, and one mediator between God and men, the man Christ Jesus."

5. Urge him to read the Bible, and furnish him with a good copy of the Scriptures.

6. Pray with him and for him.

UNITARIANS

A Unitarian does not accept the deity of Christ, the personality of the Holy Spirit, or the inspiration or binding authority of the Scriptures. Hence he has light notions of sin.

1. Show him that he cannot get to God, the Father, without faith in Jesus, the Son.

> MATTHEW 11:27. All things are delivered unto me of my Father: and no man knoweth the Son, but the Father; neither knoweth any man the Father, save the Son, and he to whomsoever the Son will reveal him.
>
> JOHN 5:22-23. For the Father judgeth no man, but hath committed all judgment unto the Son: that all men should honour the Son, even as they honour the Father. He that honoureth not the Son honoureth not the Father which hath sent him.
>
> JOHN 14:6. Jesus saith unto him, I am the way, the truth, and the life: no man cometh unto the Father, but by me.
>
> 1 JOHN 2:22-23. Who is a liar but he that denieth that Jesus is the Christ? He is antichrist, that denieth the Father and the Son. Whosoever denieth the Son, the same hath not the Father: [but] he that acknowledgeth the Son hath the Father also.

2. Show him that there is no other way to be saved except through Jesus Christ.

> JOHN 10:1-9. Verily, verily, I say unto you, He that entereth not by the door into the sheepfold, but climbeth up some other way, the same is a thief and a robber. But he that entereth in by the door is the shepherd of the sheep. To him the porter openeth; and the sheep hear his voice: and he calleth his own sheep by name, and leadeth them out. And when he putteth forth his own sheep, he goeth before them, and the sheep follow him: for they know his voice. And a stranger will they not follow, but will flee from him: for they know not the voice of strangers. This parable spake Jesus unto them: but they understood not what things they were which he spake unto them. Then said Jesus unto them again, Verily, verily, I say unto you, I am the door of the sheep. All that ever came before me are thieves and robbers: but the sheep did not hear them. I am the door: by me if any man enter in, he shall be saved, and shall go in and out, and find pasture.
>
> ACTS 4:12. Neither is there salvation in any other: for there is none other name under heaven given among men, whereby we must be saved.

3. Show him that his rejection of Christ as God's divine Son involves him in awful sin.

> JOHN 16:8-10. And when he is come, he will reprove the world

of sin, and of righteousness, and of judgment: of sin, because they believe not on me; of righteousness, because I go to my Father, and ye see me no more.

HEBREWS 10:28-29. He that despised Moses' law died without mercy under two or three witnesses: of how much sorer punishment, suppose ye, shall he be thought worthy, who hath trodden under foot the Son of God, and hath counted the blood of the covenant, wherewith he was sanctified, an unholy thing, and hath done despite unto the Spirit of grace?

1 JOHN 2:22-23. Who is a liar but he that denieth that Jesus is the Christ? He is antichrist, that denieth the Father and the Son. Whosoever denieth the Son, the same hath not the Father.

1 JOHN 5:10-12. He that believeth on the Son of God hath the witness in himself: he that believeth not God hath made him a liar; because he believeth not the record that God gave of his Son. And this is the record, that God hath given to us eternal life, and this life is in his Son. He that hath the Son hath life; and he that hath not the Son of God hath not life.

THE UNIVERSALISTS

Universalists are so-called Christians who believe that all men will be saved. They base their belief on—

1 CORINTHIANS 15:22. For as in Adam all die, even so in Christ shall all be made alive.

1 TIMOTHY 2:3-4. For this is good and acceptable in the sight of God our Saviour; who will have all men to be saved, and to come unto the knowledge of the truth.

They mistake God's loving desire for all men to be saved for his determination to save them. God desires all men to be saved; he saves only those who trust him through Christ.

1. Show him that God's desire for men to be saved does not keep men from having to seek Christ, repent of their sins, believe in Jesus as personal Saviour, and confess, obey, and follow him, to have the joys of salvation and service.

LUKE 13:3. I tell you, Nay: but, except ye repent, ye shall all likewise perish.

JOHN 3:36. He that believeth on the Son hath everlasting life: and he that believeth not the Son shall not see life; but the wrath of God abideth on him.

JOHN 5:40. Ye will not come to me, that ye might have life.

2. Show him that some men are unsaved because they refuse God's condition of salvation.

> MATTHEW 25:41, 46. Then shall he say also unto them on the left hand, Depart from me, ye cursed, into everlasting fire, prepared for the devil and his angels. . . . And these shall go away into everlasting punishment: but the righteous into life eternal.
>
> JOHN 3:36. He that believeth on the Son hath everlasting life: and he that believeth not the Son shall not see life; but the wrath of God abideth on him.
>
> ROMANS 1:16. For I am not ashamed of the gospel of Christ: for it is the power of God unto salvation to every one that believeth; to the Jew first, and also to the Greek.
>
> 2 THESSALONIANS 1:7-10. . . . the Lord Jesus shall be revealed from heaven with his mighty angels, in flaming fire taking vengeance on them that know not God, and that obey not the gospel of our Lord Jesus Christ; who shall be punished with everlasting destruction from the presence of the Lord, and from the glory of his power; when he shall come to be glorified in his saints, and to be admired in all them that believe (because our testimony among you was believed) in that day.
>
> REVELATION 20:15. And whosoever was not found written in the book of life was cast into the lake of fire.

THE SPIRITUALISTS

Spiritualists believe that living men can and do communicate with the spirits of the dead through persons called mediums. The best way to meet this cult is to face them with God's Word on their sin.

> DEUTERONOMY 18:9-12. When thou art come into the land which the Lord thy God giveth thee, thou shalt not learn to do after the abominations of those nations. There shall not be found among you any one that maketh his son or his daughter to pass through the fire, or that useth divination, or an observer of times, or an enchanter, or a witch, or a charmer, or a consulter with familiar spirits, or a wizard, or a necromancer. For all that do these things are an abomination unto the Lord: and because of these abominations the Lord thy God doth drive them out from before thee.
>
> 1 CHRONICLES 10:13-14. So Saul died for his transgression which he committed against the Lord, even against the word

of the Lord, which he kept not, and also for asking counsel of one that had a familiar spirit, to enquire of it; and enquired not of the Lord: therefore he slew him, and turned the kingdom unto David the son of Jesse.

ISAIAH 8:19-20. And when they shall say unto you, Seek unto them that have familiar spirits, and unto wizards that peep, and mutter: should not a people seek unto their God? for the living to the dead? To the law and to the testimony: if they speak not according to this word, it is because there is no light in them.

1 TIMOTHY 4:1. Now the Spirit speaketh expressly, that in the latter times some shall depart from the faith, giving heed to seducing spirits, and doctrines of devils.

Apply God's test of spirits to them—

1 JOHN 4:1-3. Beloved, believe not every spirit, but try the spirits whether they are of God: because many false prophets are gone out into the world. Hereby know ye the Spirit of God: Every spirit that confesseth that Jesus Chirst is come in the flesh is of God: and every spirit that confesseth not that Jesus Christ is come in the flesh is not of God: and this is that spirit of antichrist, whereof ye have heard that it should come; and even now already is it in the world.

Spiritualism denies the humanity of Jesus; hence, it is of the devil and is anti-Christ.

FOLLOWERS OF RUSSELL

The followers of "Pastor Russell" call themselves Millennial Dawnists. They deny the doctrines dear to Christians: both the humanity and the deity of Christ, and hence his resurrection; the Holy Spirit; and the eternal punishment of the unbeliever. The way to meet them and win them is to prove from the Scriptures the truth of those doctrines which they deny.

The following passages have to do with Christ and the Holy Spirit.

MATTHEW 28:19. Go ye therefore, and teach all nations, baptizing them in the name of the Father, and of the Son, and of the Holy Ghost.

LUKE 24:39. Behold my hands and my feet, that it is I myself: handle me, and see; for a spirit hath not flesh and bones, as ye see me have.

JOHN 1:1. In the beginning was the Word, and the Word was with God, and the Word was God.

JOHN 16:13-14. Howbeit when he, the Spirit of truth, is come, he will guide you into all truth: for he shall not speak of himself; but whatsoever he shall hear, that shall he speak: and he will shew you things to come. He shall glorify me: for he shall receive of mine, and shall shew it unto you.

JOHN 20:24-29. But Thomas, one of the twelve, called Didymus, was not with them when Jesus came. The other disciples therefore said unto him, We have seen the Lord. But he said unto them, Except I shall see in his hands the print of the nails, and put my finger into the print of the nails, and thrust my hand into his side, I will not believe. And after eight days again his disciples were within, and Thomas with them: then came Jesus, the doors being shut, and stood in the midst, and said, Peace be unto you. Then saith he to Thomas, Reach hither thy finger, and behold my hands; and reach hither thy hand, and thrust it into my side: and be not faithless, but believing. And Thomas answered and said unto him, My Lord and my God. Jesus saith unto him, Thomas, because thou hast seen me, thou hast believed: blessed are they that have not seen, and yet have believed.

ACTS 7:56. . . . and said, Behold, I see the heavens opened, and the Son of man standing on the right hand of God.

COLOSSIANS 1:16-17. For by him were all things created, that are in heaven, and that are in earth, visible and invisible, whether they be thrones, or dominions, or principalities, or powers: all things were created by him, and for him: and he is before all things, and by him all things consist.

1 TIMOTHY 2:5. For there is one God, and one mediator between God and men, the man Christ Jesus.

Use the following verses to show them that God teaches that there is a hell.

JOB 21:29-30. Have ye not asked them that go by the way? and do ye not know their tokens, that the wicked is reserved to the day of destruction? they shall be brought forth to the day of wrath.

MATTHEW 25:41, 46. Then shall he say also unto them on the left hand, Depart from me, ye cursed, into everlasting fire, prepared for the devil and his angels. . . . And these shall go away into everlasting punishment: but the righteous into life eternal.

JOHN 3:36. He that believeth on the Son hath everlasting life: and he that believeth not the Son shall not see life; but the wrath of God abideth on him.

2 THESSALONIANS 1:7-10. . . . the Lord Jesus shall be revealed from heaven with his mighty angels, in flaming fire taking vengeance on them that know not God, and that obey not the gospel of our Lord Jesus Christ: who shall be punished with everlasting destruction from the presence of the Lord, and from the glory of his power; when he shall come to be glorified in his saints, and to be admired in all them that believe (because our testimony among you was believed) in that day.

2 PETER 2:9. The Lord knoweth how to deliver the godly out of temptations, and to reserve the unjust unto the day of judgment to be punished.

REVELATION 20:15. And whosoever was not found written in the book of life was cast into the lake of fire.

REVELATION 21:8. But the fearful, and unbelieving, and the abominable, and murderers, and whoremongers, and sorcerers, and idolaters, and all liars, shall have their part in the lake which burneth with fire and brimstone: which is the second death.

THE SEVENTH-DAY ADVENTISTS

The soul-winner who seeks to win Seventh-Day Adventists will need to be able to combat their errors concerning the sabbath and concerning "soul-sleeping."

1. Seventh-Day Adventists teach that one must keep the seventh day of the week, Saturday, as the sabbath in order to be a Christian, that anyone who observes any other day cannot be saved. Wherever the word "commandment" is used in the New Testament they substitute "sabbath." Hence they make 1 John 2:4 to read, "He that saith, I know him, and keepeth not his sabbath, is a liar, and the truth is not in him." And the same with 1 John 3:23 and Revelation 22:14. They interpret "commandment" to mean the Ten Commandments, which includes the fourth, concerning the sabbath.

Show them—

(1) That the law, as a legal set of rules binding on the consciences of men, was done away with in Christ's rule of grace.

> 2 CORINTHIANS 3:7-11. But if the ministration of death, written and engraven in stones, was glorious, so that the children of Israel could not stedfastly behold the face of Moses for the glory of his countenance; which glory was to be done away: how shall not the ministration of the spirit be rather glorious? For if the ministration of condemnation be glory, much more doth the ministration of righteousness exceed in glory. For even that which was made glorious had no glory in this respect, by reason of the glory that excelleth. For if that which is done away was glorious, much more that which remaineth is glorious.

And that in Christ Jesus the child of God is dead to the law as a legal procedure.

> ROMANS 7:4. Wherefore, my brethren, ye also are become dead to the law by the body of Christ; that ye should be married to another, even to him who is raised from the dead, that we should bring forth fruit unto God.

(2) That each of the Ten Commandments except the one concerning the sabbath is reaffirmed in the New Testament (see Christ's example in Matthew 12:1-8).

(3) That belief that the sabbath obligation is binding on the Christian as a legal observance is declared to be done away with.

> COLOSSIANS 2:16-17. Let no man therefore judge you in meat, or in drink, or in respect of an holy day, or of the new moon, or of the sabbath days: which are a shadow of things to come; but the body is of Christ.

(4) That the sabbath was given as the seventh day, and Christ by his resurrection transferred it to the Lord's Day of the New Testament—the day of rest, worship, and religious service. As such it became the Christian's Lord's Day, with spiritual freedom to do God's will and work therein, and not the Jewish sabbath of strict legalistic observance. Christ's disciples met after his resurrection on the first day of the week.

MATTHEW 28:1. In the end of the sabbath, as it began to dawn toward the first day of the week, came Mary Magdalene and the other Mary to see the sepulchre.

MARK 16:1. And when the sabbath was past, Mary Magdalene, and Mary the mother of James, and Salome, had bought sweet spices, that they might come and anoint him.

LUKE 24:1. Now upon the first day of the week, very early in the morning, they came unto the sepulchre, bringing the spices which they had prepared, and certain others with them.

JOHN 20:1, 19. The first day of the week cometh Mary Magdalene early, when it was yet dark, unto the sepulchre, and seeth the stone taken away from the sepulchre. . . Then the same day at evening, being the first day of the week, when the doors were shut where the disciples were assembled for fear of the Jews, came Jesus and stood in the midst, and saith unto them, Peace be unto you.

ACTS 20:7. And upon the first day of the week, when the disciples came together to break bread, Paul preached unto them, ready to depart on the morrow; and continued his speech until midnight.

1 CORINTHIANS 16:2. Upon the first day of the week let every one of you lay by him in store, as God hath prospered him, that there be no gatherings when I come.

REVELATION 1:10. I was in the Spirit on the Lord's day, and heard behind me a great voice, as of a trumpet.

The preceding passages teach—

(1) That Christ rose on the first day of the week, "when the sabbath was past" (Mark 16:1-2).

(2) That the apostles had their meetings on the first day of the week, at which time Jesus appeared unto them and they worshiped him (John 20:19-26).

(3) That after his ascension the apostles and disciples, Christ's church, held their meetings—days for preaching, partaking of the Lord's Supper, and raising money for his kingdom—on the first day of the week (Acts 20:7; 1 Cor. 16:2).

(4) That this day was called the Lord's Day (Rev. 1:10), not the sabbath. It was a new day to take the place of the old sabbath and came the day after it—the Christian sabbath or Lord's Day.

2. The Adventists teach, also, the doctrine of "soul-sleeping," that is, that the soul between death and the resurrection has no conscious existence.

To meet this error, explain the following passages to them.

MATTHEW 27:52. And the graves were opened; and many bodies of the saints which slept arose.

LUKE 23:43, 46. And Jesus said unto him, Verily I say unto thee, To day shalt thou be with me in paradise. . . . And when Jesus had cried with a loud voice, he said, Father, into thy hands I commend my spirit: and having said thus, he gave up the ghost.

2 CORINTHIANS 5:1-9. For we know that if our earthly house of this tabernacle were dissolved, we have a building of God, an house not made with hands, eternal in the heavens. For in this we groan, earnestly desiring to be clothed upon with our house which is from heaven: if so be that being clothed we shall not be found naked. For we that are in this tabernacle do groan, being burdened: not for that we would be unclothed, but clothed upon, that mortality might be swallowed up of life. Now he that hath wrought us for the selfsame thing is God, who also hath given unto us the earnest of the Spirit. Therefore we are always confident, knowing that, whilst we are at home in the body, we are absent from the Lord: (For we walk by faith, not by sight:) we are confident, I say, and willing rather to be absent from the body, and to be present with the Lord. Wherefore we labour, that, whether present or absent, we may be accepted of him.

2 CORINTHIANS 12:2. I knew a man in Christ above fourteen years ago, (whether in the body, I cannot tell; or whether out of the body, I cannot tell: God knoweth;) such an one caught up to the third heaven.

PHILIPPIANS 1:21-24. For to me to live is Christ, and to die is gain. But if I live in the flesh, this is the fruit of my labour: yet what I shall choose I wot not. For I am in a strait betwixt two, having a desire to depart, and to be with Christ; which is far better: nevertheless to abide in the flesh is more needful for you.

The unmistakable case is that of Lazarus and the rich man.

LUKE 16:26-31. And beside all this, between us and you there is a great gulf fixed: so that they which would pass from hence to you cannot; neither can they pass to us, that would

THE DECEIVED AND DELUDED

come from thence. Then he said, I pray thee therefore, father, that thou wouldest send him to my father's house: for I have five brethren; that he may testify unto them, lest they also come into this place of torment. Abraham saith unto him, They have Moses and the prophets; let them hear them. And he said, Nay, father Abraham: but if one went unto them from the dead, they will repent. And he said unto him, If they hear not Moses and the prophets, neither will they be persuaded, though one rose from the dead.

The rich man opened his eyes in hell, cried for mercy, remembered his good things, was thirsty, and desired Lazarus to go to his father's house. If the Adventist answers that this is a parable, you can reply that he must prove it. The Bible does not intimate that it is a parable. Then, if it is a parable, Christ did not teach an untruth, even in parabolic form.

Then refer them to Matthew 17:1-13. "Behold, there appeared unto them Moses and Elias talking with him." Moses had been buried by God's own hand many hundreds of years before, and yet he appeared and talked. His soul was not asleep.

The following passages concerning the "sleeping dead" are easily explained as referring to the bodies of the dead, not to their spirits.

> JOHN 11:11, 14, 39. These things said he: and after that he saith unto them, Our friend Lazarus sleepeth; but I go, that I may awake him out of sleep. . . . Then said Jesus unto them plainly, Lazarus is dead. . . . Jesus said, Take ye away the stone. Martha, the sister of him that was dead, saith unto him, Lord, by this time he stinketh: for he hath been dead four days.
>
> 1 THESSALONIANS 4:13, 15. But I would not have you to be ignorant, brethren, concerning them which are asleep, that ye sorrow not, even as others which have no hope. . . . For this we say unto you by the word of the Lord, that we which are alive and remain unto the coming of the Lord shall not prevent them which are asleep.

Luke 15:10, "There is joy in the presence of the angels of God over one sinner that repenteth," shows that the departed Christians in heaven rejoice when men on earth are saved.

If the Adventist's heart is not hardened and you can convince him of his error, then seek by methods laid down in other chapters to bring him to Christ.

> JOHN 1:12-13. But as many as received him, to them gave he power to become the sons of God, even to them that believe on his name: which were born, not of blood, nor of the will of the flesh, nor of the will of man, but of God.
> JOHN 3:16, 36. For God so loved the world, that he gave his only begotten Son, that whosoever believeth in him should not perish, but have everlasting life. . . . He that believeth on the Son hath everlasting life: and he that believeth not the Son shall not see life; but the wrath of God abideth on him.
> JOHN 5:24. Verily, verily, I say unto you, He that heareth my word, and believeth on him that sent me, hath everlasting life, and shall not come into condemnation; but is passed from death unto life.
> ROMANS 5:1. Therefore being justified by faith, we have peace with God through our Lord Jesus Christ.
> EPHESIANS 2:8. For by grace are ye saved through faith; and that not of yourselves: it is the gift of God.

Nowhere is sabbath-keeping given as a condition of salvation.

So-called Christian Scientists

Christ Science, or "Eddyism," is the arch delusion with the greatest amount of nonsense. We need not ridicule it or fear it. We should squarely meet it in the light of God's Word and common sense.

The so-called signs and wonders of Christian Science are foretold in—

> MATTHEW 7:22-23. Many will say to me in that day, Lord, Lord, have we not prophesied in thy name? and in thy name have cast out devils? and in thy name done many wonderful works? And then will I profess unto them, I never knew you: depart from me, ye that work iniquity.
> MARK 13:22-23. For false Christs and false prophets shall rise, and shall shew signs and wonders, to seduce, if it were

possible, even the elect. But take ye heed: behold, I have foretold you all things.

2 CORINTHIANS 11:14-15. And no marvel; for Satan himself is transformed into an angel of light. Therefore it is no great thing if his ministers also be transformed as the ministers of righteousness; whose end shall be according to their works.

2 THESSALONIANS 2:8-9. And then shall that Wicked be revealed, whom the Lord shall consume with the spirit of his mouth, and shall destroy with the brightness of his coming: even him, whose coming is after the working of Satan with all power and signs and lying wonders.

"Eddyism" denies so many fundamentals taught in the Bible that to convince its followers one must go through the entire system of Christian faith in order to cover their heresies.

1. They deny God's personality. He is a great "influence," they say. Almost any Scripture passage referring to God shows him to be an intelligent, spiritual personality.

2. They deny Christ's deity and humanity, and hence his atonement for sin. Answer them with—

MATTHEW 3:17. And lo a voice from heaven, saying, This is my beloved Son, in whom I am well pleased.

JOHN 1:18. No man hath seen God at any time: the only begotten Son, which is in the bosom of the Father, he hath declared him.

JOHN 19:30-35. When Jesus therefore had received the vinegar, he said, It is finished: and he bowed his head, and gave up the ghost. The Jews therefore, because it was the preparation, that the bodies should not remain upon the cross on the sabbath day, (for that sabbath day was an high day,) besought Pilate that their legs might be broken, and that they might be taken away. Then came the soldiers, and brake the legs of the first, and of the other which was crucified with him. But when they came to Jesus, and saw that he was dead already, they brake not his legs: but one of the soldiers with a spear pierced his side, and forthwith came there out blood and water. And he that saw it bare record, and his record is true: and he knoweth that he saith true, that ye might believe.

ROMANS 6:4-5, 8-10. Therefore we are buried with him by baptism into death: that like as Christ was raised up from the dead by the glory of the Father, even so we also should walk in newness of life. For if we have been planted together in the likeness of his death, we shall be also in the likeness of his resurrection. . . . Now if we be dead with Christ, we believe that we shall also live with him: knowing that Christ being raised from the dead dieth no more; death hath no more dominion over him. For in that he died, he died unto sin once: but in that he liveth, he liveth unto God.

1 CORINTHIANS 15:1-4. Moreover, brethren, I declare unto you the gospel which I preached unto you, which also ye have received, and wherein ye stand; by which also ye are saved, if ye keep in memory what I preached unto you, unless ye have believed in vain. For I delivered unto you first of all that which I also received, how that Christ died for our sins according to the scriptures; and that he was buried, and that he rose again the third day according to the scriptures.

3. They deny the doctrine of sin. They say: "Belief in sin is an error; there is no evil. Sin is not real; it is an illusion." Show them in God's Word—

EZEKIEL 18:4. Behold, all souls are mine; as the soul of the father, so also the soul of the son is mine: the soul that sinneth it shall die.

ROMANS 5:12. Wherefore, as by one man sin entered into the world, and death by sin; and so death passed upon all men, for that all have sinned.

2 CORINTHIANS 5:21. For he hath made him to be sin for us, who knew no sin; that we might be made the righteousness of God in him.

GALATIANS 3:13. Christ hath redeemed us from the curse of the law, being made a curse for us: for it is written, Cursed is every one that hangeth on a tree.

1 PETER 2:24. . . . who his own self bare our sins in his own body on the tree, that we, being dead to sins, should live unto righteousness: by whose stripes ye were healed.

4. They put *Science and Health,* "the Bible of Eddyism," above the Holy Scriptures. They know more about that than they do about the Bible; they quote it more, carry it with them more, study it more.

Test them out on—

1 JOHN 2:22. Who is a liar but he that denieth that Jesus is the Christ? He is antichrist, that denieth the Father and the Son.

THE DECEIVED AND DELUDED

1 JOHN 4:1-3. Beloved, believe not every spirit, but try the spirits whether they are of God: because many false prophets are gone out into the world. Hereby know ye the Spirit of God: Every spirit that confesseth that Jesus Christ is come in the flesh is of God: and every spirit that confesseth not that Jesus Christ is come in the flesh is not of God: and this is that spirit of antichrist, whereof ye have heard that it should come; and even now already is it in the world.

2 JOHN 7. For many deceivers are entered into the world, who confess not that Jesus Christ is come in the flesh. This is a deceiver and an antichrist.

After you run them out of their false refuges, try to win them to Christ in the same way you would any other sinner.

28

How to Win Skeptics and Doubters

An atheist is one who does not believe in the existence of a supreme being called God. An infidel is one who denies the deity of Jesus Christ. An agnostic is one who does not know, hence repudiates all idea of God and a supreme being by any name. A skeptic is a doubter on any phase of the fundamentals concerning God and Christ and their work among men. Few people in Christian lands today are outspoken in their disbelief. There are, however, many secret unbelievers who have been reared in or, for one reason or another, driven into infidelity in some of its forms. They are difficult to reach, and to win them requires the most tactful and skilful treatment from Christian workers.

There are different degrees of disbelief. There are insincere, trifling persons who usually profess disbelief—whether as atheists, infidels, agnostics, or skeptics—to cover up sinful and rotten lives, thus seeking to appease the goading of their consciences and to give a covering to and a defense for their sins. And there are real, sincere doubters and disbelievers, whose minds are psychologically skeptical. Their rearing has encouraged such an attitude, and they stand appalled at the "mysteries of religion." Both types must be met fairly and squarely by the soul-winner.

The Light-headed, Trifling Disbeliever

In dealing with a light-headed, trifling disbeliever there are two methods which the worker may follow. He must seek the wisdom of God for guidance as to which will be more effective.

Shock him; strike him hard and fast with God's hammering word; run a "fifth rib" thrust with the Sword of the Spirit, which cuts, divides, burns, and breaks into pieces. Say to him: "Your trouble is not your doubts but your sins. You are living in secret and black sin, and you are unwilling to give it up. You are trying to satisfy your conscience by professing to do away with religion in your heart."

Put straight to his soul—

> ROMANS 1:25, 28. . . . who changed the truth of God into a lie, and worshipped and served the creature more than the Creator, who is blessed for ever. Amen. . . . And even as they did not like to retain God in their knowledge, God gave them over to a reprobate mind, to do those things which are not convenient.
>
> 2 CORINTHIANS 4:3-4. But if our gospel be hid, it is hid to them that are lost: in whom the god of this world hath blinded the minds of them which believe not, lest the light of the glorious gospel of Christ, who is the image of God, should shine unto them.

In my early ministry a young, high-spirited professional man got a group around him, asked a lot of "infidel" questions, and laughed at the group in their confusion. He saw me coming and said: "Let's try this young preacher and see if he can help us out." As I walked into the group, he put his question to me. I did not answer his question, but put my hand under the lapel of his coat and said: "Your trouble is not your infidelity. You are living a double life, untrue to your wife and deceiving her and your friends; but you are not deceiving God. Be sure your sins will find you out." I immediately went my way.

He got mad, swore, and raged that the preacher had insulted him. I met him three days afterward. He had cooled off and was in his right mind. He said: "I wanted to whip you and would if I had seen you. I was first mad at you, then at myself, and then at the devil. I want you to pray for me. You have discovered me. I want to be a Christian."

It was not long until he was saved, and since that time he has lived a consistent Christian life.

But remember that this shock method is a dangerous one to use. It is easy to make a mistake and do it in a wrong spirit.

Another way of dealing with disbelievers of this type is to *convince them* by the purity, genuineness, and strength of your Christian life. A mother, a wife, a child; a godly businessman; a doctor, lawyer, or farmer, pure in life; a deeply spiritual preacher—these may win to Christ by their walk with God and their purity of life. This is a fine method to try on all kinds of sinners. Hezekiah's prayer was: "Remember now, O Lord, I beseech thee, how I have walked before thee in truth and with a perfect heart, and have done that which is good in thy sight" (Isa. 38:3).

The logic of a great life for God cannot be answered. A young college senior said to me: "I can answer all the arguments you have made for Christ's deity, the inspiration of the Bible, the efficacy of Christ's death, but I cannot answer my mother's life. I want you to pray that I may have what she has, that which made her what she is." Life won where logic failed.

The Fair-minded, Honest Skeptic

The difficulties of honest skeptics arise, usually, out of a failure or inability to believe in certain Christian fundamentals.

1. They may not believe in the Bible as the inspired and authoritative Word of God. This is a basic difficulty. The soul-winner leans heavily and depends tremendously on the Word of God; and if this support is taken from him, he is at a greater disadvantage. The worker should be informed on the arguments for the inspiration of the Bible, its triumphant history, its fulfilled prophecy, its unity in variety of authorship, and its wonderful results in the transformation of individual and national character.

Show them what the Bible professes concerning its divine authorship.

ISAIAH 40:8. The grass withereth, the flower fadeth: but the word of our God shall stand for ever.

MATTHEW 5:18. For verily I say unto you, Till heaven and earth pass, one jot or one tittle shall in no wise pass from the law, till all be fulfilled.

JOHN 10:35. If he called them gods, unto whom the word of God came, and the scripture cannot be broken. . . .

2 TIMOTHY 3:15-17. . . . and that from a child thou hast known the holy scriptures, which are able to make thee wise unto salvation through faith which is in Christ Jesus. All scripture is given by inspiration of God, and is profitable for doctrine, for reproof, for correction, for instruction in righteousness: that the man of God may be perfect, throughly furnished unto all good works.

2 PETER 1:21. For the prophecy came not in old time by the will of man: but holy men of God spake as they were moved by the Holy Ghost.

Press on them—

JOHN 7:17. If any man will do his will, he shall know of the doctrine, whether it be of God, or whether I speak of myself.

2. They may not, or perhaps cannot, believe in the existence of an intelligent, moral being called God.

Show them where God classifies them.

PSALM 14:1. The fool hath said in his heart, There is no God. They are corrupt, they have done abominable works, there is none that doeth good.

Show them that all the world's wonders in creation, progress, and providence indicate an intelligent Creator and Preserver. Your very hand or eye speaks in its artful mechanisms for God. Read to them:

PSALM 19:1-2. The heavens declare the glory of God; and the firmament sheweth his handywork. Day unto day uttereth speech, and night unto night sheweth knowledge.

ROMANS 1:19-22. . . . because that which may be known of God is manifest in them; for God hath shewed it unto them. For the invisible things of him from the creation of the world are clearly seen, being understood by the things that are made, even his eternal power and Godhead; so that they are without excuse: because that, when they knew God, they glorified him not as God, neither were thankful; but became vain in their imaginations, and their foolish heart was darkened. Professing themselves to be wise, they became fools.

3. They may deny or doubt the deity of Jesus Christ. In trying to prove Christ's deity, show them that—

(1) The Bible ascribes to him names of God.

Acts 10:36. The word which God sent unto the children of Israel, preaching peace by Jesus Christ: (he is Lord of all:) ...

1 CORINTHIANS 2:8. ... which none of the princes of this world knew: for had they known it, they would not have crucified the Lord of glory.

(2) He receives the worship due only to God.

JOHN 5:22-23. For the Father judgeth no man, but hath committed all judgment unto the Son: that all men should honour the Son, even as they honour the Father. He that honoureth not the Son honoureth not the Father which hath sent him.

PHILIPPIANS 2:10. ... that at the name of Jesus every knee should bow, of things in heaven, and things in earth, and things under the earth.

HEBREWS 1:6. And again, when he bringeth in the firstbegotten into the world, he saith, And let all the angels of God worship him.

(3) He has the offices of God.

HEBREWS 1:3, 10. ... who being the brightness of his glory, and the express image of his person, and upholding all things by the word of his power, when he had by himself purged our sins, sat down on the right hand of the Majesty on high .... And, Thou, Lord, in the beginning hast laid the foundation of the earth; and the heavens are the works of thine hands.

(4) He performs the deeds of God.

JOHN 1:1-4. In the beginning was the Word, and the Word was with God, and the Word was God. The same was in the beginning with God. All things were made by him; and without him was not anything made that was made. In him was life; and the life was the light of men.

(5) God's Word says:

ISAIAH 7:14. Therefore the Lord himself shall give you a sign; Behold, a virgin shall conceive, and bear a son, and shall call his name Immanuel.

ISAIAH 9:6-7. For unto us a child is born, unto us a son is given: and the government shall be upon his shoulder: and his name shall be called Wonderful, Counsellor, The mighty God, The everlasting Father, The Prince of Peace. Of the increase of his government and peace there shall be no end, upon the throne of David, and upon his kingdom, to order it, and to establish it with judgment and with justice from henceforth even for ever. The zeal of the Lord of hosts will perform this.

MATTHEW 3:16-17. And Jesus, when he was baptized, went up straightway out of the water: and, lo, the heavens were opened unto him, and he saw the Spirit of God descending like a dove, and lighting upon him: and lo a voice from heaven, saying, This is my beloved Son, in whom I am well pleased.

(6) His resurrection points to his deity.

ROMANS 1:3-4. . . . concerning his Son Jesus Christ our Lord, which was made of the seed of David according to the flesh; and declared to be the Son of God with power, according to the spirit of holiness, by the resurrection from the dead.

Press on them—

JOHN 7:17. If any man will do his will, he shall know of the doctrine, whether it be of God, or whether I speak of myself.

4. They may not accept the doctrine of eternal punishment.

Make them face God's Word on this doctrine. (See the section on "Followers of Russell" in the preceding chapter.)

A man, a professed Christian, said to me: "I am thinking of joining your church. Does a man have to believe in hell in order to be a Baptist?" My answer was: "Let me see. Maybe your trouble is worse than that. You believe in heaven, do you?" "Yes," he said. "I am sure my mother and child whom you recently buried are in heaven. It is a precious doctrine to me." I asked, "On whose authority do you believe in heaven?" He said, "On Christ's," and referred to John 14:2-3. "Well," I said, "the same Christ in the same Bible says, 'Depart from me, ye cursed, into everlasting fire. . . . These shall go away into everlasting punishment: but the righteous into life eternal.' Do you believe Christ would tell you the truth about heaven and lie to you about hell? Your trouble, my friend, is that you do not believe in Christ. Your attitude is that of an infidel." He saw the direful consequences of his position and withdrew from it. All the doctrines of the New Testament stand or fall with Christ.

Push far into the souls of those who say they do not believe in hell—

> JOHN 5:24. Verily, verily, I say unto you, He that heareth my word, and believeth on him that sent me, hath everlasting life, and shall not come into condemnation; but is passed from death unto life.
>
> JOHN 7:17. If any man will do his will, he shall know of the doctrine, whether it be of God, or whether I speak of myself.

29

How to Win the Moralist

Under the influences of Christian civilization many men and women have been reared to live good, moral lives, free from many of the sins of the world, exemplary in their conduct, favoring Christianity and high standards of morality. They have absorbed many of the principles of life taught by Jesus Christ, but they have never given themselves by faith to him and acknowledged him as their Saviour. They claim to be moral. They are self-righteous. They depend on their good lives and good deeds to get them through this world and the world to come. This class was very prevalent in New Testament times and has left to history some shining marks: Nicodemus, Saul of Tarsus, Cornelius, the rich young ruler, the self-righteous Pharisee. Such people today claim that they are as good as or better than church members and that they do nothing very wrong. Soul-winners will find them in every Christian community. Some of them are not boastful, but go on silently trusting in their righteous lives and good deeds and rejecting Christ and often go down to hell like any other sinner.

In dealing with them there are several ways of approach. I have followed somewhat the following:

1. Face them with God's general statements in the Bible on the sin of self-righteousness and the futility of trying to achieve righteousness by works.

> PROVERBS 16:2. All the ways of a man are clean in his own eyes; but the Lord weigheth the spirits.
>
> ISAIAH 53:5-6. But he was wounded for our transgressions, he was bruised for our iniquities: the chastisement of our peace was upon him; and with his stripes we are healed. All we

> like sheep have gone astray; we have turned every one to his own way; and the Lord hath laid on him the iniquity of us all.
> ISAIAH 64:6. But we are all as an unclean thing, and all our righteousnesses are as filthy rags; and we all do fade as a leaf; and our iniquities, like the wind, have taken us away.
> LUKE 16:15. And he said unto them, Ye are they which justify yourselves before men; but God knoweth your hearts: for that which is highly esteemed among men is abomination in the sight of God.
> ROMANS 3:19-20. Now we know that what things soever the law saith, it saith to them who are under the law: that every mouth may be stopped, and all the world may become guilty before God. Therefore by the deeds of the law there shall no flesh be justified in his sight: for by the law is the knowledge of sin.
> GALATIANS 2:16. . . . knowing that a man is not justified by the works of the law, but by the faith of Jesus Christ, even we have believed in Jesus Christ, that we might be justified by the faith of Christ, and not by the works of the law: for by the works of the law shall no flesh be justified.
> GALATIANS 3:10. For as many as are of the works of the law are under the curse: for it is written, Cursed is every one that continueth not in all things which are written in the book of the law to do them.
> TITUS 3:5. Not by works of righteousness which we have done, but according to his mercy he saved us, by the washing of regeneration, and renewing of the Holy Ghost.

2. Show them what God said of the self-righteous in the Bible.

(1) Of Abraham.—Abraham did not claim to be self-righteous, but God explains that his righteousness did not avail in his salvation.

> ROMANS 4:2-6. For if Abraham were justified by works, he hath whereof to glory; but not before God. For what saith the scripture? Abraham believed God, and it was counted unto him for righteousness. Now to him that worketh is the reward not reckoned of grace, but of debt. But to him that worketh not, but believeth on him that justifieth the ungodly, his faith is counted for righteousness. Even as David also describeth the blessedness of the man, unto whom God imputeth righteousness without works.

(2) Of Nicodemus.

JOHN 3:1-7. There was a man of the Pharisees, named Nicodemus, a ruler of the Jews: the same came to Jesus by night, and said unto him, Rabbi, we know that thou art a teacher come from God: for no man can do these miracles that thou doest, except God be with him. Jesus answered and said unto him, Verily, verily, I say unto thee, Except a man be born again, he cannot see the kingdom of God. Nicodemus saith unto him, How can a man be born when he is old? can he enter the second time into his mother's womb, and be born? Jesus answered, Verily, verily, I say unto thee, Except a man be born of water and of the Spirit, he cannot enter into the kingdom of God. That which is born of the flesh is flesh; and that which is born of the Spirit is spirit. Marvel not that I said unto thee, Ye must be born again.

(3) Of the Pharisees.

MATTHEW 5:20. For I say unto you, That except your righteousness shall exceed the righteousness of the scribes and Pharisees, ye shall in no case enter into the kingdom of heaven.

LUKE 18:10-14. Two men went up into the temple to pray; the one a Pharisee, and the other a publican. The Pharisee stood and prayed thus with himself, God, I thank thee, that I am not as other men are, extortioners, unjust, adulterers, or even as this publican. I fast twice in the week, I give tithes of all that I possess. And the publican, standing afar off, would not lift up so much as his eyes unto heaven, but smote upon his breast, saying, God be merciful to me a sinner. I tell you, this man went down to his house justified rather than the other: for every one that exalteth himself shall be abased; and he that humbleth himself shall be exalted.

(4) Of Cornelius.

ACTS 10:1-2,4,42-43. There was a certain man in Caesarea called Cornelius, a centurion of the band called the Italian band, a devout man, and one that feared God with all his house, which gave much alms to the people, and prayed to God alway. . . . And when he looked on him, he was afraid, and said, What is it, Lord? And he said unto him, Thy prayers and thine alms are come up for a memorial before God. . . .

And he commanded us to preach unto the people, and to testify that it is he which was ordained of God to be the

the Judge of quick and dead. To him give all the prophets witness, that through his name whosoever believeth in him shall receive remission of sins.

(5) Of Saul of Tarsus.

PHILIPPIANS 3:4-11. Though I might also have confidence in the flesh. If any other man thinketh that he hath whereof he might trust in the flesh, I more: circumcised the eighth day, of the stock of Israel, of the tribe of Benjamin, an Hebrew of the Hebrews; as touching the law, a Pharisee; concerning zeal, persecuting the church; touching the righteousness which is in the law, blameless. But what things were gain to me, those I counted loss for Christ. Yea doubtless, and I count all things but loss for the excellency of the knowledge of Christ Jesus my Lord: for whom I have suffered the loss of all things, and do count them but dung, that I may win Christ, and be found in him, not having mine own righteousness, which is of the law, but that which is through the faith of Christ, the righteousness which is of God by faith: that I may know him, and the power of his resurrection, and the fellowship of his sufferings, being made conformable unto his death; if by any means I might attain unto the resurrection of the dead.

These all had to believe in Christ and receive his righteousness and turn away from their own as the basis for a hope of salvation.

3. Show them the terms of salvation laid down in the Scriptures.

(1) *Repentance* toward God for their own personal sins.

JOHN 16:8-11. And when he is come, he will reprove the world of sin, and of righteousness, and of judgment: of sin, because they believe not on me; of righteousness, because I go to my Father, and ye see me no more; of judgment, because the prince of this world is judged.

ACTS 3:19. Repent ye therefore, and be converted, that your sins may be blotted out, when the times of refreshing shall come from the presence of the Lord.

ACTS 20:21. . . . testifying both to the Jews, and also to the Greeks, repentance toward God, and faith toward our Lord Jesus Christ.

(2) *Faith* in the Lord Jesus Christ.

> JOHN 1:12-13. But as many as received him, to them gave he power to become the sons of God, even to them that believe on his name: which were born, not of blood, nor of the will of the flesh, nor of the will of man, but of God.
> JOHN 3:16,36. For God so loved the world, that he gave his only begotten Son, that whosoever believeth in him should not perish, but have everlasting life. . . . He that believeth on the Son hath everlasting life: and he that believeth not the Son shall not see life; but the wrath of God abideth on him.
> JOHN 6:29. Jesus answered and said unto them, This is the work of God, that ye believe on him whom he hath sent.
> HEBREWS 11:6. But without faith it is impossible to please him: for he that cometh to God must believe that he is, and that he is a rewarder of them that diligently seek him.

All this looks away from self and what it is or does, and looks to Christ.

4. Show them that a self-righteous claim for salvation nullifies Christ's meritorious death for us and makes his atonement the unnecessary crime of the ages.

> ROMANS 11:6. And if by grace, then is it no more of works: otherwise grace is no more grace. But if it be of works, then is it no more grace: otherwise work is no more work.
> GALATIANS 2:21. I do not frustrate the grace of God: for if righteousness come by the law, then Christ is dead in vain.
> HEBREWS 10:28-29. He that despised Moses' law died without mercy under two or three witnesses: of how much sorer punishment, suppose ye, shall he be thought worthy, who hath trodden under foot the Son of God, and hath counted the blood of the covenant, wherewith he was sanctified, an unholy thing, and hath done despite unto the Spirit of grace?

5. Press on them—

> JOHN 1:12-13. But as many as received him, to them gave he power to become the sons of God, even to them that believe on his name: which were born, not of blood, nor of the will of the flesh, nor of the will of man, but of God.
> JOHN 3:3. Jesus answered and said unto him, Verily, verily, I say unto thee, Except a man be born again, he cannot see the kingdom of God.

> EPHESIANS 2:8. For by grace are ye saved through faith; and that not of yourselves: it is the gift of God.

A charming young woman, reared in a Christian home, heard me preach on repentance as the first step every sinner must take toward God. I said no one could evade it, avoid it, or escape it, nor could there be made any substitute for repentance: not morality or baptism or money or service—nothing. "God . . . commandeth all men every where to repent." The pastor spoke to her as she stood in the congregation. She was angry and would not hear him. As I approached her, I found she was enraged by my message. She said: "I am no sinner. I do not have to repent. I have been raised in the lap of a godly home, knowing nothing but church and Sunday school. I do not have to repent." I looked deep into her soul and said: "Have you ever yielded yourself in faith to Jesus Christ and trusted him and him alone for salvation?" Her reply was prompt and spirited: "No, sir, I have not." "Then," I said, "you are a sinner deserving God's wrath and sin's eternal punishment," and quoted:

> JOHN 3:36. He that believeth on the Son hath everlasting life: and he that believeth not the Son shall not see life; but the wrath of God abideth on him.
> JOHN 16:8-9. And when he is come, he will reprove the world of sin, and of righteousness, and of judgment: of sin, because they believe not on me.

The Spirit of God took the message and barbed the arrow. She broke down in tears, followed me to the front, and sat with her face in her hands. I said, "Trust Christ now." She said: "I am too great a sinner. I am the meanest woman in this city." Immediately the light supernal broke in on her repenting soul. The Saviour entered the open door of her heart by faith and supped with her in a joyful season of grace (Rev. 3:20).

30

How to Win the Pleasure-loving

Many people, especially young men and young women, are being kept out of the kingdom of God because of their love for the pleasures of the world—they desire to have a good time. They do not wish to be put under the restrictions and limitations of church rule and obligation until they have drunk deep at the fountain of the world's pleasures. Such things as the social dance, the theater, the race track, the card game, the social glass, the moving picture, the poolroom, and club life keep them away from God and his churches. Many church members defend some of these social evils, and many indulge in them themselves and encourage young people in them. "And one shall say unto him, What are these wounds in thine hands? Then he shall answer, Those with which I was wounded in the house of my friends" (Zech. 13:6).

This pleasure-loving spirit is exceedingly difficult to handle for Christ. Multiplied thousands are passing from these pleasures into grosser sins and on, out of the reach of the gospel influences, into eternity, hopeless, Christless, and Godless. The old devil has been cycles of centuries beautifying sin—putting gaudy colors on it; making it attractive; fitting it to our carnal nature; making it appealing to our passions, tempers, and appetites; veneering and whitewashing it; camouflaging, sugar-coating it; mingling it with sweet music; putting up pretty pictures; baiting souls for perdition.

In many places religious leaders are yielding, modifying, apologizing, and compromising, and thus making matters perilous for souls and making it more difficult for the faithful to stand. We should put on the whole armor of God and stand immovably by the high standards of the gospel. A flag-bearer in the Cuban War, climbing a hill under a terrific shellfire, got a hundred yards ahead of the men being thinned by the shot and shell. An officer said, "Bring the standard back to the men." Another officer countermanded, "No, for God's sake, bring the men up to the standard." This should be the attitude of all Christ's leaders and churches as they face a world seeking to sap the very life out of Christ's kingdom by sinful pleasures. Paul's standard was: "Have no fellowship with the unfruitful works of darkness, but rather reprove them" (Eph. 5:11).

In dealing with the pleasure-mad the following methods may be helpful:

1. Do not minimize the joy of sinful pleasure. There is great joy in the world's ways, or men and women by the millions would not be going that way.

2. Show them there is also great joy, a richer joy, a safer joy, in Christianity. Show them that all sinful pleasure is destructive to mind, body, or soul, as the poisonous virus which penetrates the vitalities and breaks down tissues of life; that, on the other hand, the pleasures in Christ's salvation and service are character-building and soul-strengthening.

3. Show them how God condemns the walk in the world's ways.

> 2 CORINTHIANS 6:14-18. Be ye not unequally yoked together with unbelievers: for what fellowship hath righteousness with unrighteousness? and what communion hath light with darkness? and what concord hath Christ with Belial? or what part hath he that believeth with an infidel? and what agreement hath the temple of God with idols? for ye are the temple of the living God; as God hath said, I will dwell in them, and walk in them; and I will be their God, and they shall be my people. Wherefore come out from among them, and be ye separate, saith the Lord, and touch not the unclean thing; and I will receive you, and will be a Father unto you, and ye shall be my sons and daughters, saith the Lord Almighty.

GALATIANS 5:17-21. For the flesh lusteth against the Spirit, and the Spirit against the flesh: and these are contrary the one to the other: so that ye cannot do the things that ye would. But if ye be led of the Spirit, ye are not under the law. Now the works of the flesh are manifest, which are these; Adultery, fornication, uncleanness, lasciviousness, idolatry, witchcraft, hatred, variance, emulations, wrath, strife, seditions, heresies, envyings, murders, drunkenness, revellings, and such like: of the which I tell you before, as I have also told you in time past, that they which do such things shall not inherit the kingdom of God.

EPHESIANS 4:17-31. This I say therefore, and testify in the Lord, that ye henceforth walk not as other Gentiles walk, in the vanity of their mind, having the understanding darkened, being alienated from the life of God through the ignorance that is in them, because of the blindness of their heart: who being past feeling have given themselves over unto lasciviousness, to work all uncleanness with greediness. But ye have not so learned Christ; if so be that ye have heard him, and have been taught by him, as the truth is in Jesus: that ye put off concerning the former conversation the old man, which is corrupt according to the deceitful lusts; and be renewed in the spirit of your mind; and that ye put on the new man, which after God is created in righteousness and true holiness. Wherefore putting away lying, speak every man truth with his neighbour: for we are members one of another. Be ye angry, and sin not: let not the sun go down upon your wrath: neither give place to the devil. Let him that stole steal no more: but rather let him labour, working with his hands the thing which is good, that he may have to give to him that needeth. Let no corrupt communication proceed out of your mouth, but that which is good to the use of edifying, that it may minister grace unto the hearers. And grieve not the holy Spirit of God, whereby ye are sealed unto the day of redemption. Let all bitterness, and wrath, and anger, and clamour, and evil speaking, be put away from you, with all malice.

1 JOHN 2:15-17. Love not the world, neither the things that are in the world. If any man love the world, the love of the Father is not in him. For all that is in the world, the lust of the flesh and the lust of the eyes, and the pride of life, is not of the Father, but is of the world. And the world passeth away, and the lust thereof: but he that doeth the will of God abideth for ever.

4. Show them that they must choose between Christ and these things. "If any man love the world, the love of the Father is not in him" (1 John 2:15). "Let the wicked forsake his way, and the unrighteous man his thoughts: and let him return unto the Lord, and he will have mercy upon him; and to our God, for he will abundantly pardon" (Isa. 55:7).

5. Show them the better way of faith and service in Christ's kingdom; and after they are saved, seek to give them something in the church to do. Have adequate social life in the church and offer all the pleasure you can, free from the sin and taint of the world's standards.

A young lady in a college revival held out against God and held on to the love of the dance. Her many friends pled with her, using every possible argument and persuasion. She was stubborn and obstinate. Finally, in the last service I approached her and said: "Mary, you love the pleasures of the world, especially the social dance, don't you?" She answered, "Yes." "Do you love your mother?" The question brought back her mother to her, her love, her consecrated life and high teachings; and her eyes filled with tears as she answered, "Yes, better than life." "Now," I said, "suppose you had to choose between your mother and the dance. Which would you give up?" As quick as thought, unhesitatingly, she said, "The dance." "Now," I said, "you must choose between Christ and this love of a worldly pleasure." And as I held out my hand, I said, "Which will you choose, Christ or sin?" She saw it plainly and with a wholehearted surrender gave herself joyfully to Christ; and though that was many years ago, she is still following Christ and finds more pleasure in his service and companionship than in the "tents of wickedness."

David said: "I had rather be a doorkeeper in the house of my God, than to dwell in the tents of wickedness" (Psalm 84:10). We should patiently lead the young back from the soiling pleasures of the world to the joys of Christ's service.

31

How to Meet the Lost Man's Difficulties

In dealing with unsaved people of all ages and conditions, soul-winners will find all kinds of difficulties which an active, aggressive devil constantly puts in their way. These difficulties should be squarely met and, as far as possible, answered and removed from the way of the sinner. Some of them are used as mere excuses, as was the case in Luke 14:15-24, where "they all with one consent began to make excuse." But in many cases honest seekers find a real hindrance and need help to overcome it.

Here are some of the prevalent difficulties and suggested ways of meeting them:

1. *"I am too great a sinner; my heart is too hard."* The devil often puts these words into the minds of seekers and makes a real barrier of them.

(1) Tell them of Paul's case (1 Tim. 1:15). He was the chief of sinners, and yet God saved him.

(2) Tell them of the thief on the cross, who was a criminal and a condemned sinner, and yet Christ spoke words of life to him (Luke 23:39-43).

(3) Tell them of the harlot at Jacob's well, whom he saved and sent away as an evangel of light (John 4).

(4) Tell them of the jailer at Philippi, who cruelly treated Paul, and how God saved him (Acts 16:22-33).

(5) Tell them of the great crowd of Christ's crucifiers who, in repentance, were saved on the day of Pentecost (Acts 2:22-23, 37-41).

(6) Tell them of David's double crime of murder and adultery and how, on his repentance and confession, God forgave him (Psalm 51).

(7) Show God's promises of pardon and salvation covering every case, it matters not how hard.

PSALM 32:5. I acknowledged my sin unto thee, and mine iniquity have I not hid. I said, I will confess my transgressions unto the Lord; and thou forgavest the iniquity of my sin. Selah.

ISAIAH 1:18. Come now, and let us reason together, saith the Lord: though your sins be as scarlet, they shall be as white as snow; though they be red like crimson, they shall be as wool.

EZEKIEL 36:26-27. A new heart also will I give you, and a new spirit will I put within you: and I will take away the stony heart out of your flesh, and I will give you an heart of flesh. And I will put my spirit within you, and cause you to walk in my statutes, and ye shall keep my judgments, and do them.

MATTHEW 9:12-13. But when Jesus heard that, he said unto them, They that be whole need not a physician, but they that are sick. But go ye and learn what that meaneth, I will have mercy, and not sacrifice: for I am not come to call the righteous, but sinners to repentance.

LUKE 19:10. For the Son of man is come to seek and to save that which was lost.

JOHN 6:37. All that the Father giveth me shall come to me: and him that cometh to me I will in no wise cast out.

ROMANS 1:16. For I am not ashamed of the gospel of Christ: for it is the power of God unto salvation to every one that believeth; to the Jew first, and also to the Greek.

ROMANS 5:6-10. For when we were yet without strength, in due time Christ died for the ungodly. For scarcely for a righteous man will one die: yet peradventure for a good man some would even dare to die. But God commendeth his love toward us, in that, while we were yet sinners, Christ died for us. Much more then, being now justified by his blood, we shall be saved from wrath through him. For if, when we were enemies, we were reconciled to God by the death of his Son, much more, being reconciled, we shall be saved by his life.

HEBREWS 7:25. Wherefore he is able also to save them to the uttermost that come unto God by him, seeing he ever liveth to make intercession for them.

REVELATION 22:17. And the Spirit and the bride say, Come. And let him that heareth say, Come. And let him that is athirst come. And whosoever will, let him take the water of life freely.

Press on them Christ's words: "Him that cometh to me I will in no wise cast out" (John 6:37). "Whosoever will, let him take the water of life freely" (Rev. 22:17).

2. *"I am not good enough to be a Christian." "I cannot live the Christian life."*

> Let not conscience make you linger,
> Nor of fitness fondly dream;
> All the fitness he requireth
> Is to feel your need of Him.
>
> JOSEPH HART

(1) Show the man who wants to be good enough before he comes to Christ that Jesus died to provide a way for the ungodly and for sinners. "While we were yet sinners, Christ died for us" (Rom. 5:8). "When we were yet without strength, in due time Christ died for the ungodly" (Rom. 5:6). "I am not come," said Jesus, "to call the righteous, but sinners to repentance." Cite to him the Father's cordial reception and treatment of the unworthy and sinning prodigal when he returned penitent (Luke 15:20-24). Tell him that God sent back home justified the penitent publican who claimed no merit but was only a sinner, and at the same time condemned the self-righteous man claiming merit (Luke 18:10-14). Christ offers to make us good enough by his righteousness, which is imputed to us when we accept him (Rom. 4:4-6, 15, 20-22).

(2) The man who says he cannot stem the tide and live the Christian life, fearing he will fall, needs to have explained to him the plan of salvation: that he becomes by faith a child of God and possesses eternal life and that God is able to keep his children.

> ISAIAH 41:13. For I the Lord thy God will hold thy right hand, saying unto thee, Fear not; I will help thee.
>
> JOHN 10:28-29. And I give unto them eternal life; and they shall never perish, neither shall any man pluck them out of my hand. My Father, which gave them me, is greater than all; and no man is able to pluck them out of my Father's hand.

> 2 TIMOTHY 1:12. For the which cause I also suffer these things: nevertheless I am not ashamed: for I know whom I have believed, and am persuaded that he is able to keep that which I have committed unto him against that day.
> HEBREWS 7:25. Wherefore he is able also to save them to the uttermost that come unto God by him, seeing he ever liveth to make intercession for them.
> 1 PETER 1:5. . . . who are kept by the power of God through faith unto salvation ready to be revealed in the last time.
> JUDE 24. Now unto him that is able to keep you from falling, and to present you faultless before the presence of his glory with exceeding joy. . . .

God's uttermost is greater than the devil's last limit of power. "And Jesus came and spake unto them, saying, All power is given unto me in heaven and in earth" (Matt. 28:18). "He hath said, I will never leave thee, nor forsake thee" (Heb. 13:5).

> ISAIAH 40:29-31. He giveth power to the faint; and to them that have no might he increaseth strength. Even the youths shall faint and be weary, and the young men shall utterly fall: but they that wait upon the Lord shall renew their strength; they shall mount up with wings as eagles; they shall run, and not be weary; and they shall walk, and not faint.
> 1 CORINTHIANS 10:13. There hath no temptation taken you but such as is common to man: but God is faithful, who will not suffer you to be tempted above that ye are able; but will with the temptation also make a way to escape, that ye may be able to bear it.
> 2 CORINTHIANS 12:9-10. And he said unto me, My grace is sufficient for thee: for my strength is made perfect in weakness. Most gladly therefore will I rather glory in my infirmities, that the power of Christ may rest upon me. Therefore I take pleasure in infirmities, in reproaches, in necessities, in persecutions, in distresses for Christ's sake: for when I am weak, then am I strong.

3. *"I cannot break with my sins."*

This is the cry of a soul in the despairing grip of some great sin, as whiskey, gambling, adultery, or swearing. He needs help from God and his Word. Tell him four things:

(1) Giving up his sins is an absolute necessity, or his soul will be forever lost in hell.

> LUKE 13:3. I tell you, Nay: but, except ye repent, ye shall all likewise perish.
> ROMANS 6:23. For the wages of sin is death; but the gift of God is eternal life through Jesus Christ our Lord.
> GALATIANS 6:7-8. Be not deceived; God is not mocked: for whatsoever a man soweth, that shall he also reap. For he that soweth to his flesh shall of the flesh reap corruption; but he that soweth to the Spirit shall of the Spirit reap life everlasting.
> REVELATION 21:8. But the fearful, and unbelieving, and the abominable, and murderers, and whoremongers, and sorcerers, and idolaters, and all liars, shall have their part in the lake which burneth with fire and brimstone: which is the second death.

(2) He has been trying to give up his sins in his own strength, when he should do it in the power of Christ.

> JOHN 8:36. If the Son therefore shall make you free, ye shall be free indeed.
> PHILIPPIANS 4:13. I can do all things through Christ which strengtheneth me.
> PHILIPPIANS 4:19. But my God shall supply all your need according to his riches in glory by Christ Jesus.
> HEBREWS 7:25. Wherefore he is able also to save them to the uttermost that come unto God by him, seeing he ever liveth to make intercession for them.

(3) Christ has saved murderers, adulterers, thieves, and all sorts of sinners, and what Christ has done he can do again (John 4; 6:37). Jesus has never failed a penitent, trusting soul.

(4) The chance to win over the worst sin lies in his own affections. If he will start to give up and break with them in his own desires and love, God's power will flood his soul in delivering and keeping strength.

> ROMANS 6:12-14. Let not sin therefore reign in your mortal body, that ye should obey it in the lusts thereof. Neither yield ye your members as instruments of unrighteousness unto sin: but yield yourselves unto God, as those that are alive from

the dead, and your members as instruments of righteousness unto God. For sin shall not have dominion over you: for ye are not under the law, but under grace.

4. "The Christian life is too hard; there is too much to give up; I know I have failed at it."

The many seeming failures among Christians are due to two general causes: Either the person was not genuinely saved, or he failed in his Christian duties after he was saved.

(1) In dealing with the person who seems to have failed as a Christian, find out just where he stands—saved and neglectful, or mistaken about his salvation.

(2) If he is saved, tell him to look to Christ for strength, to pray, study the Bible, and go to work for Christ, and his failure will be turned into victory.

(3) If he is unsaved, show him that Christ does not ask him to give up anything but that which, if kept, will injure and finally ruin him. Whatever he asks us to surrender, it is for our good to surrender it.

> PSALM 84:11. For the Lord God is a sun and shield: the Lord will give grace and glory: no good thing will he withhold from them that walk uprightly.

Tell him that when he gives up his sins in his deepest soul, then God's ways are easy and pleasant.

> PROVERBS 3:17. Her ways are ways of pleasantness, and all her paths are peace.
> MATTHEW 11:30. For my yoke is easy, and my burden is light.

Tell him it is sin's ways that are hard.

> PROVERBS 13:15. Good understanding giveth favour: but the way of transgressors is hard.
> ISAIAH 57:21. There is no peace, saith my God, to the wicked.

Remind him that God offers good things as compensations for all he loses in giving up sin.

> ROMANS 8:32. He that spared not his own Son, but delivered him up for us all, how shall he not with him also freely give us all things?

PHILIPPIANS 3:7-8. But what things were gain to r counted loss for Christ. Yea doubtless, and I coun but loss for the excellency of the knowledge of C my Lord: for whom I have suffered the loss of all do count them but dung, that I may win Christ.

He will get Christ, eternal life, joy in service, and heaven.

5. "*I will lose my business and friends and be ridiculed and persecuted.*"

This fear influences many uninformed, timid souls. Show them that—

(1) They put a poor value on their souls. Their eternal welfare is far more important than their temporal affairs.

MATTHEW 16:26. For what is a man profited, if he shall gain the whole world, and lose his own soul? or what shall a man give in exchange for his soul?

(2) If business injures their souls' interests, they ought to give it up; and if friendships hang on such a basis, they are not worth having.

PSALM 1:1-2. Blessed is the man that walketh not in the counsel of the ungodly, nor standeth in the way of sinners, nor sitteth in the seat of the scornful. But his delight is in the law of the Lord; and in his law doth he meditate day and night.

PROVERBS 13:20. He that walketh with wise men shall be wise: but a companion of fools shall be destroyed.

PROVERBS 29:25. The fear of man bringeth a snare: but whoso putteth his trust in the Lord shall be safe.

JAMES 4:4. Ye adulterers and adulteresses, know ye not that the friendship of the world is enmity with God? whosoever therefore will be a friend of the world is the enemy of God.

(3) Ridicule and persecution have their compensations.

MATTHEW 5:11-12. Blessed are ye, when men shall revile you, and persecute you, and shall say all manner of evil against you falsely, for my sake. Rejoice, and be exceeding glad: for great is your reward in heaven: for so persecuted they the prophets which were before you.

MARK 10:29-30. And Jesus answered and said, Verily I say unto you, There is no man that hath left house, or brethren, or sisters, or father, or mother, or wife, or children, or lands, for my sake, and the gospel's, but he shall receive an hundred-fold now in this time, houses, and brethren, and sisters, and mothers, and children, and lands, with persecutions; and in the world to come eternal life.

ROMANS 8:18. For I reckon that the sufferings of this present time are not worthy to be compared with the glory which shall be revealed in us.

2 TIMOTHY 2:12. If we suffer, we shall also reign with him: if we deny him, he also will deny us.

1 PETER 2:20-21. For what glory is it, if, when ye be buffeted for your faults, ye shall take it patiently? but if, when ye do well, and suffer for it, ye take if patiently, this is acceptable with God. For even hereunto were ye called: because Christ also suffered for us, leaving us an example, that ye should follow his steps.

6. "I do not feel like it."

This is one of the devil's most skilful deceptions. Multitudes of lost souls have gone headlong into eternity waiting for "feeling." It never came, and they plunged into hell.

In dealing with such cases great care should be exercised. There is a feeling that the sinner must have. Salvation is a matter of experience in the deepest part of the soul. The emotional nature, the heart life, is reached by redemption. One ought to have feelings before and after he is saved, but he ought not to confuse these feelings. One is the feeling of sorrow for sin, the other the feeling of the joy of salvation. He will have the sense of sin before, and the joy of being saved after, he trusts Christ.

If he has "feeling" enough to give up his sins, that is all God requires. Let him seek till he has a sense of his own sins and feeling enough to forsake his sins; and then let him trust the Saviour, and Christ will come into his heart.

REVELATION 3:20. Behold, I stand at the door, and knock: if any man hear my voice, and open the door, I will come in to him, and will sup with him, and he with me.

Use these verses and explain them to him:

ISAIAH 55:7. Let the wicked forsake his way, and the unrighteous man his thoughts: and let him return unto the Lord,

and he will have mercy upon him; and to our God, for he will abundantly pardon.
JOHN 1:12. But as many as received him, to them gave he power to become the sons of God, even to them that believe on his name.
JOHN 3:36. He that believeth on the Son hath everlasting life: and he that believeth not the Son shall not see life; but the wrath of God abideth on him.
EPHESIANS 1:13. In whom ye also trusted, after that ye heard the word of truth, the gospel of your salvation: in whom also after that ye believed, ye were sealed with that holy Spirit of promise.
1 PETER 1:8. . . . whom having not seen, ye love; in whom, though now ye see him not, yet believing, ye rejoice with joy unspeakable and full of glory.

Do not undervalue the necessity for true repentance or fail to distinguish between the feelings before and after conversion. Tell him there will be feeling when he trusts Christ's saving power, when pardon and joy and Christ come in.

7. *"There is so much inconsistency and hypocrisy among church members."*

This is one of the most common excuses among unsaved people.

The charge is often sadly true. Carelessness, godlessness, worldliness, and often open sins of all kinds among professed Christians, constitute one of the most serious hindrances to Christ's cause. "One shall say unto him, What are these wounds in thine hands? Then he shall answer, Those with which I was wounded in the house of my friends" (Zech. 13:6). ". . . Judas, which was guide to them that took Jesus" (Acts 1:16). These are scriptural charges against professed Christians. Many of those inside the fold have denied Jesus and betrayed his cause since Peter and Judas blackened the Bible records with their deeds of shame. It will not help to deny the fact. You can only regret it and lead the sinner past its deadly influence the best you can.

It will help to say to him:

(1) Do not look to men for standards of life, but to **Christ**.

> Hebrews 12:2. . . . looking unto Jesus the author and finisher of our faith; who for the joy that was set before him endured the cross, despising the shame, and is set down at the right hand of the throne of God.

Christ is our model in life and our standard of righteousness at the judgment.

> Acts 17:30-31. And the times of this ignorance God winked at; but now commandeth all men every where to repent: because he hath appointed a day, in the which he will judge the world in righteousness by that man whom he hath ordained; whereof he hath given assurance unto all men, in that he hath raised him from the dead.

(2) That many church members are not genuinely saved. They failed to receive Christ in their hearts. Their lives show that they are counterfeits, and we must not let their mistakes damn us.

(3) That we do not always know other men's difficulties and troubles. We probably could do no better if we had their loads and burdens.

(4) That men, though saved, are not perfect. They still have their carnal minds, tempers, and passions; and if they do not keep up the fight and keep close to God in prayer, Bible study, worship, and work, their lives will not bear the proper testimony.

(5) That many are saved but do not show it much. They do not grow in strength of Christian character. Their works will be burned up, but their souls will be saved (1 Cor. 3:15). It is better to be a sorry, unfruitful Christian and be saved and go to heaven, than for consistency's sake to refuse Christ and die and go down to hell. Furthermore, men had better live with hypocrites a short time in the church than to live with them in hell forever.

(6) That he must stand alone on his own record, not another's, at the judgment.

(7) What God says about those who judge others and do the same things.

> ROMANS 14:12. So then every one of us shall give account of himself to God.
>
> MATTHEW 7:1-5. Judge not, that ye be not judged. For with what judgment ye judge, ye shall be judged: and with what measure ye mete, it shall be measured to you again. And why beholdest thou the mote that is in thy brother's eye, but considerest not the beam that is in thine own eye? Or how wilt thou say to thy brother, Let me pull out the mote out of thine eye; and, behold, a beam is in thine own eye? Thou hypocrite, first cast out the beam out of thine own eye; and then shalt thou see clearly to cast out the mote out of thy brother's eye.
>
> ROMANS 2:1-6. Therefore thou art inexcusable, O man, whosoever thou art that judgest: for wherein thou judgest another, thou condemnest thyself; for thou that judgest doest the same things. But we are sure that the judgment of God is according to truth against them which commit such things. And thinkest thou this, O man, that judgest them which do such things, and doest the same, that thou shalt escape the judgment of God? or despisest thou the riches of his goodness and forbearance and longsuffering; not knowing that the goodness of God leadeth thee to repentance? but after thy hardness and impenitent heart treasurest up unto thyself wrath against the day of wrath and revelation of the righteous judgment of God; who will render to every man according to his deeds.

(8) That there are inconsistencies and hypocrisies out of the church—in business, society, professional life, everywhere—and that his logic applied elsewhere in life would keep him out of business and society.

(9) That there are many fine, strong, consecrated, and true-living Christians. Let them be the example if he must take men as his example. Take the good dollar, and let the counterfeit go. This is common sense. Think of John instead of Peter and Judas.

(10) That he cannot be saved by the sins of other men. He is to be saved by the power of God in Christ Jesus. It is Christ's righteousness imputed to us which is the basis of

our hope, not the unrighteousness of weak and frail men.

8. *"I have unforgiveness in my heart; I have been wronged and cannot forgive."*

Unforgiveness as an excuse is one of the devil's big obstacles in the way of some souls. It steels and hardens the heart and makes it difficult for grace to enter.

(1) Tell the person who gives you this as his reason for not accepting Christ that unforgiveness is one of the worst sins. It hardens the heart, brings unhappiness, and carries with it a constant peril of something worse. It may lead to anger and often to murder, to family and community tragedies. He ought to give it up because of its perils and dangers to his own life and happiness.

(2) Tell him he must give it up or face God's wrath and the consequences of unforgiveness at the judgment. God will not forgive him unless he forgives. "But if ye forgive not men their trespasses, neither will your Father forgive your trespasses" (Matt. 6:15).

> MATTHEW 18:21-22. Then came Peter to him, and said, Lord, how oft shall my brother sin against me, and I forgive him? till seven times? Jesus saith unto him, I say not unto thee, Until seven times: but, Until seventy times seven.

Read to him the parable of the unjust steward in Matthew 18:23-35.

(3) Show what wrongs he has done to God in rejecting and crucifying Christ, disobeying his law, putting his holy blood under his feet, doing despite to the Spirit, and sinning constantly in the face of God's mercy, love, and blessings.

> EPHESIANS 4:32. And be ye kind one to another, tenderhearted, forgiving one another, even as God for Christ's sake hath forgiven you.

(4) Tell him he can forgive in Christ's strength if he will only give up his stubborn will and way.

> GALATIANS 5:22-23. But the fruit of the Spirit is love, joy, peace, longsuffering, gentleness, goodness, faith, **meekness**, temperance: against such there is no law.

PHILIPPIANS 4:13. I can do all things through Christ which strengtheneth me.

9. "I have crossed the deadline, and there is no hope for me."

Some discouraged people lose heart and think that they have "sinned away their day of grace." It is a dreadful sin to continue to reject Christ, to refuse offered mercy and continuously shut the door of the heart in the face of God's Spirit seeking to save. It does callous the soul, sear the conscience, harden the heart, and constantly make more difficult one's chance to be saved. Answer such a person:

(1) That God is long-suffering and full of mercy.

PSALM 86:5. For thou, Lord, art good, and ready to forgive; and plenteous in mercy unto all them that call upon thee.

PSALM 130:7. Let Israel hope in the Lord: for with the Lord there is mercy, and with him is plenteous redemption.

ISAIAH 55:6-7. Seek ye the Lord while he may be found, call ye upon him while he is near: let the wicked forsake his way, and the unrighteous man his thoughts: and let him return unto the Lord, and he will have mercy upon him; and to our God, for he will abundantly pardon.

2 PETER 3:9. The Lord is not slack concerning his promise, as some men count slackness; but is longsuffering to us-ward, not willing that any should perish, but that all should come to repentance.

His love is an everlasting love, and he will go to infinite limits to save a soul.

(2) That God promises to receive all who come to him, all who call on him, and that he invites whosoever will to come.

JOHN 6:37. All that the Father giveth me shall come to me: and him that cometh to me I will in no wise cast out.

ROMANS 10:13. For whosoever shall call upon the name of the Lord shall be saved.

REVELATION 22:17. And the Spirit and the bride say, Come. And let him that heareth say, Come. And let him that is athirst come. And whosoever will, let him take the water of life freely.

(3) That he saved souls which had put him off long and were confirmed sinners: Nicodemus, the self-righteous sinner; Paul, the religiously outrageous sinner; the woman with seven devils; the Gadarene with a legion of devils; the thief on the cross who accepted his last chance. He says he will save "him that cometh."

Stress God's love for him and its demonstration in Christ's death and the Spirit's persistent call; his anxiety for him to come, in that he wills the death of none; his seeking for his soul, as illustrated in the prodigal son's father (Luke 15) and in Christ's great mission, "The son of man is come to seek and to save that which was lost" (Luke 19:10). As God took back to his bounty and love the sinning, ungrateful prodigal, so will he receive any sinner who comes to himself, arises, and goes to the Father's arms.

Read to him Deuteronomy 4:30-31.

10. "I have committed the unpardonable sin."

Many weary souls mistakenly think they have committed the unpardonable sin. They are worked with by Christian workers through many revivals and are not saved, and they conclude that God has rejected them and that they have committed the sin against the Holy Spirit. This sin is stated in—

> MATTHEW 12:31-32. Wherefore I say unto you, All manner of sin and blasphemy shall be forgiven unto men: but the blasphemy against the Holy Ghost shall not be forgiven unto men. And whosoever speaketh a word against the Son of man, it shall be forgiven him: but whosoever speaketh against the Holy Ghost, it shall not be forgiven him, neither in this world, neither in the world to come.
>
> 1 JOHN 5:16. If any man see his brother sin a sin which is not unto death, he shall ask, and he shall give him life for them that sin not unto death. There is a sin unto death: I do not say that he shall pray for it.

It is very clear that this sin, for which there is no pardon in this world or the world to come, is attributing to the devil the work known to be done by the Holy Spirit. Most people who think they have committed the unpardonable sin have *a mistaken view of what this sin is.* If they have really committed it, then their case is settled and their doom is eternally fixed.

How can one tell whether or not he has committed it and God's Spirit has left him to his doom?

(1) When one has sinned against the Spirit in this fashion, he will have no desire to be a Christian; no spiritual impression will ever again come to his soul.

> JOHN 6:44. No man can come to me, except the Father which hath sent me draw him: and I will raise him up at the last day.

As long as he has the faintest desire to be a Christian, God had not left him.

(2) In case he has committed the unpardonable sin, he will be given over wholly to the devil, and his heart will be as hard as steel. Not all who have cold and hard hearts have committed this sin, but that is one of its marks.

Remind him that God goes to the limit for souls.

> JOHN 6:37. All that the Father giveth me shall come to me: and him that cometh to me I will in no wise cast out.
> ACTS 13:38-39. Be it known unto you therefore, men and brethren, that through this man is preached unto you the forgiveness of sins: and by him all that believe are justified from all things, from which ye could not be justified by the law of Moses.
> ROMANS 10:13. For whosoever shall call upon the name of the Lord shall be saved.
> 1 TIMOTHY 1:15-16. This is a faithful saying, and worthy of all acceptation, that Christ Jesus came into the world to save sinners; of whom I am chief. Howbeit for this cause I obtained mercy, that in me first Jesus Christ might shew forth all longsuffering, for a pattern to them which should hereafter believe on him to life everlasting.
> HEBREWS 7:25. Wherefore he is able also to save them to the uttermost that come unto God by him, seeing he ever liveth to make intercession for them.

> REVELATION 22:17. And the Spirit and the bride say, Come. And let him that heareth say, Come. And let him that is athirst come. And whosoever will, let him take the water of life freely.

11. "I want to be saved but can't believe."

Many souls, when they are near the Saviour, will say, "I can't believe." It is as difficult to teach one how to believe as it is to teach one how to love. In dealing with such a person, first find out just what his trouble is. It may be a confusion of mind about whom and what to believe.

(1) Show him how worthy Christ is of his richest faith and confidence. Christ's death for him, his continued love and mercy, the call of his Spirit, the blessings he bestows in life, and his many providences—all these call for trust.

(2) Show him that it is not belief in himself, but in Christ as a personal Saviour that he needs. Christ's strength is sufficient; his merit is all God asks.

(3) Ask him to answer these questions:

>   Do you believe God has saved others?
>   Do you believe he *wants* to save you?
>   Do you believe he *can* save you?
>   Do you believe he *will* save you?
>   Will you trust *him* to save you now?

(4) Show him that God's command is to believe. God's promises are based on personal trust, and all the sinner's future is involved in his faith in Christ.

> JOHN 1:12. But as many as received him, to them gave he power to become the sons of God, even to them that believe on his name.
>
> JOHN 3:16. For God so loved the world, that he gave his only begotten Son, that whosoever believeth in him should not perish, but have everlasting life.
>
> JOHN 5:24. Verily, verily, I say unto you, He that heareth my word, and believeth on him that sent me, hath everlasting life, and shall not come into condemnation; but is passed from death unto life.

ROMANS 5:1. Therefore being justified by faith, we have peace with God through our Lord Jesus Christ.

12. "I cannot repent."

The person who says he cannot repent may not understand repentance, or he may be hiding an unwillingness to give up some sin. Show him that a willing spirit will have much to do with his faith and repentance.

> PSALM 110:3. Thy people shall be willing in the day of thy power, in the beauties of holiness from the womb of the morning: thou hast the dew of thy youth.
>
> JOHN 7:17. If any man will do his will, he shall know of the doctrine, whether it be of God, or whether I speak of myself.

13. "I cannot understand—, I cannot accept—"

(1) *"The Bible is not divine, and its authority is not binding on me."*

a. Ask the person who says the Bible is not divine to explain its power over the world—its marvelous history, its fulfilment of prophecy, its unity, its mighty saving message, and the civilization it produces—if it is not divinely inspired.

b. Show what it says about its origin in—

> 1 THESSALONIANS 2:13. For this cause also thank we God without ceasing, because, when ye received the word of God which ye heard of us, ye received it not as the word of men, but as it is in truth, the word of God, which effectually worketh also in you that believe.
>
> 2 TIMOTHY 3:16. All scripture is given by inspiration of God, and is profitable for doctrine, for reproof, for correction, for instruction in righteousness.
>
> 2 PETER 1:20-21. . . . knowing this first, that no prophecy of the scripture is of any private interpretation. For the prophecy came not in old time by the will of man: but holy men of God spake as they were moved by the Holy Ghost.

(2) *"The Bible has inconsistencies and contradictions in it."*

Usually the person who says that the Bible contains inconsistencies and contradictions does so out of ignorance, and an examination will show his inability to point out these errors. Press him to prove his statement, and you will embarrass him.

Give him what God says about the critics and those who understand not.

> Isaiah 55:8-9. For my thoughts are not your thoughts, neither are your ways my ways, saith the Lord. For as the heavens are higher than the earth, so are my ways higher than your ways, and my thoughts than your thoughts.
>
> Daniel 12:10. Many shall be purified, and made white, and tried; but the wicked shall do wickedly: and none of the wicked shall understand; but the wise shall understand.
>
> 1 Corinthians 2:14. But the natural man receiveth not the things of the Spirit of God: for they are foolishness unto him: neither can he know them, because they are spiritually discerned.
>
> 2 Peter 2:12. But these, as natural brute beasts, made to be taken and destroyed, speak evil of the things that they understand not; and shall utterly perish in their own corruption.
>
> 2 Peter 3:16-18. . . . as also in all his epistles, speaking in them of these things; in which are some things hard to be understood, which they that are unlearned and unstable wrest, as they do also the other scriptures, unto their own destruction. Ye therefore, beloved, seeing ye know these things before, beware lest ye also, being led away with the error of the wicked, fall from your own stedfastness. But grow in grace, and in the knowledge of our Lord and Saviour Jesus Christ. To him be glory both now and for ever. Amen.

Use and press on him—

> Psalm 119:18. Open thou mine eyes, that I may behold wondrous things out of thy law.
>
> John 7:17. If any man will do his will, he shall know of the doctrine, whether it be of God, or whether I speak of myself.
>
> 1 Corinthians 1:18,23-24. For the preaching of the cross is to them that perish foolishness; but unto us which are saved it is the power of God. . . . But we preach Christ crucified, unto the Jews a stumblingblock, and unto the Greeks foolishness; but unto them which are called, both Jews and Greeks, Christ the power of God, and the wisdom of God.
>
> James 1:5. If any of you lack wisdom, let him ask of God, that giveth to all men liberally, and upbraideth not; and it shall be given him.

(3) *"I cannot understand the atonement or the necessity for Christ's death."*

Tell him he does not have to understand. God's ways are above his. The revealed things belong to us and the secret things to God (Isa. 55:8-9).

He does not have to understand the processes of digestion in order to eat, or gravitation to walk, or electricity to enjoy its light and use its power. Trust God for his ways. God says that man sinned and thus fell and that someone who had not violated God's law had to intervene, pay the penalty, and thus redeem him. Nicodemus could not tell from whence the wind came or where it went, but he knew it was there because he experienced it. Jesus said it is thus with one who is born of the Spirit. He may not understand all the initial process of it; he may not understand all the ultimate reach of it. But he can know it as a reality because he experiences it (John 3:8).

Show him God's question:

> ROMANS 9:20-24. Nay but, O man, who art thou that repliest against God? Shall the thing formed say to him that formed it, Why hast thou made me thus? Hath not the potter power over the clay, of the same lump to make one vessel unto honour, and another unto dishonour? What if God, willing to shew his wrath, and to make his power known, endured with much longsuffering the vessels of wrath fitted to destruction: and that he might make known the riches of his glory on the vessels of mercy, which he had afore prepared unto glory, even us, whom he hath called, not of the Jews only, but also of the Gentiles?

Go carefully through Romans 5 with him. Light may come into his heart.

(4) *"I do not believe in hell—the doctrine of eternal punishment."*

The rejection of the idea of eternal punishment is a common difficulty with certain people who have been under the influences of "Russellism," "Eddyism," and other strange and misleading cults. It is not of much avail to discuss this difficulty with one who does not believe in the deity of Christ and the binding authority of the Scriptures. Eternal punishment is a doctrine of divine revelation. The arguments from sin and its punishment here in this world have some weight, but unless the person believes in God's Word, you can do very little with him on this or any other doctrine of pure revelation. Only God knows the future; and if men refuse his plain word on their destiny, they will have to wait and see and take the consequences.

The Holy Scriptures are perfectly explicit and very plain on this unspeakably meaningful doctrine. The Old Testament has many references to eternal punishment which you can point out to the person who says he does not believe in it, such as:

> JOB 21:29-30. Have ye not asked them that go by the way? and do ye not know their tokens, that the wicked is reserved to the day of destruction? they shall be brought forth to the day of wrath.
> PSALM 9:17. The wicked shall be turned into hell, and all the the nations that forget God.
> PROVERBS 15:11. Hell and destruction are before the Lord: how much more then the hearts of the children of men?
> ISAIAH 14:9. Hell from beneath is moved for thee to meet thee at thy coming: it stirreth up the dead for thee, even all the chief ones of the earth; it hath raised up from their thrones all the kings of the nations.
> EZEKIEL 31:16. I made the nations to shake at the sound of his fall, when I cast him down to hell with them that descend into the pit: and all the trees of Eden, the choice and best of Lebanon, all that drink water, shall be comforted in the nether parts of the earth.
> DANIEL 12:2. And many of them that sleep in the dust of the earth shall awake, some to everlasting life, and some to shame and everlasting contempt.

The New Testament is full of this doctrine, there being more than 225 verses bearing in one way or another on it, such as:

MATTHEW 5:22. But I say unto you, That whosoever is angry with his brother without a cause shall be in danger of the judgment: and whosoever shall say to his brother, Raca, shall be in danger of the council: but whosoever shall say, Thou fool, shall be in danger of hell fire.

MATTHEW 10:28. And fear not them which kill the body, but are not able to kill the soul: but rather fear him which is able to destroy both soul and body in hell.

MATTHEW 11:23. And thou, Capernaum, which art exalted unto heaven, shall be brought down to hell: for if the mighty works, which have been done in thee, had been done in Sodom, it would have remained until this day.

MATTHEW 25:31-34,46. When the Son of man shall come in his glory, and all the holy angels with him, then shall he sit upon the throne of his glory: and before him shall be gathered all nations; and he shall separate them one from another, as a shepherd divideth his sheep from the goats: and he shall set the sheep on his right hand, but the goats on the left. Then shall the King say unto them on his right hand, Come, ye blessed of my Father, inherit the kingdom prepared for you from the foundation of the world. . . . And these shall go away into everlasting punishment: but the righteous into life eternal.

JOHN 3:36. He that believeth on the Son hath everlasting life: and he that believeth not the Son shall not see life; but the wrath of God abideth on him.

2 THESSALONIANS 1:7-10. . . . the Lord Jesus shall be revealed from heaven with his mighty angels, in flaming fire taking vengeance on them that know not God, and that obey not the gospel of our Lord Jesus Christ: who shall be punished with everlasting destruction from the presence of the Lord, and from the glory of his power; when he shall come to be glorified in his saints, and to be admired in all them that believe (because our testimony among you was believed) in that day.

2 PETER 2:9. The Lord knoweth how to deliver the godly out of temptations, and to reserve the unjust unto the day of judgment to be punished.

REVELATION 20:14-15. And death and hell were cast into the lake of fire. This is the second death. And whosoever was not found written in the book of life was cast into the lake of fire.

REVELATION 21:8. But the fearful, and unbelieving, and the abominable, and murderers, and whoremongers, and sorcerers, and idolaters, and all liars, shall have their part in the lake which burneth with fire and brimstone: which is the second death.

Read to him also Luke 16:19-31.

Show him that the Scripture passages above and many others, containing the words of Job, David, Isaiah, Daniel, Matthew, John, Peter, Paul, and Jesus Christ—all with the imprint of God's Holy Spirit—make clear the following tragic facts about the future destiny of unbelieving and sinning men and women:

a. That there is a spiritual state or place made and reserved by a merciful and just God for all who reject his love and mercy, as expressed in Jesus Christ, and who persist in refusing his grace; and that condition when once entered into is endless. The terms describing its duration are the same as those describing the length of life of the souls of the redeemed.

b. That this place was made for the devil and his angels and all who have the mark of "the beast," and who follow Satan instead of Christ.

c. That the sin of unbelief is sufficient of itself to doom men forever in hell.

> JOHN 3:18,36. He that believeth on him is not condemned: but he that believeth not is condemned already, because he hath not believed in the name of the only begotten Son of God. . . He that believeth on the Son hath everlasting life: and he that believeth not the Son shall not see life; but the wrath of God abideth on him.
>
> REVELATION 2:18. But the fearful, and unbelieving, and the abominable, and murderers, and whoremongers, and sorcerers, and idolaters, and all liars, shall have their part in the lake which burneth with fire and brimstone: which is the second death.

d. That when once in hell, there is no opportunity to change. Their destiny is eternally settled. "A great gulf" intervenes between the damned and the redeemed (Luke 16:22-31; Heb. 9:27).

e. That in this condition the soul is conscious and has its faculties—can see, cry, remember, reason, feel thirst, and call for mercy—and shows an interest in the eternal welfare of loved ones left in the earth (Luke 16:22-31).

f. That the bodies of the lost sinners will be raised from the dead unto damnation (Dan. 12:2).

g. That Satan and his angels are doing their utmost to carry every possible soul down to hell.

> ISAIAH 14:9. Hell from beneath is moved for thee to meet thee at thy coming: it stirreth up the dead for thee, even all the chief ones of the earth; it hath raised up from their thrones all the kings of the nations.
> GALATIANS 5:17. For the flesh lusteth against the Spirit, and the Spirit against the flesh: and these are contrary the one to the other: so that ye cannot do the things that ye would.
> EPHESIANS 6:11-12. Put on the whole armour of God, that ye may be able to stand against the wiles of the devil. For we wrestle not against flesh and blood, but against principalities, against powers, against the rulers of the darkness of this world, against spiritual wickedness in high places.
> 1 PETER 5:8. Be sober, be vigilant; because your adversary the devil, as a roaring lion, walketh about, seeking whom he may devour.

Show him that men go to hell because they do not repent and believe (John 3:18,36; Rev. 21:8).

Thus make him face God's Word in the most earnest spirit. Deal with him, not in controversy, but in love and the power of the Holy Spirit.

14. *"Not tonight; I will wait."*

Many postpone salvation for various reasons. Some put salvation off because of their age, being too young, as they or their parents think; some because of business, desiring to accumulate; some because of pleasures, desiring to enjoy the world's ways first and become Christians when they are older.

(1) On all such press God's teachings on the perils and risks involved in procrastination.

a. The peril of God's wrath.—He is a God of wrath, and his wrath hangs in awful, impending danger over every lost sinner every hour of life.

> Job 21:20. His eyes shall see his destruction, and he shall drink of the wrath of the Almighty.
> Job 36:18. Because there is wrath, beware lest he take thee away with his stroke: then a great ransom cannot deliver thee.
> Psalm 58:9. Before your pots can feel the thorns, he shall take them away as with a whirlwind, both living, and in his wrath.
> Isaiah 13:9. Behold, the day of the Lord cometh, cruel both with wrath and fierce anger, to lay the land desolate: and he shall destroy the sinners thereof out of it.
> Matthew 3:7. But when he saw many of the Pharisees and Sadducees come to his baptism, he said unto them, O generaton of vipers, who hath warned you to flee from the wrath to come?
> John 3:36. He that believeth on the Son hath everlasting life: and he that believeth not the Son shall not see life; but the wrath of God abideth on him.
> Romans 1:18. For the wrath of God is revealed from heaven against all ungodliness and unrighteousness of men, who hold the truth in unrighteousness.
> Revelation 6:15-17. And the kings of the earth, and the great men, and the rich men, and the chief captains, and the mighty men, and every bondman, and every free man, hid themselves in the dens and in the rocks of the mountains; and said to the mountains and rocks, Fall on us, and hide us from the face of him that sitteth on the throne, and from the wrath of the Lamb: for the great day of his wrath is come; and who shall be able to stand?
> Revelation 15:1; 16:19. And I saw another sign in heaven, great and marvellous, seven angels having the seven last plagues; for in them is filled up the wrath of God. . . . And the great city was divided into three parts, and the cities of the nations fell: and great Babylon came in remembrance before God, to give unto her the cup of the wine of the fierceness of his wrath.

b. The peril of the withdrawal of his Holy Spirit, who alone can bring salvation from Christ.—He may leave him without hope.

GENESIS 6:3. And the Lord said, My spirit shall not always strive with man, for that he also is flesh: yet his days shall be an hundred and twenty years.

c. The peril of a drifting and hardened heart.

HEBREWS 2:1. Therefore we ought to give the more earnest heed to the things which we have heard, lest at any time we should let them slip.

HEBREWS 3:7-8. . . . as the Holy Ghost saith, To day if ye will hear his voice, harden not your hearts, as in the provocation, in the day of temptation in the wilderness.

d. The peril of death.—It may take him unawares and unprepared at any time.

PROVERBS 27:1. Boast not thyself of to morrow; for thou knowest not what a day may bring forth.

PROVERBS 29:1. He, that being often reproved hardeneth his neck, shall suddenly be destroyed, and that without remedy.

EZEKIEL 33:11. Say unto them, As I live, saith the Lord God, I have no pleasure in the death of the wicked; but that the wicked turn from his way and live: turn ye, turn ye from your evil ways; for why will ye die, O house of Israel?

AMOS 4:12. Therefore thus will I do unto thee, O Israel: and because I will do this unto thee, prepare to meet thy God, O Israel.

e. The peril of ignoring feeling and desire.—When the Spirit of God works a desire in the heart, men should then yield to God. The desire may not last but may pass forever.

ACTS 24:24-25. And after certain days, when Felix came with his wife Drusilla, which was a Jewess, he sent for Paul, and heard him concerning the faith in Christ. And as he reasoned of righteousness, temperance, and judgment to come, Felix trembled, and answered, Go thy way for this time; when I have a convenient season, I will call for thee.

ACTS 26:28,29. Then Agrippa said unto Paul, Almost thou persuadest me to be a Christian. And Paul said, I would to God, that not only thou, but also all that hear me this day, were both almost, and altogether such as I am, except these bonds.

(2) Urge him to seek God now, for his promises to the sinner are all in the present tense.

> MATTHEW 6:33. But seek ye first the kingdom of God, and his righteousness; and all these things shall be added unto you.
> LUKE 12:19-20. And I will say to my soul, Soul, thou hast much goods laid up for many years; take thine ease, eat, drink, and be merry. But God said unto him, Thou fool, this night thy soul shall be required of thee: then whose shall those things be, which thou hast provided?
> JOHN 12:35. Then Jesus said unto them, Yet a little while is the light with you. Walk while ye have the light, lest darkness come upon you: for he that walketh in darkness knoweth not whither he goeth.
> 2 CORINTHIANS 6:2. (For he saith, I have heard thee in a time accepted, and in the day of salvation have I succoured thee: behold, now is the accepted time; behold, now is the day of salvation.)
> JAMES 4:13-14. Go to now, ye that say, To day or to morrow we will go into such a city, and continue there a year, and buy and sell, and get gain: whereas ye know not what shall be on the morrow. For what is your life It is even a vapour, that appeareth for a little time, and then vanisheth away.

(3) Remind him of the suddenness of Christ's return for judgment. Every man should be ready for his coming.

> DEUTERONOMY 32:35. To me belongeth vengeance, and recompence; their foot shall slide in due time: for the day of their calamity is at hand, and the things that shall come upon them make haste.
> MATTHEW 25:10-12. And while they went to buy, the bridegroom came; and they that were ready went in with him to the marriage: and the door was shut. Afterward came also the other virgins, saying, Lord, Lord, open to us. But he answered and said, Verily I say unto you, I know you not.
> ACTS 17:30-31. And the times of this ignorance God winked at; but now commandeth all men every where to repent: because he hath appointed a day, in the which he will judge the world in righteousness by that man whom he hath ordained; whereof he hath given assurance unto all men, in that he hath raised him from the dead.

Now is God's time to save. "Seek ye the Lord while he may be found" (Isa. 55:6).

All these difficulties, and any others which the soul-winner finds in his experience with the lost, can be met in a patient, persistent spirit of prayer and love and in the power of the Holy Spirit, if he but turn the light of God's Word on their hearts. It is the sword of the Spirit and "is quick, and powerful, and sharper than any twoedged sword, piercing even to the dividing asunder of soul and spirit, and of the joints and marrow, and is a discerner of the thoughts and intents of the heart" (Heb. 4:12). It is God's fire and hammer with which to burn and break hearts.

32

How to Deal with Those Under Conviction

The Holy Spirit works conviction in the hearts of men through the Word of God and through Christian testimony (John 16:8-11). When a man is under conviction of sin, he feels that he is a sinner in God's sight; there is in his soul a deep sense of the weight of his sins. It is the beginning of the work of grace in his soul, and out of this sense of sin come godly sorrow, contrition, repentance, faith, and confession. Conviction affects men differently, according to their temperament and the environment which has conditioned their reactions. Some experience great anxiety; agony floods their souls. They may go for days in a state of excitement before peace comes as a result of trust and surrender. Others are not so visibly moved; they have a deep sense of sin without much outward manifestation. But when they turn to Christ, joy floods their lives, and peace is regnant in their hearts.

One of the great values of preaching in the Spirit's power is the conviction of sin which results. Evangelistic presentation of the gospel will always bring conviction to the hearts of some. Private and personal appeal, prayer in the Spirit, the reading of God's Word, and consecrated testimony in a life devoted to God, are other vital agencies of conviction.

Those under conviction must be dealt with wisely and earnestly.

1. Point them to the Lamb of God, who takes away their sins.

(1) *Christ as God's sacrifice and priest.*—Show the one under conviction that Christ died in his place under God's

law ("the soul that sinneth, it shall die"), that he paid the full penalty and price for his soul, and that he replaces his sins with his own righteousness and merit in God's sight (Gal. 2:16; Rom. 4:5-6).

> ISAIAH 53:5-7,10-12. But he was wounded for our transgressions, he was bruised for our iniquities: the chastisement of our peace was upon him; and with his stripes we are healed. All we like sheep have gone astray; we have turned every one to his own way; and the Lord hath laid on him the iniquity of us all. He was oppressed, and he was afflicted, yet he opened not his mouth: he is brought as a lamb to the slaughter, and as a sheep before her shearers is dumb, so he openeth not his mouth. . . . Yet it pleased the Lord to bruise him; he hath put him to grief: when thou shalt make his soul an offering for sin, he shall see his seed, he shall prolong his days, and the pleasure of the Lord shall prosper in his hand. He shall see of the travail of his soul, and shall be satisfied: by his knowledge shall my righteous servant justify many; for he shall bear their iniquities. Therefore will I divide him a portion with the great, and he shall divide the spoil with the strong; because he hath poured out his soul unto death: and he was numbered with the transgressors; and he bare the sin of many, and made intercession for the transgressors.
>
> JOHN 1:29. The next day John seeth Jesus coming unto him, and saith, Behold the Lamb of God, which taketh away the sin of the world.
>
> GALATIANS 1:4. . . . who gave himself for our sins, that he might deliver us from this present evil world, according to the will of God and our Father.
>
> GALATIANS 6:14. But God forbid that I should glory, save in the cross of our Lord Jesus Christ, by whom the world is crucified unto me, and I unto the world.

(2) Christ as risen, regnant Lord and Master, able to save and keep saved.

> JOHN 5:24. Verily, verily, I say unto you, He that heareth my word, and believeth on him that sent me, hath everlasting life, and shall not come into condemnation; but is passed from death unto life.
>
> JOHN 6:37. All that the Father giveth me shall come to me: and him that cometh to me I will in no wise cast out.
>
> JOHN 10:28. And I give unto them eternal life; and they shall

never perish, neither shall any man pluck them out of my hand.

JOHN 11:26. And whosoever liveth and believeth in me shall never die. Believest thou this?

JOHN 14:19. Yet a little while, and the world seeth me no more; but ye see me: because I live, ye shall live also.

ACTS 2:36. Therefore let all the house of Israel know assuredly, that God hath made that same Jesus, whom ye have crucified, both Lord and Christ.

ROMANS 1:16-17. For I am not ashamed of the gospel of Christ: for it is the power of God unto salvation to every one that believeth; to the Jew first, and also to the Greek. For therein is the righteousness of God revealed from faith to faith: as it is written, The just shall live by faith.

ROMANS 10:9. . . . that if thou shalt confess with thy mouth the Lord Jesus, and shalt believe in thine heart that God hath raised him from the dead, thou shalt be saved.

HEBREWS 7:25. Wherefore he is able also to save them to the uttermost that come unto God by him, seeing he ever liveth to make intercession for them.

1 PETER 1:5. . . . who are kept by the power of God through faith unto salvation ready to be revealed in the last time.

JUDE 24. Now unto him that is able to keep you from falling and to present you faultless before the presence of his glory with exceeding joy. . . .

2. Lead them to a personal acceptance of Christ as their own Saviour.

(1) They must forsake, in their hearts' affection, sin in all forms known to them.

ISAIAH 55:6-7. Seek ye the Lord while he may be found, call ye upon him while he is near: let the wicked forsake his way, and the unrighteous man his thoughts: and let him return unto the Lord, and he will have mercy upon him; and to our God, for he will abundantly pardon.

EZEKIEL 33:11. Say unto them, As I live, saith the Lord God, I have no pleasure in the death of the wicked; but that the wicked turn from his way and live: turn ye, turn ye from your evil ways; for why will ye die, O house of Israel?

MATTHEW 3:2. . . . and saying, Repent ye: for the kingdom of heaven is at hand.

LUKE 13:3. I tell you, Nay: but, except ye repent, ye shall all likewise perish.

ACTS 3:19. Repent ye therefore, and be converted, that your sins may be blotted out, when the times of refreshing shall come from the presence of the Lord.

(2) They must accept Christ in their inmost souls by faith, believe in him with their hearts.

JOHN 1:12. But as many as received him, to them gave he power to become the sons of God, even to them that believe on his name.

JOHN 3:16,18,36. For God so loved the world, that he gave his only begotten Son, that whosoever believeth in him should not perish, but have everlasting life. . . . He that believeth on him is not condemned: but he that believeth not is condemned already, because he hath not believed in the name of the only begotten Son of God. . . . He that believeth on the Son hath everlasting life: and he that believeth not the Son shall not see life; but the wrath of God abideth on him.

JOHN 5:24. Verily, verily, I say unto you, He that heareth my word, and believeth on him that sent me, hath everlasting life, and shall not come into condemnation; but is passed from death unto life.

ACTS 10:43. To him give all the prophets witness, that through his name whosoever believeth in him shall receive remission of sins.

ACTS 13:39. And by him all that believe are justified from all things, from which ye could not be justified by the law of Moses.

ROMANS 5:1-2. Therefore being justified by faith, we have peace with God through our Lord Jesus Christ: by whom also we have access by faith into this grace wherein we stand, and rejoice in hope of the glory of God.

ROMANS 10:8-10. But what saith it? The word is nigh thee, even in thy mouth, and in thy heart: that is, the word of faith, which we preach; that if thou shalt confess with thy mouth the Lord Jesus, and shalt believe in thine heart that God hath raised him from the dead, thou shalt be saved. For with the heart man believeth unto righteousness; and with the mouth confession is made unto salvation.

EPHESIANS 2:8-9. For by grace are ye saved through faith; and that not of yourselves: it is the gift of God: not of works, lest any man should boast.

REVELATION 3:20. Behold, I stand at the door, and knock: if any man hear my voice, and open the door, I will come in to him, and will sup with him, and he with me.

Make it clear that it is not by works of righteousness, not by moral fitness or merit, not by ordinance of any kind, not by church membership, not by subscribing to a creed or the performance of any patriotic, meritorious, or praiseworthy deed, that they are to be saved; but only by the merit, righteousness, blood, life, and power of Jesus Christ as God's crucified, risen, and reigning Son. Show them that they cannot merit salvation, they cannot buy it with money, good deeds, penance, or self-sacrifice of any sort. They obtain its grace only by prayer, repentance, and faith in Jesus Christ.

3. Show them the meaning of this salvation resulting from their penitent trust in Christ.

(1) It is spiritual and has to do with the soul and heart (John 3:3-13; Rom. 10:9-10).

(2) It is a regeneration, a quickening, a re-creation from God, changing the heart-life, the psychic nature; an impartation of the divine nature, resulting in a new creature.

JOHN 1:12-13. But as many as received him, to them gave he power to become the sons of God, even to them that believe on his name: which were born, not of blood, nor of the will of the flesh, nor of the will of man, but of God.

JOHN 3:3-7. Jesus answered and said unto him, Verily, verily, I say unto thee, Except a man be born again, he cannot see the kingdom of God. Nicodemus saith unto him, How can a man be born when he is old? can he enter the second time into his mother's womb, and be born? Jesus answered, Verily, verily, I say unto thee, Except a man be born of water and of the Spirit, he cannot enter into the kingdom of God. That which is born of the flesh is flesh; and that which is born of the Spirit is spirit. Marvel not that I said unto thee, Ye must be born again.

ROMANS 5:10. For if, when we were enemies, we were reconciled to God by the death of his Son, much more, being reconciled, we shall be saved by his life.

GALATIANS 6:15. For in Christ Jesus neither circumcision availeth any thing, nor uncircumcision, but a new creature.

EPHESIANS 2:4-5, 10. But God, who is rich in mercy, for his great love wherewith he loved us, even when we were dead in sins, hath quickened us together with Christ, (by grace ye are saved;) .... For we are his workmanship, created in Christ Jesus unto good works, which God hath before ordained that we should walk in them.

EPHESIANS 4:22-24. ... that ye put off concerning the former conversation the old man, which is corrupt according to the deceitful lusts; and be renewed in the spirit of your mind; and that ye put on the new man, which after God is created in righteousness and true holiness.

COLOSSIANS 2:13-15. And you, being dead in your sins and the uncircumcision of your flesh, hath he quickened together with him, having forgiven you all trespasses; blotting out the handwriting of ordinances that was against us, which was contrary to us, and took it out of the way, nailing it to his cross; and having spoiled principalities and powers, he made a shew of them openly, triumphing over them in it.

TITUS 3:4-7. But after that the kindness and love of God our Saviour toward man appeared, not by works of righteousness which we have done, but according to his mercy he saved us, by the washing of regeneration, and renewing of the Holy Ghost; which he shed on us abundantly through Jesus Christ our Saviour; that being justified by his grace, we should be made heirs according to the hope of eternal life.

JAMES 1:18. Of his own will begat he us with the word of truth, that we should be a kind of firstfruits of his creatures.

1 PETER 1:22-23. Seeing ye have purified your souls in obeying the truth through the Spirit unto unfeigned love of the brethren, see that ye love one another with a pure heart fervently: being born again, not of corruptible seed, but of incorruptible, by the word of God, which liveth and abideth for ever.

2 PETER 1:4. ... whereby are given unto us exceeding great and precious promises: that by these ye might be partakers of the divine nature, having escaped the corruption that is in the world through lust.

(3) It is the possession of eternal life.

JOHN 3:36. He that believeth on the Son hath everlasting life: and he that believeth not the Son shall not see life; but the wrath of God abideth on him.

JOHN 5:24. Verily, verily, I say unto you, He that heareth my word, and believeth on him that sent me, hath everlasting life, and shall not come into condemnation; but is passed from death unto life.

And no power on earth or in hell can take this life away from them.

JOHN 10:27-29. My sheep hear my voice, and I know them, and they follow me: and I give unto them eternal life; and they shall never perish, neither shall any man pluck them out of my hand. My Father, which gave them me, is greater than all; and no man is able to pluck them out of my Father's hand.

ROMANS 8:35-39. Who shall separate us from the love of Christ? shall tribulation, or distress, or persecution, or famine, or nakedness, or peril, or sword? As it is written, For thy sake we are killed all the day long; we are accounted as sheep for the slaughter. Nay, in all these things we are more than conquerors through him that loved us. For I am persuaded, that neither death, nor life, nor angels, nor principalities, nor powers, nor things present, nor things to come, nor height, nor depth, nor any other creature, shall be able to separate us from the love of God, which is in Christ Jesus our Lord.

1 PETER 1:3-5. Blessed be the God and Father of our Lord Jesus Christ, which according to his abundant mercy hath begotten us again unto a lively hope by the resurrection of Jesus Christ from the dead, to an inheritance incorruptible, and undefiled, and that fadeth not away, reserved in heaven for you, who are kept by the power of God through faith unto salvation ready to be revealed in the last time.

JUDE 24. Now unto him that is able to keep you from falling and to present you faultless before the presence of his glory with exceeding joy. . . .

(4) It carries with it tremendous and meaningful privileges, opportunities, and responsibilities.

a. Sonship with God.

JOHN 1:12-13. But as many as received him, to them gave he power to become the sons of God, even to them that believe on his name: which were born, not of blood, nor of the will of the flesh, nor of the will of man, but of God.

ROMANS 8:14-16. For as many as are led by the Spirit of God, they are the sons of God. For ye have not received the spirit of bondage again to fear; but ye have received the Spirit of adoption, whereby we cry, Abba, Father. The Spirit itself beareth witness with our spirit, that we are the children of God.

2 CORINTHIANS 6:18. . . . and will be a Father unto you, and ye shall be my sons and daughters, saith the Lord Almighty.

REVELATION 21:7. He that overcometh shall inherit all things; and I will be his God, and he shall be my son.

b. Brothership and heirship with Jesus Christ.

JOHN 17:10. And all mine are thine, and thine are mine; and I am glorified in them.

ROMANS 8:17, 32. . . . and if children, then heirs; heirs of God, and joint-heirs with Christ; if so be that we suffer with him, that we may be also glorified together. . . . He that spared not his own Son, but delivered him up for us all, how shall he not with him also freely give us all things?

PHILIPPIANS 4:19. But my God shall supply all your need according to his riches in glory by Christ Jesus.

c. Vital union and fellowship with God's people.

JOHN 17:21-23. . . . that they all may be one; as thou, Father, art in me, and I in thee, that they also may be one in us: that the world may believe that thou hast sent me. And the glory which thou gavest me I have given them; that they may be one, even as we are one: I in them, and thou in me, that they may be made perfect in one; and that the world may know that thou hast sent me, and hast loved them, as thou hast loved me.

ROMANS 12:5. So we, being many, are one body in Christ, and every one members one of another.

GALATIANS 3:28. There is neither Jew nor Greek, there is neither bond nor free, there is neither male nor female: for ye are all one in Christ Jesus.

EPHESIANS 5:30-32. For we are members of his body, of his flesh, and of his bones. For this cause shall a man leave his father and mother, and shall be joined unto his wife, and they two shall be one flesh. This is great mystery: but I speak concerning Christ and the church.

d. Access to the Father's heart and bounty.

ROMANS 8:28. And we know that all things work together

for good to them that love God, to them who are the called according to his purpose.

COLOSSIANS 1:27. . . . to whom God would make known what is the riches of the glory of this mystery among the Gentiles; which is Christ in you, the hope of glory.

COLOSSIANS 2:2-3. . . . that their hearts might be comforted, being knit together in love, and unto all riches of the full assurance of understanding, to the acknowledgment of the mystery of God, and of the Father, and of Christ; in whom are hid all the treasures of wisdom and knowledge.

COLOSSIANS 3:24. . . . knowing that of the Lord ye shall receive the reward of the inheritance: for ye serve the Lord Christ.

Part Five

SCRIPTURE PASSAGES FOR WORKERS

33

Vital Scriptures for the Heart of the Soul-Winner

The weepers win; the weepless won't. A burdened heart is an unfailing condition of successful evangelism.

> PSALM 126:5-6. They that sow in tears shall reap in joy. He that goeth forth and weepeth, bearing precious seed, shall doubtless come again with rejoicing, bringing his sheaves with him.

The highest earthly and heavenly wisdom is found in winning souls to Christ.

> PROVERBS 11:30. The fruit of the righteous is a tree of life; and he that winneth souls is wise.

Here is God's ground for persistence in soul-winning. Press the battle to the getting-in place; lay siege to souls.

> ISAIAH 28:5-6. In that day shall the Lord of hosts be for a crown of glory, and for a diadem of beauty, unto the residue of his people. And for a spirit of judgment to him that sitteth in judgment, and for strength to them that turn the battle to the gate.

A spiritual appropriation of the following promise will save the nerves of humanity from all fret, worry, and wasting anxiety. It has preserved the life of the author of this book for fifteen years. Try it.

> ISAIAH 30:15. For thus saith the Lord God, the Holy One of Israel; In returning and rest shall ye be saved; in quietness and in confidence shall be your strength: and ye would not.

This is the promise of upholding power to those who live a strenuous life for Christ.

ISAIAH 40:31. But they that wait upon the Lord shall renew their strength; they shall mount up with wings as eagles; they shall run, and not be weary; and they shall walk, and not faint.

God holds your hand with his big right hand. Christ holds you by his right hand. Go and fear not.

ISAIAH 41:10. Fear thou not; for I am with thee: be not dismayed; for I am thy God: I will strengthen thee; yea, I will help thee; yea, I will uphold thee with the right hand of my righteousness.

Doubt not; the harvest is sure if God's Word is given out from a compassionate, reliant heart.

ISAIAH 55:10-11. For as the rain cometh down, and the snow from heaven, and returneth not thither, but watereth the earth, and maketh it bring forth and bud, that it may give seed to the sower, and bread to the eater: so shall my word be that goeth forth out of my mouth: it shall not return unto me void, but it shall accomplish that which I please, and it shall prosper in the thing whereto I sent it.

God is on the road to meet you if you work righteousness joyfully and keep him ever in mind.

ISAIAH 64:5. Thou meetest him that rejoiceth and worketh righteousness, those that remember thee in thy ways: behold, thou art wroth; for we have sinned: in those is continuance, and we shall be saved.

Prayer and faith bring God to, and link him with, every earthly task for his glory. They make defeat impossible. In some respects this is the greatest promise in the range of revelation.

JEREMIAH 33:3. Call unto me, and I will answer thee, and shew thee great and mighty things, which thou knowest not.

Limitless possibilities lie within easy reach of the people who know God.

DANIEL 11:32. And such as do wickedly against the covenant shall be corrupt by flatteries: but the people that do know their God shall be strong, and do exploits.

The secret of soul-winning power is found in following Christ.

> MATTHEW 4:19. And he saith unto them, Follow me, and I will make you fishers of men.

These are Christ's marching orders to every child of God and to every church of Christ, and the guarantee of his constant presence:

> MATTHEW 28:18-20. And Jesus came and spake unto them, saying, All power is given unto me in heaven and in earth. Go ye therefore, and teach all nations, baptizing them in the name of the Father, and of the Son, and of the Holy Ghost: teaching them to observe all things whatsoever I have commanded you: and, lo, I am with you alway, even unto the end of the world. Amen.

This is "taking" faith:

> MARK 11:24. Therefore I say unto you, What things soever ye desire, when ye pray, believe that ye receive them, and ye shall have them.

Prayer brings power, unlimited power, to the soul-winning task.

> LUKE 11:13. If ye then, being evil, know how to give good gifts unto your children: how much more shall your heavenly Father give the Holy Spirit to them that ask him?

This promise, when spiritually accepted, brings Pentecost:

> ACTS 1:8. But ye shall receive power, after that the Holy Ghost is come upon you: and ye shall be witnesses unto me both in Jerusalem, and in all Judaea, and in Samaria, and unto the uttermost part of the earth.

Our only chance to win is in Christ's strengthening.

> PHILIPPIANS 4:13. I can do all things through Christ which strengtheneth me.

Our source of supply is inexhaustible, and it is in Christ's loving hands.

PHILIPPIANS 4:19. But my God shall supply all your need according to his riches in glory by Christ Jesus.

With these great promises in the heart and claimed by faith, no one need fail in "taking men alive" for Christ.

34

The Unbeliever's Peril and Destiny

His Spiritual Condition Before God

Sin operates in earliest childhood.

PSALM 51:5. Behold, I was shapen in iniquity; and in sin did my mother conceive me.

PSALM 58:3. The wicked are estranged from the womb: they go astray as soon as they be born, speaking lies.

There is no perfect man this side of heaven.

ECCLESIASTES 7:20. For there is not a just man upon earth, that doeth good, and sinneth not.

This is God's version of the unbeliever's heart:

JEREMIAH 17:9. The heart is deceitful above all things, and desperately wicked: who can know it?

All humanity is in the same boat.

ROMANS 3:23. For all have sinned, and come short of the glory of God.

The unbeliever is dead in sin when God's quickening power finds him.

EPHESIANS 2:1. And you hath he quickened, who were dead in trespasses and sins.

By nature we are the children of the devil, by grace the children of God.

EPHESIANS 2:3. . . . among whom also we all had our conversation in times past in the lusts of our flesh, fulfilling the desires of the flesh and of the mind; and were by nature the children of wrath, even as others.

Unspeakably horrible is the sinner's plight—Godless, Christless, hopeless.

EPHESIANS 2:12. . . . that at that time ye were without Christ, being aliens from the commonwealth of Israel, and strangers from the covenants of promise, having no hope, and without God in the world.

In the light of these passages it is clear that men are born neither saints nor saved. Neither culture, nor education, nor good environment, nor reformation, nor ordinance can save them. It takes regeneration to reach the seat of their sins and cleanse their souls.

HIS PERIL

God's destruction comes suddenly, without warning.

DEUTERONOMY 32:35. To me belongeth vengeance, and recompence; their foot shall slide in due time: for the day of their calamity is at hand, and the things that shall come upon them make haste.

The oldest book in human history warns the sinner.

JOB 21:29-30. Have ye not asked them that go by the way? and do ye not know their tokens, that the wicked is reserved to the day of destruction? they shall be brought forth to the day of wrath.

Every last man stands on slippery glass in the darkness every hour he is out of Christ.

PROVERBS 29:1. He, that being often reproved hardeneth his neck, shall suddenly be destroyed, and that without remedy.

JEREMIAH 23:12. Wherefore their way shall be unto them as slippery ways in the darkness: they shall be driven on, and fall therein: for I will bring evil upon them, even the year of their visitation, saith the Lord.

Condemnation rests on every unbelieving soul.

JOHN 3:18. He that believeth on him is not condemned: but he that believeth not is condemned already, because he hath not believed in the name of the only begotten Son of God.

God's impending, imminent wrath rests over every man out of Christ.

JOHN 3:36. He that believeth on the Son hath everlasting life: and he that believeth not the Son shall not see life; but the wrath of God abideth on him.

HIS DESTINY

Isaiah and David tell of doom ahead.

PSALM 9:17. The wicked shall be turned into hell, and all the nations that forget God.

ISAIAH 14:9. Hell from beneath is moved for thee to meet thee at thy coming: it stirreth up the dead for thee, even all the chief ones of the earth; it hath raised up from their thrones all the kings of the nations.

Daniel, the great statesman counsels men to get ready for eternity.

DANIEL 12:2. And many of them that sleep in the dust of the earth shall awake, some to everlasting life, and some to shame and everlasting contempt.

Christ himself speaks with heaven's emphasis about eternal doom.

MATTHEW 25:41,46. Then shall he say also unto them on the left hand, Depart from me, ye cursed, into everlasting fire, prepared for the devil and his angels. . . . And these shall go away into everlasting punishment: but the righteous into life eternal.

Paul, God's topmost man, records God's will concerning the unbeliever.

2 THESSALONIANS 1:7-10. . . . the Lord Jesus shall be revealed from heaven with his mighty angels, in flaming fire taking vengeance on them that know not God, and that obey not the gospel of our Lord Jesus Christ: who shall be punished with everlasting destruction from the presence of the Lord, and from the glory of his power; when he shall come to be glorified in his saints, and to be admired in all them that believe (because our testimony among you was believed) in that day.

Peter, the great apostle, makes it plain.

> 2 PETER 2:9. The Lord knoweth how to deliver the godly out of temptations, and to reserve the unjust unto the day of judgment to be punished.

John says that the unmixed, undiluted wine of God's indignant wrath will be upon the soul of the unprepared sinner.

> REVELATION 14:10. The same shall drink of the wine of the wrath of God, which is poured out without mixture into the cup of his indignation; and he shall be tormented with fire and brimstone in the presence of the holy angels, and in the presence of the Lamb.

God's records must have our names, or the second death will take us eternally.

> REVELATION 20:15. And whosoever was not found written in the book of life was cast into the lake of fire.

The unbeliever must take his place in hell with earth's worst and most sinful crowd.

> REVELATION 21:8. But the fearful, and unbelieving, and the abominable, and murderers, and whoremongers, and sorcerers, and idolaters, and all liars, shall have their part in the lake which burneth with fire and brimstone: which is the second death.

In the face of these passages—from Job, the oldest inspired writer, to John on Patmos, the last voice from heaven in inspiration, including David, Isaiah, Daniel, Paul, Peter, and Jesus Christ himself—plainly telling, warning, exhorting, how can any man disbelieve in hell, or rest until his soul is safe from its awful doom?

35

God's Attitude Toward the Lost

God turns his face of grace and mercy to every lost man.

> 2 CHRONICLES 30:9. For if ye turn again unto the Lord, your brethren and your children shall find compassion before them that lead them captive, so that they shall come again into this land: for the Lord your God is gracious and merciful, and will not turn away his face from you, if ye return unto him.

God's love reaches to the depths of spiritual corruption in men's souls.

> ISAIAH 38:17. Behold, for peace I had great bitterness: but thou hast in love to my soul delivered it from the pit of corruption: for thou cast all my sins behind thy back.

His mercy will abundantly pardon every returning sinner.

> ISAIAH 55:7. Let the wicked forsake his way, and the unrighteous man his thoughts: and let him return unto the Lord, and he will have mercy upon him; and to our God, for he will abundantly pardon.

God loves the sinner's soul to the very gates of hell.

> JEREMIAH 31:3. The Lord hath appeared of old unto me, saying, Yea, I have loved thee with an everlasting love: therefore with lovingkindness have I drawn thee.

God and Christ proved their love in what the Father gave up and what the Son took up on Calvary for us.

> JOHN 3:16. For God so loved the world, that he gave his only begotten Son, that whosoever believeth in him should not perish, but have everlasting life.

The climactic proof of Christ's love for sinners is found on Calvary.

> ROMANS 5:8. But God commendeth his love toward us, in that, while we were yet sinners, Christ died for us.

Nothing in the grave of the past, nothing in the womb of the future, can intervene between the saved soul and the saving Christ.

> ROMANS 8:35-39. Who shall separate us from the love of Christ? shall tribulation, or distress, or persecution, or famine, or nakedness, or peril, or sword? As it is written, For thy sake we are killed all the day long; we are accounted as sheep for the slaughter. Nay, in all these things we are more than conquerors through him that loved us. For I am persuaded, that neither death, nor life, nor angels, nor principalities, nor powers, nor things present, nor things to come, nor height, nor depth, nor any other creature, shall be able to separate us from the love of God, which is in Christ Jesus our Lord.

He loved one sinner enough to go through the garden, past the cross, and down into the tomb for his soul.

> GALATIANS 2:20. I am crucified with Christ: nevertheless I live; yet not I, but Christ liveth in me: and the life which I now live in the flesh I live by the faith of the Son of God, who loved me, and gave himself for me.

The washing of his blood cleanses from every stain of sin in the believing soul.

> REVELATION 1:5. . . . and from Jesus Christ, who is the faithful witness, and the first begotten of the dead, and the prince of the kings of the earth. Unto him that loved us, and washed us from our sins in his own blood. . . .

Viewing these verses, no sinner out of hell need delay coming to Christ nor fear to find mercy when he comes.

> O Love that wilt not let me go,
>   I rest my weary soul in Thee;
> I give Thee back the life I owe,
> That in Thine ocean depths its flow
>   May richer, fuller be.
>
> O Light that followest all my way,
>   I yield my flickering torch to Thee;
> My heart restores its borrowed ray,
> That in Thy sunshine's glow its day
>   May brighter, fairer be.

O Joy that seeketh me through pain,
  I cannot close my heart to Thee;
I trace the rainbow through the rain,
And feel the promise is not vain
  That morn shall tearless be.

O cross that liftest up my head,
  I dare not ask to hide from Thee;
I lay in dust life's glory dead,
And from the ground there blossoms red
  Life that shall endless be.

GEORGE MATHESON

36

God's Provision for the Sinner's Redemption

God, in his infinite love, has planned for the sinner's redemption, and to that end he has provided:

A Beneficent Creation

In God's heavens we see his handiwork, a perfect bow, looking to man's salvation.

> PSALM 19:1. The heavens declare the glory of God; and the firmament sheweth his handywork.

God reveals himself as a redeeming God throughout creation.

> ROMANS 1:19-20. . . . because that which may be known of God is manifest in them; for God hath shewed it unto them. For the invisible things of him from the creation of the world are clearly seen, being understood by the things that are made, even his eternal power and Godhead; so that they are without excuse.

God created all things by Jesus Christ in order to show forth his eternal purposes of redemption.

> EPHESIANS 3:9-11. . . . and to make all men see what is the fellowship of the mystery, which from the beginning of the world hath been hid in God, who created all things by Jesus Christ: to the intent that now unto the principalities and powers in heavenly places might be known by the church the manifold wisdom of God, according to the eternal purpose which he purposed in Christ Jesus our Lord.

His cross is to reconcile all creation to his divine headship.

> COLOSSIANS 1:16-20. For by him were all things created, that are in heaven, and that are in earth, visible and invisible,

whether they be thrones, or dominions, or principalities, or powers: all things were created by him, and for him: and he is before all things, and by him all things consist. And he is the head of the body, the church: who is the beginning, the firstborn from the dead; that in all things he might have the preeminence. For it pleased the Father that in him should all fulness dwell; and, having made peace through the blood of his cross, by him to reconcile all things unto himself; by him, I say, whether they be things in earth, or things in heaven.

An Illuminating Revelation

God's Word gives the soul light in which to walk.

PSALM 119:105. Thy word is a lamp unto my feet, and a light unto my path.

The constructive agencies in character-building are found in this revealed Word.

ACTS 20:32. And now, brethren I commend you to God, and to the word of his grace, which is able to build you up, and to give you an inheritance among all them which are sanctified.

Wisdom in salvation and instruction in righteousness are found in this lamp of the soul.

2 TIMOTHY 3:15-17. . . . and that from a child thou hast known the holy scriptures, which are able to make thee wise unto salvation through faith which is in Christ Jesus. All scripture is given by inspiration of God, and is profitable for doctrine, for reproof, for correction, for instruction in righteousness: that the man of God may be perfect, throughly furnished unto all good works.

National Dispensations

1. *The Jews.*—God called, separated, and providentially blessed Abraham's seed that they might be the exemplifiers of his grace, establish his laws in the earth, and be the

channel through which his Son would come to bring salvation.

> GALATIANS 3:8-9. And the scripture, foreseeing that God would justify the heathen through faith, preached before the gospel unto Abraham, saying, In thee shall all nations be blessed. So then they which be of faith are blessed with faithful Abraham.

2. *The Gentiles.*—God offered his salvation, prepared in the Jewish stock, to the Gentiles—all men in all ages.

> ROMANS 11:18. Boast not against the branches. But if thou boast, thou bearest not the root, but the root thee.
> ROMANS 15:12. And again, Esaias saith, There shall be a root of Jesse, and he that shall rise to reign over the Gentiles; in him shall the Gentiles trust.
> GALATIANS 3:13-14. Christ hath redeemed us from the curse of the law, being made a curse for us: for it is written, Cursed is every one that hangeth on a tree: that the blessing of Abraham might come on the Gentiles through Jesus Christ; that we might receive the promise of the Spirit through faith.

Personal Manifestation

The following verses show the personal manifestation of God's Son, who by life and death gave himself to save us from our sins.

> JOHN 1:1,4,9,14. In the beginning was the Word, and the Word was with God, and the Word was God. . . . In him was life; and the life was the light of men. . . . That was the true Light, which lighteth every man that cometh into the world. . . . And the Word was made flesh, and dwelt among us, (and we beheld his glory, the glory as of the only begotten of the Father,) full of grace and truth.
> JOHN 1:29. The next day John seeth Jesus coming unto him, and saith, Behold the Lamb of God, which taketh away the sin of the world.
> GALATIANS 4:4-5. But when the fulness of the time was come, God sent forth his Son, made of a woman, made under the law, to redeem them that were under the law, that we might receive the adoption of sons.
> PHILIPPIANS 2:6-8. . . . who, being in the form of God, thought it not robbery to be equal with God: but made himself of no reputation, and took upon him the form of a servant, and

was made in the likeness of men: and being found in fashion as a man, he humbled himself, and became obedient unto death, even the death of the cross.

HEBREWS 2:14. Forasmuch then as the children are partakers of flesh and blood, he also himself likewise took part of the same; that through death he might destroy him that had the power of death, that is, the devil.

A Quickening Inspiration

God's divine power quickens and gives life's inspiring glow to the soul dead in trespasses and sins.

JOHN 1:13. . . . which were born, not of blood, nor of the will of the flesh, nor of the will of man, but of God.

JOHN 3:5-6. Jesus answered, Verily, verily, I say unto thee, Except a man be born of water and of the Spirit, he cannot enter into the kingdom of God. That which is born of the flesh is flesh; and that which is born of the Spirit is spirit.

JOHN 16:8-10. And when he is come, he will reprove the world of sin, and of righteousness, and of judgment: of sin, because they believe not on me; of righteousness, because I go to my Father, and ye see me no more.

EPHESIANS 2:5. . . . even when we were dead in sins, hath quickened us together with Christ, (by grace ye are saved;).

COLOSSIANS 2:13. And you, being dead in your sins and the uncircumcision of your flesh, hath he quickened together with him, having forgiven you all trespasses.

A Spiritual Organization

In his wonderful provision for the world's redemption and spiritual progress, God gave his glorious churches for the growth of our souls and the exercise of our powers and as centers for worship, work, and worldwide service.

MATTHEW 16:18. And I say also unto thee, That thou art Peter, and upon this rock I will build my church; and the gates of hell shall not prevail against it.

ACTS 2:47. . . . praising God, and having favour with all the people. And the Lord added to the church daily such as should be saved.

EPHESIANS 3:10. . . . to the intent that now unto the principalities and powers in heavenly places might be known by the church the manifold wisdom of God.

EPHESIANS 5:25. Husbands, love your wives, even as Christ also loved the church, and gave himself for it.

COLOSSIANS 1:24. ... who now rejoice in my sufferings for you, and fill up that which is behind of the afflictions of Christ in my flesh for his body's sake, which is the church.

1 THESSALONIANS 2:14. For ye, brethren, became followers of the churches of God which in Judaea are in Christ Jesus: for ye also have suffered like things of your own countrymen, even as they have of the Jews.

A Providential Combination

He assures our troubled hearts that all providences, expressed as the goodness of God, are calling us to him and working together for our eternal good, if we are his called and show our calling by our love for him.

ROMANS 2:4. Or despisest thou the riches of his goodness and forbearance and longsuffering; not knowing that the goodness of God leadeth thee to repentance?

ROMANS 8:28. And we know that all things work together for good to them that love God, to them who are the called according to his purpose.

A Preserving Predestination

He teaches us the watchful care of unchanging love and omnipotent power, which enables us without any doubt to realize his age-long purpose for us. He guarantees for all who believe a safe passage through life, death, resurrection, and the judgment, and a home with him forever.

ROMANS 8:29-31,35-39. For whom he did foreknow, he also did predestinate to be conformed to the image of his Son, that he might be the firstborn among many brethren. Moreover whom he did predestinate, them he also called: and whom he called, them he also justified: and whom he justified, them he also glorified. What shall we then say to these things? If God be for us, who can be against us? . . . Who shall separate us from the love of Christ? shall tribulation, or distress, or persecution, or famine, or nakedness, or peril, or sword? As it is written, For thy sake we are killed all the day long; we are accounted as sheep for the slaughter. Nay, in all these things we are more than conquerors through him that loved us. For I am persuaded, that neither death, nor life, nor angels, nor principalities, nor powers, nor things present, nor things to come, nor height, nor depth, nor any other creature, shall be able to separate us from the love of God, which is in Christ Jesus our Lord.

EPHESIANS 1:5, 11-12. . . . having predestinated us unto the adoption of children by Jesus Christ to himself, according to the good pleasure of his will. . . . in whom also we have obtained an inheritance, being predestinated according to the purpose of him who worketh all things after the counsel of his own will: that we should be to the praise of his glory, who first trusted in Christ.

A Glorious Resurrection

Our Father assures us of the resurrection of our bodies to an incorruptible immortality and their adoption into an endless sonship.

ROMANS 8:11. But if the Spirit of him that raised up Jesus from the dead dwell in you, he that raised up Christ from the dead shall also quicken your mortal bodies by his Spirit that dwelleth in you.

ROMANS 8:22-23. For we know that the whole creation groaneth and travaileth in pain together until now. And not only they, but ourselves also, which have the firstfruits of the Spirit, even we ourselves groan within ourselves, waiting for the adoption, to wit, the redemption of our body.

1 CORINTHIANS 15:20, 22-23, 42-44, 51-57. But now is Christ risen from the dead, and become the firstfruits of them that slept. . . . For as in Adam all die, even so in Christ shall all be made alive. But every man in his own order: Christ the firstfruits; afterward they that are Christ's at his coming. . . . So also is the resurrection of the dead. It is sown in corruption; it is raised in incorruption: it is sown in dishonour; it is raised in glory: it is sown in weakness; it is raised in power: it is sown a natural body; it is raised a spiritual body. There is a natural body, and there is a spiritual body. . . . Behold, I shew you a mystery; We shall not all sleep, but we shall all be changed, in a moment, in the twinkling of an eye, at the last trump: for the trumpet shall sound, and the

dead shall be raised incorruptible, and we shall be changed. For this corruptible must put on incorruption, and this mortal must put on immortality. So when this corruptible shall have put on incorruption, and this mortal shall have put on immortality, then shall be brought to pass the saying that is written, Death is swallowed up in victory. O death, where is thy sting? O grave, where is thy victory? The sting of death is sin; and the strength of sin is the law. But thanks be to God, which giveth us the victory through our Lord Jesus Christ.

1 THESSALONIANS 4:16-17. For the Lord himself shall descend from heaven with a shout, with the voice of the archangel, and with the trump of God: and the dead in Christ shall rise first: then we which are alive and remain shall be caught up together with them in the clouds, to meet the Lord in the air: and so shall we ever be with the Lord.

A Guaranteed Destination

God's final and glorious work shall be housing his people in their eternal mansions with him where their light shall be the face of the Lamb.

JOHN 10:27-29. My sheep hear my voice, and I know them, and they follow me: and I give unto them eternal life; and they shall never perish, neither shall any man pluck them out of my hand. My Father, which gave them me, is greater than all; and no man is able to pluck them out of my Father's hand.

JOHN 14:2-4. In my Father's house are many mansions: if it were not so, I would have told you. I go to prepare a place for you. And if I go and prepare a place for you, I will come again, and receive you unto myself; that where I am, there ye may be also. And whither I go ye know, and the way ye know.

1 THESSALONIANS 4:17. Then we which are alive and remain shall be caught up together with them in the clouds, to meet the Lord in the air: and so shall we ever be with the Lord.

1 PETER 1:3-5. Blessed be the God and Father of our Lord Jesus Christ, which according to his abundant mercy hath begotten us again unto a lively hope by the resurrection of Jesus Christ from the dead, to an inheritance incorruptible, and undefiled, and that fadeth not away, reserved in heaven for you, who are kept by the power of God through faith unto salvation ready to be revealed in the last time.

2 PETER 1:10-11. Wherefore the rather, brethren, give diligence to make your calling and election sure: for if ye do these things, ye shall never fall: for so an entrance shall be ministered unto you abundantly into the everlasting kingdom of our Lord and Saviour Jesus Christ.

37

The Salvation of the Soul

God is at work both before and during the salvation of the sinner. But the sinner is more than a passive recipient; he has his part to fulfil in the process of salvation.

WHAT GOD DOES BEFORE SALVATION

1. He foreknows, predestinates, and elects.

ISAIAH 46:9-10. Remember the former things of old: for I am God, and there is none else; I am God, and there is none like me, declaring the end from the beginning, and from ancient times the things that are not yet done, saying, My counsel shall stand, and I will do all my pleasure.

JOHN 6:37. All that the Father giveth me shall come to me; and him that cometh to me I will in no wise cast out.

ROMANS 8:29. For whom he did foreknow, he also did predestinate to be conformed to the image of his Son, that he might be the firstborn among many brethren.

ROMANS 8:33. Who shall lay any thing to the charge of God's elect? It is God that justifieth.

ROMANS 9:11. . . . that the purpose of God according to election might stand, not of works, but of him that calleth. . . .

EPHESIANS 1:5-11. . . . having predestinated us unto the adoption of children by Jesus Christ to himself, according to the good pleasure of his will. . . in whom also we have obtained an inheritance, being predestinated according to the purpose of him who worketh all things after the counsel of his own will.

COLOSSIANS 3:12. Put on therefore, as the elect of God, holy and beloved, bowels of mercies, kindness, humbleness of mind, meekness, longsuffering.

1 THESSALONIANS 1:4. . . . knowing, brethren beloved, your election of God.

1 PETER 1:2. . . . elect according to the foreknowledge of God the Father, through sanctification of the Spirit, unto

[260]

obedience and sprinkling of the blood of Jesus Christ: Grace unto you, and peace, be multiplied.

2 PETER 1:10. Wherefore the rather, brethren, give diligence to make your calling and election sure: for if ye do these things, ye shall never fall.

2. He calls—by his providences, his goodness, Christ, his people, his divine Word, and his Holy Spirit.

MATTHEW 9:13. But go ye and learn what that meaneth, I will have mercy, and not sacrifice: for I am not come to call the righteous, but sinners to repentance.

ACTS 2:39. For the promise is unto you, and to your children, and to all that are afar off, even as many as the Lord our God shall call.

ROMANS 8:30. Moreover whom he did predestinate, them he also called: and whom he called, them he also justified: and whom he justified, them he also glorified.

HEBREWS 3:1. Wherefore, holy brethren, partakers of the heavenly calling, consider the Apostle and High Priest of our profession, Christ Jesus.

HEBREWS 9:15. And for this cause he is the mediator of the new testament, that by means of death, for the redemption of the transgressions that were under the first testament, they which are called might receive the promise of eternal inheritance.

REVELATION 22:17. And the Spirit and the bride say, Come. And let him that heareth say, Come. And let him that is athirst come. And whosoever will, let him take the water of life freely.

3. He convinces and convicts of sin.

JOHN 16:8-9. And when he is come, he will reprove the world of sin, and of righteousness, and of judgment: of sin, because they believe not on me.

ACTS 2:37. Now when they heard this, they were pricked in their heart, and said unto Peter and to the rest of the apostles, Men and brethren, what shall we do?

ACTS 9:8-9. And Saul arose from the earth; and when his eyes were opened, he saw no man: but they led him by the hand, and brought him into Damascus. And he was three days without sight, and neither did eat nor drink.

ACTS 16:29-31. Then he called for a light, and sprang in, and came trembling, and fell down before Paul and Silas, and brought them out, and said, Sirs, what must I do to be saved? And they said, Believe on the Lord Jesus Christ, and thou shalt be saved, and thy house.

ACTS 24:25. And as he reasoned of righteousness, temperance, and judgment to come, Felix trembled, and answered, Go thy way for this time; when I have a convenient season, I will call for thee.

4. He quickens.

ROMANS 4:17. . . . God, who quickeneth the dead, and calleth those things which be not as though they were.

EPHESIANS 2:1,5. And you hath he quickened, who were dead in trespasses and sins. . . . even when we were dead in sins, hath quickened us together with Christ, (by grace ye are saved;). . . .

5. He worketh godly sorrow.

2 CORINTHIANS 7:9-10. Now I rejoice, not that ye were made sorry, but that ye sorrowed to repentance: for ye were made sorry after a godly manner, that ye might receive damage by us in nothing. For godly sorrow worketh repentance to salvation not to be repented of: but the sorrow of the world worketh death.

6. He giveth repentance.

ACTS 5:31. Him hath God exalted with his right hand to be a Prince and a Saviour, for to give repentance to Israel, and forgiveness of sins.

2 TIMOTHY 2:25. . . . In meekness instructing those that oppose themselves; if God peradventure will give them repentance to the acknowledging of the truth.

HEBREWS 12:17. For ye know how that afterward, when he would have inherited the blessing, he was rejected: for he found no place of repentance, though he sought it carefully with tears.

WHAT THE SINNER DOES IN SALVATION

1. He hears the word of truth.

ROMANS 10:8,17. But what saith it? The word is nigh thee, even in thy mouth, and in thy heart: that is, the word of faith, which we preach. . . . So then faith cometh by hearing, and hearing by the word of God.

2. He feels the weight of his sins and repents.

ACTS 3:19. Repent ye therefore, and be converted, that your sins may be blotted out, when the times of refreshing shall come from the presence of the Lord.

ACTS 20:21. . . . testifying both to the Jews, and also to the Greeks, repentance toward God, and faith toward our Lord Jesus Christ.

3. He prays for help.

LUKE 18:13. And the publican, standing afar off, would not lift up so much as his eyes unto heaven, but smote upon his breast, saying, God be merciful to me a sinner.

ROMANS 10:12-13. For there is no difference between the Jew and the Greek: for the same Lord over all is rich unto all that call upon him. For whosoever shall call upon the name of the Lord shall be saved.

4. He receives Christ by faith into his own soul.

JOHN 1:12. But as many as received him, to them gave he power to become the sons of God, even to them that believe on his name.

JOHN 3:16. For God so loved the world, that he gave his only begotten Son, that whosoever believeth in him should not perish, but have everlasting life.

JOHN 3:36. He that believeth on the Son hath everlasting life: and he that believeth not the Son shall not see life; but the wrath of God abideth on him.

JOHN 5:24. Verily, verily, I say unto you, He that heareth my word, and believeth on him that sent me, hath everlasting life, and shall not come into condemnation; but is passed from death unto life.

ACTS 8:37. And Philip said, If thou believest with all thine heart, thou mayest. And he answered and said, I believe that Jesus Christ is the Son of God.

ROMANS 5:1. Therefore being justified by faith, we have peace with God through our Lord Jesus Christ.

EPHESIANS 2:8. For by grace are ye saved through faith; and that not of yourselves: it is the gift of God.

REVELATION 3:20. Behold, I stand at the door, and knock: if any man hear my voice, and open the door, I will come in to him, and will sup with him, and he with me.

5. He confesses Christ as his Saviour.

MATTHEW 10:32-33. Whosoever therefore shall confess me before men, him will I confess also before my Father which is in heaven. But whosoever shall deny me before men, him will I also deny before my Father which is in heaven.

ROMANS 10:9-10. . . . that if thou shalt confess with thy mouth the Lord Jesus, and shalt believe in thine heart that God hath raised him from the dead, thou shalt be saved. For with the heart man believeth unto righteousness; and with the mouth confession is made unto salvation.

WHAT GOD DOES IN SALVATION

1. He pronounces the believing sinner justified through Christ's atoning death.

LUKE 18:14. I tell you, this man went down to his house justified rather than the other: for every one that exalteth himself shall be abased; and he that humbleth himself shall be exalted.

ACTS 13:39. And by him all that believe are justified from all things, from which ye could not be justified by the law of Moses.

ROMANS 3:24, 26, 28. . . . being justified freely by his grace through the redemption that is in Christ Jesus: . . . to declare, I say, at this time his righteousness: that he might be just, and the justifier of him which believeth in Jesus. . . . Therefore we conclude that a man is justified by faith without the deeds of the law.

ROMANS 5:1. Therefore being justified by faith, we have peace with God through our Lord Jesus Christ.

ROMANS 8:30. Moreover whom he did predestinate, them he also called: and whom he called, them he also justified: and whom he justified, them he also glorified.

1 CORINTHIANS 6:11. And such were some of you: but ye are washed, but ye are sanctified, but ye are justified in the name of the Lord Jesus, and by the Spirit of our God.

2. He pardons the sinner and forgives all his sins.

ISAIAH 55:7. Let the wicked forsake his way, and the unrighteous man his thoughts: and let him return unto the Lord, and he will have mercy upon him; and to our God, for he will abundantly pardon.

THE SALVATION OF THE SOUL

JEREMIAH 33:8. And I will cleanse them from all their iniquity, whereby they have sinned against me; and I will pardon all their iniquities, whereby they have sinned, and whereby they have transgressed against me.

ACTS 26:18. . . . to open their eyes, and to turn them from darkness to light, and from the power of Satan unto God, that they may receive forgiveness of sins, and inheritance among them which are sanctified by faith that is in me.

EPHESIANS 1:7. In whom we have redemption through his blood, the forgiveness of sins, according to the riches of his grace.

3. He washes and cleanses the sinner's soul from all iniquity and makes it pure by the blood of Christ.

PSALM 51:7. Purge me with hyssop, and I shall be clean: wash me, and I shall be whiter than snow.

ISAIAH 1:18. Come now, and let us reason together, saith the Lord: though your sins be as scarlet, they shall be as white as snow; though they be red like crimson, they shall be as wool.

1 JOHN 1:7. But if we walk in the light, as he is in the light, we have fellowship one with another, and the blood of Jesus Christ his Son cleanseth us from all sin.

REVELATION 1:5. . . . and from Jesus Christ, who is the faithful witness, and the first begotten of the dead, and the prince of the kings of the earth. Unto him that loved us, and washed us from our sins in his own blood.

REVELATION 7:14. And I said unto him, Sir, thou knowest. And he said to me, These are they which came out of great tribulation, and have washed their robes, and made them white in the blood of the Lamb.

4. He puts away the sinner's sins, casting them behind his back, and remembers them against him no more.

PSALM 103:12. As far as the east is from the west, so far hath he removed our transgressions from us.

ISAIAH 38:17. Behold, for peace I had great bitterness: but thou hast in love to my soul delivered it from the pit of corruption: for thou hast cast all my sins behind thy back.

ISAIAH 53:5,11. But he was wounded for our transgressions, he was bruised for our iniquities: the chastisement of our peace was upon him; and with his stripes we are healed. . . . He shall see of the travail of his soul, and shall be satisfied: by his knowledge shall my righteous servant justify many; for he shall bear their iniquities.

JEREMIAH 31:34. And they shall teach no more every man his neighbour, and every man his brother, saying, Know the Lord; for they shall all know me, from the least of them unto the greatest of them, saith the Lord: for I will forgive their iniquity, and I will remember their sin no more.

JOHN 1:29. The next day John seeth Jesus coming unto him, and saith, Behold the Lamb of God, which taketh away the sin of the world.

HEBREWS 8:12. For I will be merciful to their unrighteousness, and their sins and their iniquities will I remember no more.

5. He regenerates him by a spiritual birth and gives him a new nature, imparting to him of the divine nature and life.

JOHN 1:12-13. But as many as received him, to them gave he power to become the sons of God, even to them that believe on his name: which were born, not of blood, nor of the will of the flesh, nor of the will of man, but of God.

JOHN 3:3. Jesus answered and said unto him, Verily, verily, I say unto thee, Except a man be born again, he cannot see the kingdom of God.

1 CORINTHIANS 4:15. For though ye have ten thousand instructors in Christ, yet have ye not many fathers: for in Christ Jesus I have begotten you through the gospel.

2 CORINTHIANS 5:17. Therefore if any man be in Christ, he is a new creature: old things are passed away; behold, all things are become new.

GALATIANS 6:15. For in Christ Jesus neither circumcision availeth any thing, nor uncircumcision, but a new creature.

EPHESIANS 4:24. . . . and that ye put on the new man, which after God is created in righteousness and true holiness.

COLOSSIANS 3:3-4. For ye are dead, and your life is hid with Christ in God. When Christ, who is our life, shall appear, then shall ye also appear with him in glory.

JAMES 1:18. Of his own will begat he us with the word of truth, that we should be a kind of firstfruits of his creatures.

1 PETER 1:23. . . . being born again, not of corruptible seed, but of incorruptible, by the word of God, which liveth and abideth for ever.

2 PETER 1:4. . . . whereby are given unto us exceeding great and precious promises: that by these ye might be partakers of the divine nature, having escaped the corruption that is in the world through lust.

This new life is eternal. The saved man possesses it now and is passed out of death and from under condemnation and judgment.

> JOHN 3:36. He that believeth on the Son hath everlasting life: and he that believeth not the Son shall not see life; but the wrath of God abideth on him.
>
> JOHN 5:24. Verily, verily, I say unto you, He that heareth my word, and believeth on him that sent me, hath everlasting life, and shall not come into condemnation; but is passed from death unto life.
>
> ROMANS 8:1. There is therefore now no condemnation to them which are in Christ Jesus, who walk not after the flesh, but after the Spirit.

He is now a child of God by faith.

> GALATIANS 3:26. For ye are all the children of God by faith in Christ Jesus.

6. God sanctifies his soul. It is holy, possessing the imputed righteousness of Christ.

> ROMANS 4:3-6. For what saith the scripture? Abraham believed God, and it was counted unto him for righteousness. Now to him that worketh is the reward not reckoned of grace, but of debt. But to him that worketh not, but believeth on him that justifieth the ungodly, his faith is counted for righteousness. Even as David also describeth the blessedness of the man, unto whom God imputeth righteousness without works.
>
> 1 CORINTHIANS 1:2. Unto the church of God which is at Corinth, to them that are sanctified in Christ Jesus, called to be saints, with all that in every place call upon the name of Jesus Christ our Lord, both theirs and ours. . . .
>
> 1 PETER 1:2. . . . elect according to the foreknowledge of God the Father, through sanctification of the Spirit, unto obedience and sprinkling of the blood of Jesus Christ: Grace unto you, and peace, be multiplied.
>
> 1 JOHN 3:9. Whosoever is born of God doth not commit sin; for his seed remaineth in him: and he cannot sin, because he is born of God.

7. He puts his seal, the image of his Son, on his soul.

> 2 CORINTHIANS 1:22. . . . who hath also sealed us, and given the earnest of the Spirit in our hearts.

EPHESIANS 1:13-14. In whom ye also trusted, after that ye heard the word of truth, the gospel of your salvation: in whom also after that ye believed, ye were sealed with the holy Spirit of promise, which is the earnest of our inheritance until the redemption of the purchased possession, unto the praise of his glory.

EPHESIANS 4:30. And grieve not the holy Spirit of God, whereby ye are sealed unto the day of redemption.

8. He puts in him the Holy Spirit, who testifiies to his sonship and guides, comforts, and uses him.

ROMANS 8:14-17. For as many as are led by the Spirit of God, they are the sons of God. For ye have not received the spirit of bondage again to fear; but ye have received the Spirit of adoption, whereby we cry, Abba, Father. The Spirit itself beareth witness with our spirit, that we are the children of God: and if children, then heirs; heirs of God, and joint-heirs with Christ; if so be that we suffer with him, that we may be also glorified together.

38

The Salvation of the Life

In the previous chapter we saw how the sinner can come to God and find salvation, life, and sonship. He is in good standing in the family of God if he has taken the steps indicated. But Jesus tells us that he came, not only to give life, but to give it more abundantly (John 10:10); that not only does the saved soul have wells of everlasting water (John 4:14), but within him shall flow rivers of living water (John 7:38), making him always to abound in the work of the Lord (1 Cor. 15:58). He says we were foreordained and created unto good works (Eph. 2:10) and that he has given us such spiritual supplies and equipment that we need not fail in any task or battle for him (Eph. 6:10-18; Phil. 4:19).

With this high expectation the saved man should follow on to know God (Hos. 6:3), remembering that "the people that do know their God shall be strong, and do exploits" (Dan. 11:32).

In this important matter Christ's churches should be alert to furnish the needed opportunities for growth on the part of the new converts. Many act as if they feel their work is over when they have led lost souls to Christ and open confession of him. But this is only the first step. Wise leadership at this point will save a world of waste and eternal loss. It is a long, patient, but exceedingly valuable service to lead the newly saved into strength and ripeness of Christian character and acceptable service in Christ's church and kingdom.

The steps to successful and faithful service are indicated in the Scriptures, as follows:

Public Confession of Christ

God does not honor secret discipleship. He does not want his children to be ashamed of their parentage.

MATTHEW 10:32-33. Whosoever therefore shall confess me before men, him will I confess also before my Father which is in heaven. But whosoever shall deny me before men, him will I also deny before my Father which is in heaven.

MARK 8:38. Whosoever therefore shall be ashamed of me and of my words in this adulterous and sinful generation; of him also shall the Son of man be ashamed, when he cometh in the glory of his Father with the holy angels.

ROMANS 10:9-10. . . . that if thou shalt confess with thy mouth the Lord Jesus, and shalt believe in thine heart that God hath raised him from the dead, thou shalt be saved. For with the heart man believeth unto righteousness; and with the mouth confession is made unto salvation.

Obedience in Baptism and Church Membership

The saved man owes it to Christ to follow him in baptism and to serve him in his church. "If you love me," he says, "keep my commandments" (John 14:15).

MATTHEW 3:5-6,15-16. Then went out to him Jerusalem, and all Judaea, and all the region round about Jordan, and were baptized of him in Jordan, confessing their sins. . . . And Jesus answering said unto him, Suffer it to be so now: for thus it becometh us to fulfil all righteousness. Then he suffered him. And Jesus, when he was baptized, went up straightway out of the water: and, lo, the heavens were opened unto him, and he saw the Spirit of God descending like a dove, and lighting upon him.

MATTHEW 28:18-20. And Jesus came and spake unto them, saying, All power is given unto me in heaven and in earth. Go ye therefore, and teach all nations, baptizing them in the name of the Father, and of the Son, and of the Holy Ghost: teaching them to observe all things whatsoever I have commanded you: and, lo, I am with you alway, even unto the end of the world. Amen.

ACTS 2:41-42,46-47. Then they that gladly received his word were baptized: and the same day there were added unto them about three thousand souls. And they continued stedfastly in the apostles' doctrine and fellowship, and in breaking of bread, and in prayers. . . . And they, continuing daily with one accord in the temple, and breaking bread from house to house, did eat their meat with gladness and singleness of heart, praising God, and having favour with all the people. And the Lord added to the church daily such as should be saved.

ACTS 8:37-38. And Philip said, if thou believest with all thine heart, thou mayest. And he answered and said, I believe that Jesus Christ is the Son of God. And he commanded the chariot to stand still: and they went down both into the water, both Philip and the eunuch; and he baptized him.

ACTS 20:28. Take heed therefore unto yourselves, and to all the flock, over the which the Holy Ghost hath made you overseers, to feed the church of God, which he hath purchased with his own blood.

ROMANS 6:4-6. Therefore we are buried with him by baptism into death: that like as Christ was raised up from the dead by the glory of the Father, even so we also should walk in newness of life. For if we have been planted together in the likeness of his death, we shall be also in the likeness of his resurrection: knowing this, that our old man is crucified with him, that the body of sin might be destroyed, that henceforth we should not serve sin.

EPHESIANS 5:28-32. So ought men to love their wives as their own bodies. He that loveth his wife loveth himself. For no man ever yet hated his own flesh; but nourisheth and cherisheth it, even as the Lord the church. For we are members of his body, of his flesh, and of his bones. For this cause shall a man leave his father and mother, and shall be joined unto his wife, and they two shall be one flesh. This is a great mystery: but I speak concerning Christ and the church.

Baptism does not save or help save, but it proclaims Christ's death, burial, and resurrection, the great act and doctrine by which men are saved. It pictures the sinner's identification with Christ's death and entrance into new life. He publicly puts a grave between himself and his former life of sin. Baptism is a vital step in one's progress in the upward way, and no one confessing Christ as Saviour ought to put off this happy obedience to his blessed command.

Surrender of Life and Talent to the Service of God

By every right of ownership Christ is entitled to our best service.

1 CHRONICLES 29:5. . . . the gold for things of gold, and the silver for things of silver, and for all manner of work to be made by the hands of artificers. And who then is willing to consecrate his service this day unto the Lord?

NEHEMIAH 4:6. So built we the wall; and all the wall was joined together unto the half thereof: for the people had a mind to work.

PSALM 110:3. Thy people shall be willing in the day of thy power, in the beauties of holiness from the womb of the morning: thou hast the dew of thy youth.

MATTHEW 6:33. But seek ye first the kingdom of God, and his righteousness; and all these things shall be added unto you.

ROMANS 12:1-2. I beseech you therefore, brethren, by the mercies of God, that ye present your bodies a living sacrifice, holy, acceptable unto God, which is your reasonable service. And be not conformed to this world: but be ye transformed by the renewing of your mind, that ye may prove what is that good, and acceptable, and perfect, will of God.

1 CORINTHIANS 6:19-20. What? know ye not that your body is the temple of the Holy Ghost which is in you, which ye have of God, and ye are not your own? For ye are bought with a price: therefore glorify God in your body, and in your spirit, which are God's.

2 CORINTHIANS 8:5. And this they did, not as we hoped, but first gave their own selves to the Lord, and unto us by the will of God.

GALATIANS 2:20. I am crucified with Christ: nevertheless I live; yet not I, but Christ liveth in me: and the life which I now live in the flesh I live by the faith of the Son of God, who loved me, and gave himself for me.

PHILIPPIANS 1:21. For to me to live is Christ, and to die is gain.

Purity of Life and Separation from the World's Ways

PSALM 24:3-4. Who shall ascend into the hill of the Lord? or who shall stand in his holy place? He that hath clean hands, and a pure heart; who hath not lifted up his soul unto vanity, nor sworn deceitfully.

ROMANS 12:1-2. I beseech you therefore, brethren, by the mercies of God, that ye present your bodies a living sacrifice, holy, acceptable unto God, which is your reasonable service. And be not conformed to this world: but be ye transformed by the renewing of your mind, that ye may prove what is that good, and acceptable, and perfect, will of God.

2 CORINTHIANS 6:15-17. And what concord hath Christ with Belial? or what part hath he that believeth with an infidel? And what agreement hath the temple of God with idols? for ye are the temple of the living God; as God hath said, I will dwell in them, and walk in them; and I will be their God, and they shall be my people. Wherefore come out from among them, and be ye separate, saith the Lord, and touch not the unclean thing; and I will receive you.

GALATIANS 5:16-26. This I say then, Walk in the Spirit, and ye ye shall not fulfil the lust of the flesh. For the flesh lusteth against the Spirit, and the Spirit against the flesh: and these are contrary the one to the other: so that ye cannot do the things that ye would. But if ye be led of the Spirit, ye are not under the law. Now the works of the flesh are manifest, which are these; Adultery, fornication, uncleanness, lasciviousness, idolatry, witchcraft, hatred, variance, emulations, wrath, strife, seditions, heresies, envyings, murders, drunkenness, revellings, and such like: of the which I tell you before, as I have also told you in time past, that they which do such things shall not inherit the kingdom of God. But the fruit of the Spirit is love, joy, peace, longsuffering, gentleness, goodness, faith, meekness, temperance: against such there is no law. And they that are Christ's have crucified the flesh with the affections and lusts. If we live in the Spirit, let us also walk in the Spirit. Let us not be desirous of vain glory, provoking one another, envying one another.

EPHESIANS 4:20-32. But ye have not so learned Christ; if so be that ye have heard him, and have been taught by him, as the truth is in Jesus: that ye put off concerning the former conversation the old man, which is corrupt according to the deceitful lusts; and be renewed in the spirit of your mind; and that ye put on the new man, which after God is created in righteousness and true holiness. Wherefore putting away lying, speak every man truth with his neighbour: for we are members one of another. Be ye angry, and sin not: let not the sun go down upon your wrath: neither give place to the devil. Let him that stole steal no more: but rather let him labour, working with his hands the thing which is good, that he may have to give to him that needeth. Let no corrupt communciation proceed out of your mouth, but that which is good to the use of edifying, that it may minister grace unto the hearers. And grieve not the holy Spirit of God, whereby ye are sealed unto the day of redemption. Let all bitterness, and wrath, and anger, and clamour, and evil speaking, be put away from you, with all malice: and be ye kind one to another, tenderhearted, forgiving one another, even as God for Christ's sake hath forgiven you.

EPHESIANS 5:7-11. Be not ye therefore partakers with them. For ye were sometimes darkness, but now are ye light in the Lord: walk as children of light: (for the fruit of the Spirit is in all goodness and righteousness and truth;) proving what is acceptable unto the Lord. And have no fellowship with the unfruitful works of darkness, but rather reprove them.

PHILIPPIANS 3:13-14. Brethren, I count not myself to have apprehended: but this one thing I do, forgetting those things which are behind, and reaching forth unto those things which are before, I press toward the mark for the prize of the high calling of God in Christ Jesus.

1 THESSALONIANS 3:12-13. And the Lord make you to increase and abound in love one toward another, and toward all men, even as we do toward you: to the end he may stablish your hearts unblameable in holiness before God, even our Father, at the coming of our Lord Jesus Christ with all his saints.

1 JOHN 1:5-7. This then is the message which we have heard of him, and declare unto you, that God is light, and in him is no darkness at all. If we say that we have fellowship with him, and walk in darkness, we lie, and do not the truth: but if we walk in the light, as he is in the light, we have fellowship one with another, and the blood of Jesus Christ his Son cleanseth us from all sin.

1 JOHN 2:15. Love not the world, neither the things that are in the world. If any man love the world, the love of the Father is not in him.

Receiving the Fulness of the Holy Spirit's Power

The fulness of the Holy Spirit's power is for every disciple who will pay the price for it.

LUKE 11:13. If ye then, being evil, know how to give good gifts unto your children: how much more shall your heavenly Father give the Holy Spirit to them that ask him?

LUKE 24:49. And, behold, I send the promise of my Father upon you: but tarry ye in the city of Jerusalem, until ye be endued with power from on high.

Acts 1:8. But ye shall receive power, after that the Holy Ghost is come upon you: and ye shall be witnesses unto me both in Jerusalem, and in all Judaea, and in Samaria, and unto the uttermost part of the earth.

Acts 2:39. For the promise is unto you, and to your children, and to all that are afar off, even as many as the Lord our God shall call.

Acts 5:32. And we are his witnesses of these things; and so is also the Holy Ghost, whom God hath given to them that obey him.

Acts 6:3. Wherefore, brethren, look ye out among you seven men of honest report, full of the Holy Ghost and wisdom, whom we may appoint over this business.

Acts 9:17. And Ananias went his way, and entered into the house, and putting his hands on him said, Brother Saul, the Lord, even Jesus, that appeared unto thee in the way as thou camest, hath sent me, that thou mightest receive thy sight, and be filled with the Holy Ghost.

Ephesians 5:18. And be not drunk with wine wherein is excess; but be filled with the Spirit.

A Meditative Study of, and a Spiritual Insight into, the Word of God

Deuteronomy 11:18-21. Therefore shall ye lay up these my words in your heart and in your soul, and bind them for a sign upon your hand, that they may be as frontlets between your eyes. And ye shall teach them your children, speaking of them when thou sittest in thine house, and when thou walkest by the way, when thou liest down, and when thou risest up. And thou shalt write them upon the door posts of thine house, and upon thy gates: that your days may be multiplied, and the days of your children, in the land which the Lord sware unto your fathers to give them, as the days of heaven upon the earth.

Joshua 1:8. This book of the law shall not depart out of thy mouth; but thou shalt meditate therein day and night, that thou mayest observe to do according to all that is written therein: for then thou shalt make thy way prosperous, and then thou shalt have good success.

Psalm 1:1-2. Blessed is the man that walketh not in the counsel of the ungodly, nor standeth in the way of sinners, nor sitteth in the seat of the scornful. But his delight is in the law of the Lord; and in his law doth he meditate day and night.

PSALM 119:11. Thy word have I hid in mine heart, that I might not sin against thee.

PSALM 119:18. Open thou mine eyes, that I may behold wondrous things out of thy law.

PSALM 119:97. O how love I thy law! it is my meditation all the day.

1 CORINTHIANS 2:14. But the natural man receiveth not the things of the Spirit of God: for they are foolishness unto him: neither can he know them, because they are spiritually discerned.

2 TIMOTHY 3:14-17. But continue thou in the things which thou hast learned and hast been assured of, knowing of whom thou hast learned them; and that from a child thou hast known the holy scriptures, which are able to make thee wise unto salvation through faith which is in Christ Jesus. All scripture is given by inspiration of God, and is profitable for doctrine, for reproof, for correction, for instruction in righteousness: that the man of God may be perfect, throughly furnished unto all good works.

The Christian should every day soulfully study some part of God's Word. Christ says, "It is written, Man shall not live by bread alone, but by every word that proceedeth out of the mouth of God" (Matt. 4:4).

JOHN 5:39. Search the scriptures; for in them ye think ye have eternal life: and they are they which testify of me.

ACTS 20:32. And now, brethren, I commend you to God, and to the word of his grace, which is able to build you up, and to give you an inheritance among all them which are sanctified.

COLOSSIANS 3:16. Let the word of Christ dwell in you richly in all wisdom; teaching and admonishing one another in psalms and hymns and spiritual songs, singing with grace in your hearts to the Lord.

1 PETER 2:2. As newborn babes, desire the sincere milk of the word, that ye may grow thereby.

The Establishment and Maintenance of a Prayer Life

Our spiritual power and our joy in the service of God will be largely determined by our prayer life.

JEREMIAH 33:3. Call unto me, and I will answer thee, and shew thee great and mighty things, which thou knowest not.
MATTHEW 6:6. But thou, when thou prayest, enter into thy closet, and when thou hast shut thy door, pray to thy Father which is in secret; and thy Father which seeth in secret shall reward thee openly.
MARK 11:24. Therefore I say unto you, What things soever ye desire, when ye pray, believe that ye receive them, and ye shall have them.
LUKE 11:9-13. And I say unto you, Ask, and it shall be given you; seek, and ye shall find; knock, and it shall be opened unto you. For every one that asketh receiveth; and he that seeketh findeth; and to him that knocketh it shall be opened. If a son shall ask bread of any of you that is a father, will he give him a stone? or if he ask a fish, will he for a fish give him a serpent? Or if he shall ask an egg, will he offer him a scorpion? If ye then, being evil, know how to give good gifts unto your children: how much more shall your heavenly Father give the Holy Spirit to them that ask him?
LUKE 18:1. And he spake a parable unto them to this end, that men ought always to pray, and not to faint.
LUKE 21:36. Watch ye therefore, and pray always, that ye may be accounted worthy to escape all these things that shall come to pass, and to stand before the Son of man.
ROMANS 12:12. . . . rejoicing in hope; patient in tribulation; continuing instant in prayer.
EPHESIANS 6:18. . . . praying always with all prayer and supplication in the Spirit, and watching thereunto with all perserverance and supplication. for all saints.
PHILIPPIANS 4:6-7. Be careful for nothing; but in every thing by prayer and supplication with thanksgiving let your requests be made known unto God. And the peace of God, which passeth all understanding, shall keep your hearts and minds through Christ Jesus.
COLOSSIANS 4:2. Continue in prayer, and watch in the same with thanksgiving.
1 THESSALONIANS 5:17-18. Pray without ceasing. In everything give thanks: for this is the will of God in Christ Jesus concerning you.
JAMES 5:13-16. Is any among you afflicted? let him pray. Is any merry? let him sing psalms. Is any sick among you? let him call for the elders of the church; and let them pray over him, anointing him with oil in the name of the Lord. And the prayer of faith shall save the sick, and the Lord shall raise him up; and

if he have committed sins, they shall be forgiven him. Confess your faults one to another, and pray one for another, that ye may be healed. The effectual fervent prayer of a righteous man availeth much.

Attendance Upon the Worship in God's House

Worship in God's house is very essential to the healthy growth and spiritual power of a child of God. He finds here—

1. A congenial place of worship.
2. A place of prayer and the study of God's Word.
3. A place to observe the Lord's Supper.
4. A place to serve and glorify Christ.

ISAIAH 58:13-14. If thou turn away thy foot from the sabbath, from doing thy pleasure on my holy day; and call the sabbath a delight, the holy of the Lord, honourable; and shalt honour him, not doing thine own ways, nor finding thine own pleasure, nor speaking thine own words: then shalt thou delight thyself in the Lord; and I will cause thee to ride upon the high places of the earth, and feed thee with the heritage of Jacob thy father: for the mouth of the Lord hath spoken it.

ACTS 2:42. And they continued stedfastly in the apostles' doctrine and fellowship, and in breaking of bread, and in prayers.

EPHESIANS 3:21. Unto him be glory in the church by Christ Jesus throughout all ages, world without end. Amen.

HEBREWS 10:25. . . . not forsaking the assembling of ourselves together, as the manner of some is; but exhorting one another: and so much the more, as ye see the day approaching.

Systematic, Proportionate, Cheerful, Liberal Giving to Christ's Cause and His Churches

MALACHI 3:10. Bring ye all the tithes into the storehouse, that there may be meat in mine house, and prove me now herewith, saith the Lord of hosts, if I will not open you the windows of heaven, and pour you out a blessing, that there shall not be room enough to receive it.

2 CORINTHIANS 9:6-8. But this I say, He which soweth sparingly shall reap also sparingly; and he which soweth bountifully shall reap also bountifully. Every man according as he purposeth in his heart, so let him give: not grudgingly, or of

necessity: for God loveth a cheerful giver. And God is able to make all grace abound toward you; that ye, always having all sufficiency in all things, may abound to every good work.

Co-operation in God's Worldwide Redemptive Program

MATTHEW 4:19. And he saith unto them, Follow me, and I will make you fishers of men.
MATTHEW 22:9. Go ye therefore into the highways, and as many as ye shall find, bid to the marriage.
MATTHEW 28:18-20. And Jesus came and spake unto them, saying, All power is given unto me in heaven and in earth. Go ye therefore, and teach all nations, baptizing them in the name of the Father, and of the Son, and of the Holy Ghost: teaching them to observe all things whatsoever I have commanded you: and, lo, I am with you alway, even unto the end of the world. Amen.
JOHN 4:34-36. Jesus saith unto them, My meat is to do the will of him that sent me, and to finish his work. Say not ye, There are yet four months, and then cometh harvest? behold, I say unto you, Lift up your eyes, and look on the fields; for they are white already to harvest. And he that reapeth receiveth wages, and gathereth fruit unto life eternal: that both he that soweth and he that reapeth may rejoice together.
ACTS 1:8. But ye shall receive power, after that the Holy Ghost is come upon you: and ye shall be witnesses unto me both in Jerusalem, and in all Judaea, and in Samaria, and unto the uttermost part of the earth.

We should co-operate with our lives, talents, and possessions in giving Christ's truth to "every creature" in all the world. The finest and fastest way to "grow in grace, and in the knowledge of our Lord and Saviour Jesus Christ" (2 Peter 3:18) is to win souls.

39

The Christian's Heavenly Rainbow

God's Presence in Death

PSALM 23:4. Yea, though I walk through the valley of the shadow of death, I will fear no evil: for thou art with me; thy rod and thy staff they comfort me.

ISAIAH 43:2. When thou passest through the waters, I will be with thee; and through the rivers, they shall not overflow thee: when thou walkest through the fire, thou shalt not be burned; neither shall the flame kindle upon thee.

An Abundant Entrance

2 PETER 1:11. For so an entrance shall be ministered unto you abundantly into the everlasting kingdom of our Lord and Saviour Jesus Christ.

The Glorious Hope

MATTHEW 24:44. Therefore be ye also ready: for in such an hour as ye think not the Son of man cometh.

ACTS 1:11. ... which also said, Ye men of Galilee, why stand ye gazing up into heaven? this same Jesus, which is taken up from you into heaven, shall so come in like manner as ye have seen him go into heaven.

1 THESSALONIANS 4:16. For the Lord himself shall descend from heaven with a shout, with the voice of the archangel, and with the trump of God: and the dead in Christ shall rise first.

Resurrection Body

1 CORINTHIANS 15:52-57. ... in a moment, in the twinkling of an eye, at the last trump: for the trumpet shall sound, and the dead shall be raised incorruptible, and we shall be changed. For this corruptible must put on incorruption, and this mortal must put on immortality. So when this corruptible

shall have put on incorruption, and this mortal shall have put on immortality, then shall be brought to pass the saying that is written, Death is swallowed up in victory. O death, where is thy sting? O grave, where is thy victory? The sting of death is sin; and the strength of sin is the law. But thanks be to God, which giveth us the victory through our Lord Jesus Christ.

Judgment Passed

JOHN 5:24. Verily, verily, I say unto you, He that heareth my word, and believeth on him that sent me, hath everlasting life, and shall not come into condemnation; but is passed from death unto life

ROMANS 8:1. There is therefore now no condemnation to them which are in Christ Jesus, who walk not after the flesh, but after the Spirit.

Welcome Plaudit

MATTHEW 25:21. His lord said unto him, Well done, thou good and faithful servant: thou hast been faithful over a few things, I will make thee ruler over many things: enter thou into the joy of thy lord.

MATTHEW 25:34. Then shall the King say unto them on his right hand, Come, ye blessed of my Father, inherit the kingdom prepared for you from the foundation of the world.

Reunion

1 THESSALONIANS 4:17. Then we which are alive and remain shall be caught up together with them in the clouds, to meet the Lord in the air: and so shall we ever be with the Lord.

REVELATION 7:14. And I said unto him, Sir, thou knowest. And he said to me, These are they which came out of great tribulation, and have washed their robes, and made them white in the blood of the Lamb.

The Star-filled Crown

DANIEL 12:3. And they that be wise shall shine as the brightness of the firmament; and they that turn many to righteousness as the stars for ever and ever.

2 Timothy 4:8. Henceforth there is laid up for me a crown of righteousness, which the Lord, the righteous judge, shall give me at that day: and not to me only, but unto all them also that love his appearing.

Eternal Companionship and Service

John 14:3. And if I go and prepare a place for you, I will come again, and receive you unto myself; that where I am, there ye may be also.

1 Thessalonians 4:17. Then we which are alive and remain shall be caught up together with them in the clouds, to meet the Lord in the air: and so shall we ever be with the Lord.

Revelation 7:15-17. Therefore are they before the throne of God, and serve him day and night in his temple: and he that sitteth on the throne shall dwell among them. They shall hunger no more, neither thirst any more; neither shall the sun light on them, nor any heat. For the Lamb which is in the midst of the throne shall feed them, and shall lead them unto living fountains of waters: and God shall wipe away all tears from their eyes.

A Holy Exhortation While We Wait for His Coming and Labor for His Glory

Titus 2:11-15. For the grace of God that bringeth salvation hath appeared to all men, teaching us that, denying ungodliness and worldly lusts, we should live soberly, righteously, and godly, in this present world; looking for that blessed hope, and the glorious appearing of the great God and our Saviour Jesus Christ; who gave himself for us, that he might redeem us from all iniquity, and purify unto himself a peculiar people, zealous of good works. These things speak, and exhort, and rebuke with all authority. Let no man despise thee.

1 John 3:1-3. Behold, what manner of love the Father hath bestowed upon us, that we should be called the sons of God: therefore the world knoweth us not, because it knew him not. Beloved, now are we the sons of God, and it doth not yet appear what we shall be: but we know that, when he shall appear, we shall be like him; for we shall see him as he is. And every man that hath this hope in him purifieth himself, even as he is pure.

Revelation 22:20-21. He which testifieth these things saith, Surely I come quickly. Amen. Even so, come, Lord Jesus. The grace of our Lord Jesus Christ be with you all. Amen.

Conclusion
The Call of the Cross

JOHN 12:32. And I, if I be lifted up from the earth, will draw all men unto me.

ACTS 26:16-19. But rise, and stand upon thy feet: for I have appeared unto thee for this purpose, to make thee a minister and a witness both of these things which thou hast seen, and of those things in which I will appear unto thee; delivering thee from the people, and from the Gentiles, unto whom now I send thee, to open their eyes, and to turn them from darkness to light, and from the power of Satan unto God, that they may receive forgiveness of sins, and inheritance among them which are sanctified by faith that is in me. Whereupon, O king Agrippa, I was not disobedient unto the heavenly vision.

ROMANS 10:21. But to Israel he saith, All day long I have stretched forth my hands unto a disobedient and gainsaying people.

EPHESIANS 6:6. . . . not with eyeservice, as menpleasers; but as the servants of Christ, doing the will of God from the heart.

THE CALL

We have sought to find the Saviour's way of leading lost souls out of spiritual darkness and death into the joys of eternal life and the power and rewards of blessed service. The author wishes to probe the soul of the reader with these burning, pungent questions:

Are you doing the will of God in your life? Have you given a full, heartful response to Christ's call for your service? Is he calling you into a larger, more sacrificial life of surrender and service? Has he appeared in the prayer hour, in some time of spiritual communion, in the impressive "small voice" of his Spirit, calling you to give up to his will and way? Have you adopted the New Testament map of the world and heard God calling you into his life-plans for you? Have you been obedient to the "heavenly vision"? Are you among the "servants of Christ doing the will of God from the heart" (Eph. 6:6)? If you have learned to win one to Christ, can't you now enter a life of soul-winning? Are you willing to face God's will and give him a complete answer? Has he the first claim on your time and talent? Does he not need you in his widening and ripening harvest fields? Where else can you invest your life with larger returns to his glory and your joy than in his soul-winning service? In view of Christ's death for you and his heavenly preparations for your eternal happiness, can you refuse him his way with your life in this brief earthly period? What are you going to do with your life? What are you going to do with God's will concerning your service?

The Need

One of the greatest needs of God's kingdom today is for more evangelistic, trained preachers. They must serve as pastors of churches; be home and foreign missionaries; do sane, New Testament evangelism; help man our Christian schools; edit our religious papers; and do the other imperial tasks in Christ's kingdom.

There is a growing need for laymen trained in gospel singing and in Sunday school, Training Union, and laymen's work—men who will prepare themselves and give their time and talents to building and promoting the kingdom of God throughout the churches.

The harvest fields are ripe for the service of trained women —in mission service, in educational institutions, in gospel singing, in Sunday school leadership, in places of trust and responsibility in all the activities of Christ's kingdom.

All phases of life call for men and women to give themselves wholly to do God's will in bringing a lost world to Christ. Do you not see some place in this wide catalogue for your life and service? Does he not call you to a place in this ripe harvest field? Answer him according to his will and not according to your choice.

The Peril

If God is really calling you into some special service, you run a dangerous risk not to obey him. Your refusal to do his will imperils everything you hold dear except your eternal salvation.

You endanger your peace of soul. You cannot have the "peace of God, which passeth all understanding" while you withhold your life and talents from God.

Your refusal to surrender fully to God menaces your joy of heart. "The joy of the Holy Spirit" cannot come into your life while you refuse God his full way in your life.

You imperil your power with men every day you fail in a full surrender to God's will.

Your disobedience threatens the destiny of lost men. Immortal souls hang on your decision.

Christ's glory is involved in this matter. He will not wear a full crown as far as you are concerned if you fail him with your best and all.

You run the terrible risk of being a "spiritual castaway" as long as you go contrary to God's will and plan for your life.

Every day of your disobedience you invite the chastening rod of God on you and yours. You may offend his long-suffering love.

The Reward

The greatest joy in any life is found in a full surrender to God's will. Your heart and conscience will be at peace when you know you are doing his will. The joy of victory and power will rest upon you when you realize that his will is being done. Power is promised those who obey him. The best results in soul-winning are found in the lives of those who have their life-plan patterned after God's.

The Challenge

You face difficulties, to be sure. You will face more and more in disobedience. If you do God's will, you will face your difficulties with God; if you refuse, you will face them alone. You say, "I am ignorant." That can be remedied; there are schools all about. You say, "I am poor." There are things worse than poverty or ignorance. Disobedience to God's will is worse than either or both. You say, "It's too late; I have waited too long." If God thinks so, why does he not withhold your call and leave your heart alone? He knows best. Follow him. His way is best and leads to final victory. *Surrender.*

Bibliography

THE HOLY SPIRIT

Broomall, Wick. *The Holy Spirit*. New York: The American Tract Society, 1940.
Calkins, Raymond. *Holy Spirit*. New York: Abingdon Press, 1930.
Candlish, James S. *Work of the Holy Spirit*. Edinburg: T & T. Clark.
Conner, W. T. *The Work of the Holy Spirit*. Nashville: Broadman Press, 1949.
Dana, H. E. *Holy Spirit in Acts*. Kansas City, Kansas: Central Seminary Press, 1943.
Denham, W. E. *Comforter*. New York: Fleming H. Revell Co., 1935.
Erdman, Charles R. *Spirit of Christ*. New York: George H. Doran Co., 1926.
Gray, James M. *The Holy Spirit in Doctrine and Life*. New York: Fleming H. Revell Co., 1936.
Green, James Benjamin. *Studies in the Holy Spirit*. New York: Fleming H. Revell Co., 1936.
Murray, Andrew. *Spirit of Christ*. New York: Anson D. F. Randolph & Co., 1888.
Rouse, W. T. *Holy Spirit*. Nashville: Sunday School Board, 1935.
Smith, Oswald J. *The Enduement of Power*. London: Marshall, Morgan, & Scott.
Stafford, T. P. *Study of the Holy Spirit*. Philadelphia: The Judson Press, 1920.

PRAYER

Blanchard, Charles A. *Getting Things from God*. Chicago: The Bible Institute Colportage Association, 1915.
Bounds, Edward M. *Power Through Prayer*. London: Marshall Brothers, Ltd.
Bounds, Edward M. *Purpose in Prayer*. New York: Fleming H. Revell, 1920.
Bounds, Edward M. *Weapon of Prayer*. New York: Fleming H. Revell.
Bushwell, James Oliver, Jr. *Problems in the Prayer Life*. Chicago: The Bible Institute Colportage Association, 1928. (Moody Press)

Buttrick, George A. *Prayer.* New York: Abindgon-Cokesbury, 1942.
Campbell, Donald J. *Place of Prayer in the Christian Religion.* New York: The Methodist Book Concern, 1915. (Abingdon-Cokesbury)
Carroll, B. H. *Messages on Prayer.* Nashville: Broadman Press, 1942.
Chadwick, Samuel. *Path of Prayer.* New York: Abingdon Press, 1931.
Fosdick, Harry Emerson. *The Meaning of Prayer.* New York: Association Press, 1915-1924.
Frost, J. M. *Men Who Prayed.* Philadelphia: Sunday School Times, 1914.
Gordon, Samuel Dickey. *Quiet Talks on Prayer.* New York: Fleming H. Revell Co., 1904.
Hallesby, Ole Christian. *Prayer.* Minnesota: Augsburg, 1931.
Harkness, Georgia. *Prayer and the Common Life.* Nashville: Abingdon-Cokesbury Press, 1948.
Hastings, James. *Christian Doctrine of Prayer.* New York: Charles Scribner & Sons, 1915.
Laubach, Frank Charles. *Prayer, the Mightiest Force in the World.* New York: Fleming H. Revell Co., 1946.
McKnight, Ozro. *He Prayed.* Kansas City, Missouri: Western Baptist Publishing Co., 1933.
Murray, Andrew. *With Christ in the School of Prayer.* Philadelphia: Henry Altemus, 1895.
O'Rear, Arthur T. *The Most Dynamic Thing in the World.* Nashville: Cokesbury, 1925.
Whyte, Alexander. *Lôrd, Teach Us to Pray.* London: Hodder & Stoughton, 1922.

EVANGELISM

Archibald, Arthur C. *New Testament Evangelism—How It Works Today.* Philadelphia: The Judson Press, 1946.
Bader, Jesse M. *The Message and Method of the New Evangelism.* New York: Round Table Press, Inc. 1937.
Bailey, Ambrose Moody. *Evangelism in a Changing World.* New York: Round Table Press, Inc., 1936.
Barton, L. E. *Helps for Soul-Winners.* Published by author, 1945.
Blackwood, Andrew W. *Evangelism in the Home Church.* New York: Abingdon-Cokesbury, 1942.
Bryan, Dawson Charles. *A Workable Plan of Evangelism.* New York: Abingdon-Cokesbury, 1945.
Conant, J. E. *Every Member Evangelism.* New York: Harper & Brothers, 1922.

Currie, Joseph. *To Seek and To Save*. London: Marshall, Morgan & Scott, Ltd., 1948.
Dawson, David M. *More Power in Soul-Winning*. Grand Rapids, Michigan: Zondervan Publishing House, 1947.
De Blois, Austen Kennedy. *Evangelism in the New Age*. Philadelphia: The Judson Press, 1933.
Dobbins, Gaines S. *A Winning Witness*. Nashville: Sunday School Board, 1938.
Dobbins, Gaines S. *Evangelism According to Christ*. Nashville: Broadman Press, 1949.
Ellis, H. W. *Fishing for Men*. Kansas City, Missouri: Western Baptist Publishing Co., 1945.
Fairbairn, Charles V. *God's Plan for World Evangelism*. Winona Lake, Indiana: Light and Life Press, 1946.
Hamilton, William W. *A Bible Revival*. Nashville: Broadman Press, 1940.
Hughes, Edwin Holt. *Evangelism and Change*. New York: The Methodist Book Concern, 1938.
Lowry, Oscar. *Scripture Memorizing for Successful Soul-Winning*. Fleming H. Revell, 1934. Reprints by Zondervan, 1951.
Muncy, W. L. *New Testament Evangelism for Today*. Kansas City, Kansas: Central Seminary Press, 1941.
Pearce, William P. *Revival Thermometer; or Gauging One's Spiritual Worth*. Dayton, Ohio: United Brethren Publishing Co., 1905.
Powell, Sidney W. *Toward the Great Awakening*. New York: Abingdon-Cokesbury Press, 1949.
Powell, Sidney W. *Where Are the People?* New York: Abingdon-Cokesbury Press, 1942.
Sangster, W. E. *Let Me Commend*. Nashville: Abingdon-Cokesbury Press, 1948.
Scarborough, Lee R. *Products of Pentecost*. New York: Fleming H. Revell, 1924.
Scarborough, Lee R. *How Jesus Won Men*. New York: George H. Doran Co., 1926.
Schaad, Julius Augustus. *Evangelism in the Church*. New York: The National Council Church Missions House, Trade name for Protestant Episcopal Church in the U.S.A., 1924.
Sharp, C. J. *New Testament Evangelism*. Cincinnati: Standard Publishing Co., 1941.
Whitesell, F. D. *Basic New Testament Evangelism*. Grand Rapids: Zondervan Publishing House, 1949.
Whitesell, F. D. *Sixty-five Ways to Give Evangelistic Invitations*. Grand Rapids, Michigan: Zondervan, 1945.

Work, Edgar W. *Every Minister His Own Evangelist.* New York: Fleming H. Revell Co., 1927.

EVANGELISTS

Beardsley, Frank G. *Heralds of Salvation.* New York: American Tract Society, 1939.
Belden, Albert D. *George Whitefield: The Awakener.* Nashville: Abingdon-Cokesbury, 1931.
Brown, Elijah P. *The Real Billy Sunday.* Dayton, Ohio: Otterbein Press, 1914.
Dana, H. E. *Lee Rutland Scarborough: A Life of Service.* Nashville: Broadman Press, 1942.
Day, Richard Ellsworth. *Man of Like Passions.* Grand Rapids, Michigan: Zondervan, 1942.
Ellis, William T. *Billy Sunday: The Man and His Message.* L. T. Myers, 1914. Winston.
English, Eugene S. *Robert G. Lee, A Chosen Vessel.* Grand Rapids, Michigan: Zondervan, 1949. (iz)

AUTOBIOGRAPHY

Finney, Charles G. *Memoirs of Charles G. Finney.* New York: Fleming H. Revell, 1908.
Hardy, Edwin Noah. *George Whitefield, The Matchless Soul-Winner.* New York: American Tract Society, 1938.
James, Powhatan W. *George W. Truett, A Biography.* Nashville: Broadman Press, 1939.
Miller, Basil. *God's Great Soul-Winners.* Anderson, Indiana: Warner, 1937.
Moody, Paul Dwight. *My Father, An Intimate Portrait of Dwight Moody.* Boston: Little, Brown & Co., 1938.
Smith, Gipsy. *His Life and Work, by Himself.* New York: Fleming H. Revell, 1925.
Spurgeon, Charles H. *Autobiography of Charles H. Spurgeon.* Philadelphia: American Baptist Publication Society.
Winslow, Ola Elizabeth. *Jonathan Edwards: A Biography.* New York: Macmillan Co. 1940.

REVIVALS

Anonymous. *Modern Evangelistic Movements.* By two univerity men. New York: Thomas and Cowan, 1924
Beardsley, Frank G. *Religious Progress Through Religious Revivals.* New York: American Tract Society, 1943.
Bready, John Wesley. *England: Before and After Wesley.* New York: Harper & Brothers. 1938.

Broughton, Len G. *Revival of a Dead Church.* New York: Fleming H. Revell, 1900.
Candler, Warren Akin. *Great Revivals and the Great Republic.* Nashville: Abingdon-Cokesbury, 1904.
Cox, Enos Kincheloe. *The Answer by Fire.* Grand Rapids, Michigan: W. B. Eerdmans. 1936.
Doe, Walter P. *Revivals: How to Secure Them.* New York: E. B. Treat, 1895.
Finney, Charles G. *Lectures on Revivals of Religion.* Oberlin, Ohio: E. J. Goodrich, 1868. Revival Lectures, 1914, Revell.
Gewehr, Wesley N. *The Great Awakening in Virginia.* Durham, North Carolina: Duke University Press, 1930.
Hervey, George W. *Manual of Revivals.* New York: Funk and Wagnalls Co., 1895.
Hughes, Philip E. *Revive Us Again.* London: Marshall, Morgan & Scott, 1947.
McConnell, F. M. *Winning Souls and Strengthening Churches.* Dallas: Irwin, 1913.
Orr, J. Edwin. *Church Must First Repent.* London: Marshall, Morgan & Scott, 1938.
Smith, Oswald J. *Revival We Need.* London: Marshall, Morgan & Scott. (Christian Alliance Pub.)
Strickland, Arthur B. *Great American Revival.* Cincinnati: Standard Press, 1934.
Sweet, William W. *Revivalism in America: Its Origin, Growth, and Decline.* New York: Charles Scribner & Sons, 1944.
Torrey, R. A. *How to Promote and Conduct a Successful Revival.* New York: Fleming H. Revell, 1901.
Tyson, W. A. *Revival.* Nashville: Abingdon-Cokesbury Press, 1925.
Weddell, John W. *Revival in the Local Church.* Philadelphia: American Baptist Publication Society, 1910.
Wells, Robert J. and Rice, John R. *How to Have a Revival.* Wheaton, Illinois: Sword of the Lord Publishers, 1946.